FLORENCE
A Traveler's Anthology

FLORENCE
A Traveler's Anthology

EDITED BY TOBY COLE

Lawrence Hill & Company
WESTPORT, CONNECTICUT

Library of Congress Cataloging in Publication Data

Main entry under title:

Florence: a traveler's anthology.

Bibliography: p.
Includes index.
1. Florence (Italy)—Literary collections.
I. Cole, Toby
PN6071.F49F59   ✓945'.51   81-80430
ISBN 0-88208-126-8   AACR2

945.5
F65

This is for Minna and Milton Abernethy and Marina Jouffroy.

*The author wishes to thank the following for their courtesy in
granting permission to reprint from copyrighted materials:*

"Introduction" from *The Stones of Florence*. Reprinted by permission of the author, Mary McCarthy.
"Machiavellian History" from Felix Gilbert's Introduction to *History of Florence* by Niccolo Machiavelli.
    Reprinted by permission of the publisher Harper & Row, Publishers, Inc., copyright 1960 by Felix Gilbert.
"The Decameron's Singular Destiny" by Ugo Foscolo from *Critical Perspectives on the Decameron*. Reprinted
    by permission of the publisher Hodder & Stoughton Educational.
"Giotto: Herald of the Renaissance" from *The Italian Painters of the Renaissance* by Bernard Berenson, 1930.
    Reprinted by permission of the publisher Oxford University Press.
"The Finest Church in Christiandom" from *The Stones of Florence*. Reprinted by permission of the author, Mary
    McCarthy.
"Masaccio: Master of the Significant" from *The Italian Painters of the Renaissance* by Bernard Berenson, 1930.
    Reprinted by permission of the publisher Oxford University Press.
"The Mona Lisa of Leonardo da Vinci" from "Kenneth Clark on the Mona Lisa." Reprinted by permission of
    the publisher The Burlington Magazine, London, March, 1973.
"Stendhal" from *Rome, Naples and Florence* by Stendhal. Reprinted by permission of the publisher George
    Braziller Inc.
"Herman Melville" excerpts from *Journal of a Visit to Europe and the Levant, October 11, 1856–May 6, 1857*
    ed. by Howard C. Horsford (copyright 1955 by Princeton University Press), footnotes pp. 217-222. Reprinted
    by permission of Princeton University Press.
"Then and Now." Excerpt from *Then and Now* by Somerset Maugham, copyright 1946 by Somerset Maugham.
    Reprinted by permission of Doubleday & Company, Inc.
"A Room With a View" from *A Room With a View* by E. M. Forster. Published 1923 by Alfred A. Knopf, Inc.
"Aaron's Rod" from *Aaron's Rod* by D. H. Lawrence. Copyright 1922 by Thomas Seltzer, Inc., copyright
    renewed 1950 by Frieda Lawrence. Reprinted by permission of Viking Penguin Inc.
"World So Wide" from *World So Wide* by Sinclair Lewis. Copyright 1950, 1951 by the Estate of Sinclair Lewis.
    Reprinted by permission of Random House, Inc.
"The Flood, November 4, 1966," originally appeared under the title "A Letter from Florence." From *Stories
    and True Stories* by Francis Steegmuller. Reprinted by permission of the publisher Little, Brown and
    Company, copyright 1967 Francis Steegmuller. This article first appeared in *The New Yorker*.

Contents

Foreword

Florence—"the mother country of western civilization"—is a relative newcomer on the traveler's itinerary. Since the Middle Ages Rome and Venice have been way stations for pilgrims to the Holy Land and students bound for schools of medicine, law, philosophy and the natural sciences in the universities of Italy. For hundreds of years the two cities were sought out for their ancient relics. In our day, Rome and Venice have become the ultimate in pleasurable pursuits.

But Florence, improbably, was "discovered" in the nineteenth century. As recently as two hundred years ago literati Joseph Addison, Horace Walpole, Thomas Gray and Oliver Goldsmith left their calling cards but garnered no lasting impressions. On the Grand Tour, James Boswell spent little time in Florence and was apparently unmoved. This curious indifference to the "little treasure city," as Henry James would later call it, may be attributed partly to Florence's then remote geographic site and partly to the prevalent English attitude towards painting, which was not considered a "gentlemanly" vocation. An early English guide, anticipating the Michelin, graded art works, awarding the Venus five stars and Michelangelo's holy family none!

During the decades of the nineteenth century Florence's incomparable ambience became a lure to England's most renowned poets and writers. They were joined in their flight by American expatriates and Russian exiles, one of them Dostoyevsky, who wrote a large part of *The Idiot* in Florence. In celebration of this earthly "paradise," as Shelley called it, several of our finest English poems were composed. A selection of the poetry and prose inspired by the city appears in the following pages. These are preceded by fervent descriptive accounts of the supreme art city from the travel journals of illustrious nineteenth-century French, English and American writers which roused the curiosity of their countrymen. Florence now modishly vies with Rome and Venice for the favor of the multitude.

The aim of this modest volume is to encourage the tourist to venture beyond Florence's stony surface and well-worn guidebook landmarks to discover the quintessential city. This collection should help to implement the quest. In Part I, passages highlight the city's cataclysmic history sequentially as seen through its predominant figures, victors and vanquished in the internecine feuds which insistently ravaged the civil life of Florence from its beginnings. The selections were extracted from rare and scholarly works, several by early Florentine pioneers in historiography who chronicled what their fellow citizens "did, heard and saw" in the very cauldron of tempestuous struggles against tyranny. The city's legacy to the modern world—what we now know about painting, sculpture, architecture, art criticism and scientific method—is illuminated in Part 2 by some of the foremost interpreters of Renaissance Florence. A more popular bequest is the new world's name, America, for Amerigo Vespucci, Florentine navigator, representative of the Medici banking house, who charted South America's coastline to tell us it was not part of Asia, and, with characteristic Florentine resourcefulness, by computing longitudes arrived at an almost exact, the first, figure for the earth's equatorial circumference. An Epilogue describes the two great catastrophes Florence has suffered at the hands of men and nature in the twentieth century: the Nazi occupation and consequent devastation of the city and the Flood of November 4, 1966.

In the making of this anthology I have been privileged to consult historians of the city and art specialists. I prize the interest shown in this work by Ruth Chavasse most especially, Rosemary Devonshire Jones, Robert Proctor, Philip Rylands and thank Sally Scully McNeil for her collaboration on the chronology of Florence. The resources of the Marciana Library in Venice were made available to me by Stefania Rossi and those at Villa I Tatti's Biblioteca Berenson in Settignano by Craig Hugh Smyth. I salute the unnamed and unsung workers in the New York Public Library at Fifth and Forty-Second, who make it one of the best in the world. Claudio Rosa and Maria Grazia provided technical help, and I am most grateful to Donald J. Davidson and my publisher, Lawrence Hill, for valuable editorial assistance. Last, but by no means least, I declare an incalculable debt to those authors, past and present, who compose this volume and helped me discover Florence.

Toby Cole

A Chronology of Florence

62 B.C.   Legendary founding of Florence by Julius Caesar, leader of expedition against Cataline, self-declared consul of the Etrurian settlement of Fiesole. Tradition has two clans settle Florence: *Neri* (Blacks), the noble descendants of the Roman Army; *Bianchi* (Whites), commoners descended from early inhabitants of Fiesole. According to legend, the city was destroyed by Totila, last king of the Ostrogoths, and later rebuilt by Charlemagne.

1082   Florence is beseiged by German Emperor Henry IV, who is contesting Pope's defender, Countess Matilda of Tuscany (1052-1115).

1138   Consuls are elected, the beginning of republican communal institutions in Florence.

c. 1200   Florence gains autonomy from Holy Roman Empire.

1200   First Podestà, chief magistrate of city and executive institution until end of century, when the Signory is established.

1215   Buondelmonte Buondelmonti is assassinated by the Amadei family, one cause of the vendetta between the Guelph and Ghibelline parties. Strife continues for 150 years.

1232–1310 *Arnolfo di Cambio*

1252   First gold florin is coined; it becomes Europe's standard gold coin.

1260   Ghibellines gain a decisive victory over Florentine Guelphs at Monteperti. Ghibellines remain in charge until final expulsion from Florence, in 1266.

1265–1321 *Dante Alighieri*
c. 1266–1337 *Giotto*

1292   Ordinances of Justice, establishment of merchant oligarchy or guild regime; popular reaction under Giano della Bella; fall of second democracy.

1292   Arnolfo di Cambio begins work on the Duomo.

1299   Palazzo Vecchio is built to protect the Signory from the attacks of the nobles.

1300–1325 City walls, originally built 1160, are enlarged to contain population growth, become outermost line of of defense. *Neri* and *Bianchi* leaders are banished.

1302   Dante (White Guelph), absent from Florence on a diplomatic mission to Rome, receives sentence of heavy fine and banishment for two years; second sentence is death by burning for "contumacy."

> **1304–1374** *Francesco Petrarca*,
> founder of *Studia humanitatis*, or humanism

1312   City beseiged by German Emperor Henry VII; siege raised, 1313.

> **1313–1375** *Giovanni Boccaccio*
> **1314–1321** Dante writes *The Divine Comedy*

1315   Disastrous defeat of Florentine and Tuscan Guelphs by Ghibellines at Montecatini.

1320–1323 Castruccio Castracani, Lord of Lucca, is victorious over Florence.

1333   Flood, ninety-six-hour storm (described by Villani), sweeps away all bridges.

1339   Edward II of England bankrupt, topples Bardi and Peruzzi banking houses; internal Florentine crisis.

1342–1343 Walter of Brienne, French knight, self-styled "Duke of Athens," is elected Podestà, but exiled after trying to establish income tax.

1348–1353 Famine and bubonic plague; 96,000 Florentines perish.

> **1348–1353** Boccaccio writes *The Decameron*
> **1377–1446** *Filippo Brunelleschi*

1378–1382 Revolt of the Ciompi, the poorest woolworkers, led by Michele di Lando; last attempt to establish democracy; Albizzi family leads merchant oligarchy, which manipulates constitution behind the scenes.

> **1378–1455** *Fra Angelico*
> **1386–1466** *Donatello*
> **1401–1428** *Masaccio*

1402   Defeat of Giangalleazzo Visconti; beginning of fifty years of "civic humanism"; Coluccio Salutati (1331–1406), chancellor of

Florence since 1375; vindication of his program of *libertas* and the liberal arts.

1404–1472 *Alberti,*
prototype of Burckhardt's "Renaissance man"

1420–1436 Brunelleschi builds the Dome of Duomo.

1423–1429 Wars of Venice and Florence against the Visconti of Milan; Florence absorbs Arezzo, Pistoia, Volterra, Pisa.

1427 Catasto, income tax, levied, for which records of over 100,000 households survive.

1434–1464 Rise of the Medici. Cosimo de' Medici (1389–1464), wealthy merchant, takes over behind-the-scenes control of Florence from the Albizzi family.

1444–1510 *Alessandro Botticelli*

1464–1469 Cosimo's son, Piero, assumes the manipulation of the Florentine constitution.

1452–1519 *Leonardo da Vinci*

1462 Cosimo endows Platonic Academy, headed by Ficino; it influences Copernicus, Kepler, et al.

1469–1527 *Machiavelli*

1469–1492 Rule of Lorenzo ("*il Magnifico*") de' Medici (b. 1449), grandson of Cosimo, son of Piero.

1475–1564 *Michelangelo*

1478 The Pazzi conspiracy: Pazzi family attempts to assassinate Lorenzo de' Medici, succeeds only in killing his brother Giuliano.

1492 Death of Lorenzo; he is succeeded by ineffectual son Piero.

1494 Charles VIII, King of France, invades Italy. Piero de' Medici is expelled from Florence; Medici treasures are dispersed. Republic is re-established under influence of Dominican monk and charismatic preacher, Fra Girolamo Savonarola (1452–1498).

1494–1512 Republican regime.

1498 Savonarola burned as heretic.

1500–1571 *Benvenuto Cellini*
1511–1571 *Giorgio Vasari*

1513 The Medici are returned to power by force of arms: Lorenzo II rules from 1513 to 1519 (his daughter Catherine marries Henry II of France); Lorenzo il Magnifico's son, Cardinal Giovanni de' Medici (1475–1521), becomes Pope Leo X. Machiavelli, secretary under the Republic, is exiled.

1523   Giulio de' Medici (1478–1534) (son of Lorenzo il Magnifico's murdered brother, Giuliano) becomes Pope Clement VII.

1527   Plague: 30,000 Florentines, or one fourth of the population, perish. The Medici are expelled. The last republic is instituted and lasts till 1530 (surrendered to Holy Roman Emperor, Charles V, 1529).

1529   Bishops of Tuscany excommunicate Clement VII; inscription on the Ponte Vecchio reads: "Jesus Christ, King of the Florentine people, elected by popular decree."

1530   The Medici in power again; Alessandro de' Medici appointed hereditary ruler (1530–1537).

1537–1574 Cosimo II de' Medici becomes ruler of Florence. Creation of Tuscan territorial state. Medici Grand Dukes rule for next 250 years.

1564–1642 *Galileo Galilei*

1577   Flood, the worst since 1333; parts of city are submerged under seventeen feet of water.

1621   The second Duke Cosimo dies, succeeded by eleven-year-old Ferdinand II under the regency of Christine of Lorraine and Maria Maddalena of Austria.

1633   Galileo sentenced to indefinite imprisonment by the Holy Roman Inquisition, suffers humiliating abjuration.

1737   The Medici line is extinguished; rule of Tuscany passes to Austrian-Habsburg Empire.

1801   Napoleonic treaty, Tuscany transformed into Kingdom of Etruria; virtual destruction of Holy Roman Empire begins.

1815   Congress of Vienna returns Florence to old regime (Tuscany virtually under rule of Austria).

1861   Unification of Italy; Florence annexed to the Kingdom of Sardinia.

1865–1870 Florence is capital of Italy (until annexation of Rome, 1871).

1922   Mussolini's march on Rome; Fascists take over government of Italy.

1940   Italy enters the Second World War on the side of the Japanese-German Axis, declaring war against the United States and Great Britain.

1944   Allies reach Rome and Florence; Florence is liberated from Nazis by Allies and partisans.

1966   Devastating flood.

Introduction

Mary McCarthy

The Florentines consider themselves and are considered by other Italians the most civilized people in Italy, just as the Tuscan peasant is regarded as the most skilled and intelligent of Italian farmers. *"Questi primitivi,"* the Tuscan poor people say pityingly of workers imported from the South and from the islands of Sicily and Sardinia, and they pity them not only for their unskilled hands but because these unfortunates, not having lived with the "Davidde" (the Florence pet name for the "David" of Michelangelo) and the *"cupolone"* (Brunelleschi's dome), do not understand *"le cose dell'arte."* The literacy rate in Tuscany is by far the highest found in Italy, and the poorest Florentine maidservant can be found in the kitchen spelling out the crimes and *"le cose dell'arte"* in the morning newspaper.

That quality called *"fiorentinità"* (and Florence is the only Italian town whose name naturally turns into a substantive denoting an abstract quality) means taste and fine workmanship, as "Paris" does in France. The world knows it in shoes, umbrellas, handbags, jewellery, trousseau linens, and the firms of Ferragamo, Gucci, Bucellati, Emilia Bellini, with their seats on Via Tornabuoni and Via della Vigna Nuova and branches in Rome, Milan, New York, awaken faint reminiscences of the old banking firms of the Peruzzi, the Bardi, the Pazzi. *Fiorentinità* is made by the Florentine workman in his coverall and by those firms of spinster sisters like the Sorelle Materassi of Aldo Palazzeschi's novel with their needles, scissors, and embroidery hoops and their big maid called Niobe. If it is synonymous with civilization and refinement, it cannot be separated from the poor and their way of talking, thinking, and seeing, which is always realistic and equalizing. The Florentine speech is full of diminutives; everything is turned into a "little" something or other, which has the curious effect of at once deprecating and dignifying it. Old-fashioned expletives (*"Accidenti!,"* which means something like "I'll be blowed," *"Diamine!,"* or "the dickens!," *"Per bacco!,"* or "You don't say!") give Florentine talk a countrified flavor. *"Per cortesia,"* among the poor people, is the common preface to an inquiry. A *"pisolino"* (somewhat humorous, meaning "a little nod") is the common word for a nap; a drink of hot water and lemon is a *"canarino"* (canary bird). Nature becomes human when the peasants look at her; around Florence they call the two kinds of cypresses, the tall male and the blowsy female, the "man" and the "woman."

Florence today is a city of craftsmen, farmers, and professors, and every Florentine has something in him of each of these. In a sense, there is no class of unskilled workers, for every occupation is treated as a skill, with its own refinement, dignity, and status – even un- employment. "What did your husband do?" *"Era un disoccupato, signora."* In the same way, upper-class idlers, such as are found in Rome and Venice, are extremely rare here, which explains the ab- sence of night life. There is no *jeunesse dorée*; children of the upper- classes are busy studying at the University: law, archaeology, archi- tecture, political science.

The Florentines today are probably more like what they were in the Middle Ages and the early Renaissance than were the Florentines of any intervening period; the revival of crafts and small industries and the restoration of free institutions after Fascism may have something to do with this. These eternal Florentines have no need to be senti- mental about the past, which does not seem remote but as near and indifferently real as the clock on the tower of Palazzo Vecchio to the housewife who puts her head out the window to time her spaghetti by it. There have been many changes, of course, in these centuries, but they are like the changes a man sees in his own lifetime. The diet eaten by Pontormo in his crazy tall house is almost precisely the diet of the Florentine people today: boiled meat, a *frittata* of eggs, a fish from the Arno, cabbage, *minestra*, beet salad, capers, lettuce salad, three pennyworth of bread, the bitter green salad called *radicchio*, pea soup, two cooked apples, asparagus with eggs, *ricotta*, artichokes, cherries, melon (*popone* in Tuscan), the small sour plums called *susine*, grapes, a young pigeon, two pennyworth of almonds, dried figs, beet greens with butter, a chicken. If he were alive now, he might have eaten, besides, white haricot beans with tuna fish from Elba, the broad beans called *mangia-tutto*, Tuscan *ravioli* (little green *gnocchi* made with beet greens and *ricotta*), rabbit, and the long string beans called *serpenti*.

The merit of this fare is that it is inexpensive and healthy. In Pontormo's *Supper at Emmaus*, the bill, or what appears to be the bill – a scroll of paper with figures on it – is shown lying on the floor. This sardonic touch is as characteristically Florentine as *radicchio* and *popone*. The economy of the Florentines, reprehended as avarice by Dante, is an ingrained trait, which was made even more pronounced, doubtless, by the general misery during the Medici period. Farmers are naturally economical, and the farmer in every Florentine scrimps, saves, and stretches. When the capital was moved to Florence at the time of the unification of Italy, a Roman paper printed a cartoon showing three Florentines seated at a dinner table with a single boiled egg in the center. "What shall we do with the leftover?" was the caption. Such jokes are still told of the Florentines, and they tell them of themselves. At an expensive seaside resort, during a recent heat wave, all the Florentines checked out of the hotel one morning. "They must have heard that the heat wave was over in Florence; someone sent them a penny postcard," observed a non-Florentine. A lady who lived in Fiesole was invited by a Florentine countess to drop in at her house "any time you feel like it; if you want to do p.p. . . . ." To the countess, this invitation was the summit of hospitality.

Eggs, cigarettes, and postage stamps are still bought cautiously, one at a time, by the poorer Florentines, and a cabbage is sold by quarters. The habit of careful division, of slicing every whole into portions, is an instinct with the Tuscans that is confirmed by their very geography. Tuscany produces a "little of everything," as the Florentines love to explain: iron, tin, copper, zinc, lead, marble, hides, oil, wheat, corn, sugar, milk, wool, flax, timber, fruit, fish, meat, fowl, and water. This little, if carefully distributed, meant self-sufficiency and independence; it was a kind of proof, from the Creator, that Tuscany was a "natural kingdom" or completely furnished model world which could survive, as in some fairy-tale pact, so long as a principle of limit was recognized. The idea of rightful shares has been rooted literally in the soil here since the early Middle Ages. The *mezzadria* system of farming (half to the peasant and half to the landlord), which introduced an even division into agriculture, emancipated the Tuscan peasant from slavery centuries in advance of the rest of Italy and Europe. This no doubt explains the superiority of the

Tuscan peasant and the sharpness of his intelligence. Similarly, in the thirteenth century, a then-revolutionary code governing mining and the rights to mineral deposits was enacted in Massa Maritima, in the Maremma. The *mezzadria*, incidentally, which has become the general practice throughout Italy, now no longer satisfies either the landowner or the peasant; it is not as equal as it sounds. Nevertheless, it made the peasant a free man and instilled in him those qualities of foresightedness, thrift, and neatness that are not found in slaves or serfs.

The pride of the Florentines, as proverbial as their avarice, is particularly irritating to materialistic people because it appears to be based on nothing concrete, except the past, to which the Florentines themselves seem all but indifferent or wryly jesting. What have they got to be so proud of? No money, no film stars, no big business, no "top" writers or painters, not even an opera company. A few critics and professors – "sharp eyes and bad tongues," which was a Renaissance summing up of the Florentines.

The professor in every Florentine is a critic, and that critical spirit is the hidden source of Florentine pride. *"O, signore, per noi tutti gli stranieri son ugualmente odiosi,"* said a manicurist, bluntly, to Bernard Berenson, who was trying to enlist her against the Germans before the First World War. "Oh sir, for us all foreigners are equally hateful." *"Noi fiorentini"* – this phrase, so often used, grates on the nerves of many strangers, who take it to be a boast. But it is only a definition or simple statement of identity, just as the manicurist's remark was not rude but explanatory.

The manicurist was a poor girl and not ashamed of it. This is the distinction, the real originality, of the Florentines in the modern world, where poverty is a source of shame and true natural pride, as opposed to boastfulness, very rare. Florence is a town of poor people, and those who are not poor are embarrassed by the fact and try to hide it. Professors, farmers, and craftsmen have one thing in common; they are generally short of ready money. The Milanese-type industrialist with his bulging crocodile wallet and the Roman-type speculator hardly exist in Florence. The aristocracy here is a gentry preoccupied with crops and rainfall. Every Friday during the growing season, the counts and *marchesi* gather in Palazzo Vecchio, the seat of the agricultural administration, to trade and barter and exchange information, just as the peasants do who come in from the country with their samples to meet in the square below; on Wednesday, which is market day in Siena, the Florentine nobles who have vineyards in the Chianti or the Val d'Elsa gather there as well, in the Palazzo Comunale on the square. These men, whatever else they may be – erudite archivists, amateur historians, collectors of scientific instruments, pious sons of the Church, automobile salesmen – are, above all, farmers, and their wives, too, who set an excellent table, spend a good deal of time in conference with the *fattore* (land agent) and the accountant, having inherited estates themselves to manage.

On the whole, stocks and shares hold little interest for the Florentines, who care only for the land, that is, for "real" property. Like Michelangelo and Cellini, Florentines of every station are absorbed in acquiring real estate: a little apartment that can be rented to foreigners; a farm that will supply the owner with oil, wine, fruit, and flowers for the house. Upper-class families return from a weekend on their country estates, their *millecento* packed with flowers wrapped in double thicknesses of damp newspaper to last the week in town, just as the poor people do who go by bus on Sunday to visit their relations in the country. The aristocracy is fond of shooting, and many a handsome old villa is furnished as a hunting lodge with a gamekeeper dressed in green; fishing in the Arno and the tributary mountain streams is a passion with the artisans and white-collar workers, whose bending rods make a Sunday pattern all along the river. Both sports rest on the same principle: taking something free from Nature.

Like the wise woman who lived in the portico of Santissima Annunziata and sewed pretty patches on her clothes, the modern Florentines are extremely gifted in repair work – mending and fixing old things to make them last. The restoration of works of art, which is mending at its most delicate and perilous, is one of the great crafts of modern Florence; to the workshops and laboratories of the Uffizi, spread out through the old quarters of the city, come pictures and frescoes, marbles, and wooden polychromes from the Florentine churches and from remote parishes in the *contado* to be put back into condition by Florentine specialists and professors. The Florentine "way" of restoration, less drastic than the German method as practiced in London and New York, is one of the new wonders of the art world; art scholars and historians of English and American universities, critics and curators come to watch how it is done. To them, the workmen in white smocks, like doctors, operating on frescoes that have been detached from damp churches and cloisters, revive the old Florence and the workshops around the Duomo. Climbing up ladders on to shaky scaffolds in the Bardi Chapel of Santa Croce, where the Giottos are being restored, the foreign professors marvel over the work and over the new, "modern" Giotto who is revealed by the removal of the nineteenth-century overpainting—a resplendent, transfigured Giotto, whom Ruskin never knew, having given nearly all his praises, it is now found, alas, to the *oeuvre* of the nineteenth-century restorer, Bianchi, who painted, *in toto*, the figure of Saint Louis of Toulouse, considered by Ruskin the essential Giotto . . .

These Giottos of the Bardi Chapel have been brought back, almost, from the dead, and the other innovations of modern, postwar Florence – the new Museum of the Belvedere with its wonderful collection of detached frescoes restored to life and the new Trinità bridge standing *come era* – appear as veritable miracles. One of Cosimo I's building projects was the Santa Trinità bridge, which was rebuilt, after a flood, by Ammannati, who also extended the Pitti Palace for Cosimo, botching, in the enlargement, Brunelleschi's original design. Ammannati's bridge, the most beautiful in Florence, the most beautiful perhaps in the world, was destroyed by the Germans during the last war and has been rebuilt, as it was. The rebuilders, working from photographs and from Ammannati's plans, became conscious of a mystery attaching to the full, swelling, looping curve of the three arches – the slender bridge's most exquisite feature – which conforms to no line or figure in geometry and seems to have been drawn, free hand, by a linear genius, which Ammannati was not. Speculation spread, throughout the city, among professors and art critics, on the enigma of the curve. Some said it was a catenary curve, drawn, that is, from the looping or suspension of a chain; some guessed that it might have been modeled on the curve of a violin body. Just before the bridge's opening, however, a new theory was offered and demonstrated, very convincingly, with photographs in the newspaper; this theory assigns the design of the bridge to Michelangelo, whom Cosimo I was consulting, through Vasari, at this period. The original of the curve was found, where no one had thought of looking for it, in the Medici Tombs, on the sarcophagi that support the figures of Night and Day, Twilight and Dawn. Thus, if the argument is correct (and it has been widely accepted), a detail of a work of sculpture, done for the glorification of a despotic line in their private chapel, was translated outdoors and became the property of the whole Florentine people. Sculpture returned to architecture, like a plant reverting to type, and a curve of beauty, thrice repeated, which was as mysterious in its final origin as though it came from a god and not from an architect's drawing board, upholds the traffic of the city.

Every time, no doubt, a bridge has been rebuilt in Florence, from the day the statue of Mars was put back "the wrong way" on Ponte Vecchio, dispute must have clouded the process. The dispute over Ponte Santa Trinità has lasted ever since the war's end and is not finished yet. First came the question of whether the old bridge should be rebuilt at all. Why not a modern one? When this was settled, the old quarries in the Boboli Garden from which the golden stone had been cut were reopened; one-sixth the original stone was retrieved from the Arno. Difficulties then followed with the masons, who had to be restrained from cutting the new stone "better" (i.e., with the clean edges made possible by modern machinery). Patience began to run out, as Michelangelo's had when he wrote: "I have undertaken to raise the dead, to try and harness these mountains, and to introduce the art of quarrying into this neighborhood." Once the stone had been cut, the matching of the color was criticized; the flooring in the Arno was criticized. A sluice was opened up in the river, inadvertently, and endangered the bridge's underpinnings when it was almost finished, and had already been opened to foot traffic. The fall rains would do the rest, said the pessimists, scanning the sky, and indeed, for a few anxious days, it appeared that they might be right, that the whole frail lovely structure might be swept away if the sluice were not closed in time. Rebuilding the bridge as it was, was really a case of "undertaking to raise the dead," and pride in this Florentine feat, unique in the modern world, made everyone apprehensive of a fall. And the more beautiful the resurrected bridge appeared, rising like an apparition from the green river, the more the population squabbled, warned, caviled, lest it not be perfect. The redemption of a work of art is a kind of Second Creation. Yet what is involved is simply painstaking repair work, not essentially different from the housewife's darning or the furniture-mending of the small workshops of the Oltrarno. Around the saving character of the Florentines, their historic vice, cluster the local virtues: the wise division of space, substantiality, simplicity, economy, and restraint. If high-flying Daedalus is their real patron, Poverty is their attendant virtue, the homemade cross of San Giovanni dei Fiorentini that guides him, the precursor, through the desert.

The two modern writers who have best caught the spirit of Florence are Aldo Palazzeschi whose *Sorelle Materassi* tells of two old-maid

sisters who have a fine-linen and embroidery business specializing in
trousseaux and hope chests – putting away for the future – and whose
own bureau drawers are stuffed with ancient trim for their own Sunday
wear (tassels, fringe, scarves, veils, little collars forty or sixty years
old, boleros, little jackets with dangles, Spanish combs and tortoise
hairpins), and Vasco Pratolini whose *Cronache di Poveri Amanti* tells
of the poor people of Santa Croce quarter: artisans, pushcart vendors,
prostitutes, and pairs and pairs of young lovers. In the back streets of
the Santa Croce quarter, the farthest remove from the smart linen
shops of Via Tornabuoni, two characteristic sounds can be heard,
when the traffic is momentarily silent, two sounds that *are* modern
Florence: the clack-clack of a sewing machine and the tinkle of a
young girl practicing on an old piano.

PART 1

TYRANNY AND HUMANISM

FLORENCE

The brightness of the world, o thou once free,
And always fair, rare land of courtesy!
O Florence! with the Tuscan fields and hills,
And famous Arno, fed with all their rills;
Thou brightest star of star-bright Italy!
Rich, ornate, populous, all treasures thine,
The golden corn, the olive, and the vine.
Fair cities, gallant mansions, castles old,
And forests, where beside his leafy hold
The sullen boar hath heard the distant horn,
And whets his tusks against the gnarled thorn:
Palladian palace with its storied halls;
Fountains where Love lies listening to their falls;
Gardens, where flings the bridge its airy span,
And Nature makes her happy home with man;
Where many a gorgeous flower is duly fed
With its own rill, on its own spangled bed,
And wreathes the marble urn; or leans its head,
A mimic mourner, that with veil withdrawn
Weeps liquid gems, the presents of the dawn;
Thine all delights, and every muse is thine;
And more than all, embrace and intertwine
Of all with all in gay and twinkling dance!
Mid gods of Greece and warriors of romance,
See! Boccace sits, unfolding on his knees
The new-found roll of old Maeonides;
But from his mantle's fold, and near the heart,
Peers Ovid's holy book of Love's sweet smart!

Samuel Taylor Coleridge

Florentine History

Niccolo Machiavelli
(1469–1527)

Among the great and wonderful institutions of the republics and principalities of antiquity that have now gone into disuse, was that by means of which towns and cities were from time to time established; and there is nothing more worthy the attention of a great prince, or of a well-regulated republic, or that confers so many advantages upon a province, as the settlement of new places, where men are drawn together for mutual accommodation and defense. This may easily be done by sending people to reside in recently acquired or uninhabited countries. Besides causing the establishment of new cities, these removals render a conquered country more secure, and keep the inhabitants of a province properly distributed. Thus, deriving the greatest attainable comfort, the inhabitants increase rapidly, are more prompt to attack others, and defend themselves with greater assurance. This custom, by the unwise practice of princes and republics, having gone into desuetude, the ruin and weakness of territories has followed; for this ordination is that by which alone empires are made secure, and countries become populated. Safety is the result of it; because the colony which a prince establishes in a newly acquired country is like a fortress and a guard to keep the inhabitants in fidelity and obedience. Neither can a province be wholly occupied and preserve a proper distribution of its inhabitants without this regulation; for all districts are not equally healthy, and hence some will abound to overflowing, while others are void; and if there be no method of withdrawing them from places in which they increase too rapidly, and planting them where they are too few the country would soon be wasted; for one part would become a desert, and the other a dense and wretched population. And as nature cannot repair this disorder, it is

necessary that industry should effect it; for unhealthy localities become wholesome when a numerous population is brought into them.
With cultivation the earth becomes fruitful, and the air is purified with
fires—remedies which nature cannot provide. The city of Venice
proves the correctness of these remarks. Being placed in a marshy and
unwholesome situation, it became healthy only by the number of
industrious individuals who were drawn together. Pisa, too, on account of its unwholesome air, was never filled with inhabitants till the
Saracens, having destroyed Genoa and rendered her rivers unnavig-
able, caused the Genoese to migrate thither in vast numbers, and thus
render her populous and powerful. Where the use of colonies is not
adopted, conquered countries are held with great difficulty; districts
once uninhabited still remain so, and those which populate quickly are
not relieved. Hence it is that many places in the world, and particularly in Italy, in comparison of ancient times, have become deserts.
This has wholly arisen and proceeded from the negligence of princes,
who have lost all appetite for true glory, and of republics which no
longer possess institutions that deserve praise. In ancient times, by
means of colonies, new cities frequently arose, and those already
begun were enlarged, as was the case with Florence, which had its
beginning from Fiesole, and its increase from colonies.

It is exceedingly probable, as Dante and Giovanni Villani show,
that the city of Fiesole, being situate upon the summit of the mountain, in order that her markets might be more frequented, and afford
greater accommodation for those who brought merchandise, would
appoint the place in which to hold them, not upon the hill, but in the
plain, between the foot of the mountain and the river Arno. I imagine
these markets to have occasioned the first erections that were made in
those places, and to have induced merchants to wish for commodious
warehouses for the reception of their goods, and which, in time,
became substantial buildings. And afterward, when the Romans,
having conquered the Carthaginians, rendered Italy secure from
foreign invasion, these buildings would greatly increase; for men
never endure inconveniences unless some powerful necessity compels
them. Thus, although the fear of war induces a willingness to occupy
places strong and difficult of access, as soon as the cause of alarm is
removed, men gladly resort to more convenient and easily attainable
localities. Hence the security to which the reputation of the Roman
republic gave birth caused the inhabitants, having begun in the manner described, to increase so much as to form a town; this was at first

called the Villa Arnina. After this occurred the civil wars between
Marius and Sylla; then those of Caesar and Pompey; and next those of
the murderers of Caesar, and the parties who undertook to avenge his
death. Therefore, first by Sylla, and afterward by the three Roman
citizens, who, having avenged the death of Caesar, divided the empire
among themselves, colonies were sent to Fiesole, which, either in part
or in whole, fixed their habitations in the plain, near to the then rising
town. By this increase the place became so filled with dwellings that it
might with propriety be enumerated among the cities of Italy.

There are various opinions concerning the derivation of the word
Florentia. Some suppose it to come from Florinus, one of the principal
persons of the colony; others think it was originally not Florentia, but
Fluentia, and suppose the word derived from *fluente*, or flowing of the
Arno; and in support of their opinion, adduce a passage from Pliny,
who says "The Fluentini are near the flowing of the Arno." This,
however, may be incorrect, for Pliny speaks of the locality of the
Florentini, not of the name by which they were known. And it seems
as if the word Fluentini were a corruption, because Frontinus and
Cornelius Tacitus, who wrote at nearly the same period as Pliny, call
them Florentia and Florentini; for in the time of Tiberius, they were
governed like the other cities of Italy. Besides, Cornelius refers to the
coming of ambassadors from the Florentines to beg of the emperor
that the waters of the Chiane might not be allowed to overflow their
country; and it is not at all reasonable that the city should have two
names at the same time. Therefore I think that, however derived, the
name was always Florentia, and that whatever the origin might be, it
occurred under the Roman empire and began to be noticed by writers
in the times of the first emperors.

When the Roman empire was afflicted by the barbarians, Florence
was destroyed by Totila, king of the Ostrogoths; and after a period of
two hundred and fifty years, rebuilt by Charlemagne; from whose
time, till the year 1215, she participated in the fortune of the rest of
Italy; and, during this period, first the descendants of Charles, then
the Berengarii, and lastly the German emperors, governed her.
. . . Nor could the Florentines, during those ages, increase in numbers, or effect anything worthy of memory, on account of the influence of those to whom they were subject. Nevertheless, in the year
1010, upon the feast of St. Romolo, a solemn day with the Fiesolani,
they took and destroyed Fiesole, which must have been performed
either with consent of the emperors, or during the interim from the

death of one to the creation of his successor, when all assumed a larger share of liberty. But when the pontiffs acquired greater influence, and the authority of the German emperors was in its wane, all the places of Italy governed themselves with less respect for the prince; so that, in the time of Henry III the mind of the country was divided between the emperor and the church. However, the Florentines kept themselves united till the year 1215, rendering obedience to the ruling power, and anxious only to preserve their own safety. But as the diseases which attack our bodies are more dangerous and mortal in proportion as they are delayed, so Florence, though late to take part in the sects of Italy, was afterward the more afflicted by them. The cause of her first division is well known, having been recorded by Dante and many other writers; I shall, however, briefly notice it.

Among the most powerful families of Florence were the Buondelmonti and the Uberti; next to these were the Amidei and the Donati. Of the Donati family there was a rich widow who had a daughter of exquisite beauty, for whom, in her own mind, she had fixed upon Buondelmonti, a young gentleman, the head of the Buondelmonti family, as her husband; but either from negligence or because she thought it might be accomplished at any time, she had not made known her intention, when it happened that the cavalier betrothed himself to a maiden of the Amidei family. This grieved the Donati widow exceedingly; but she hoped, with her daughter's beauty, to disturb the arrangement before the celebration of the marriage; and from an upper apartment, seeing Buondelmonti approach her house alone, she descended, and as he was passing she said to him, "I am glad to learn you have chosen a wife, although I had reserved my daughter for you"; and, pushing the door open, presented her to his view. The cavalier, seeing the beauty of the girl, which was very uncommon, and considering the nobility of her blood, and her portion not being inferior to that of the lady whom he had chosen, became inflamed with such an ardent desire to possess her that, not thinking of the promise given or the injury he committed in breaking it, or of the evils which his breach of faith might bring upon himself, said, "Since you have reserved her for me, I should be very ungrateful indeed to refuse her, being yet at liberty to choose"; and without any delay married her. As soon as the fact became known, the Amidei and the Uberti, whose families were allied, were filled with rage, and having assembled with many others, connections of the parties, they concluded that the injury could not be tolerated without disgrace and that the only vengeance proportionate to the enormity of the offense would be to put Buondelmonti to death. And although some took into consideration the evils that might ensue upon it, Mosca Lamberti said that those who talk of many things effect nothing, using that trite and common adage, *Cosa fatta capo ha.** Thereupon, they appointed to the execution of the murder Mosca himself, Stiatti Uberti, Lambertuccio Amidei, and Oderigo Fifanti, who, on the morning of Easter day, concealed themselves in a house of the Amidei, situate between the old bridge and S. Stefano's, and as Buondelmonti was passing upon a white horse, thinking it as easy a matter to forget an injury as reject an alliance, he was attacked by them at the foot of the bridge, and slain close by a statue of Mars. This murder divided the whole city; one party espousing the cause of the Buondelmonti, the other that of the Uberti; and as these families possessed men and means of defense, they contended with each other for many years, without one being able to destroy the other.

Florence continued in these troubles till the time of Frederick II who, being king of Naples, endeavored to strengthen himself against the church and, to give greater stability to his power in Tuscany, favored the Uberti and their followers, who, with his assistance, expelled the Buondelmonti; thus our city, as all the rest of Italy had long time been, became divided into Guelphs and Ghibellines. Besides the noble families on each side, each party was joined by many of the higher ranks of the people, so that the whole city was corrupted with this division. The Guelphs being expelled, took refuge in the Upper Val d'Arno, where part of their castles and strongholds were situated, and where they strengthened and fortified themselves against the attacks of their enemies. But upon the death of Frederick, the most unbiased men, and those who had the greatest authority with the people, considered that it would be better to effect the reunion of the city than, by keeping her divided, cause her ruin. They therefore induced the Guelphs to forget their injuries and return and the Ghibellines to lay aside their jealousies and receive them with cordiality.

*A thing done has a head (i.e., is finished).

Machiavellian History

Felix Gilbert

Machiavelli's *Florentine History* ends with the death of Lorenzo de'
Medici, the Magnificent, in 1492. As he was dying, lightning struck
the pinnacle of the Florentine cathedral, and Heaven gave many other
signs that dangers and ruin were to come over Italy.

When the events recounted on the last pages of the *Florentine
History* happened, Machiavelli was a young man of twenty-three. His
first-known political utterance is a letter written five years after the
death of the Magnificent. With ironical and contemptuous detachment
Machiavelli described two sermons which Girolamo Savonarola, the
dominating figure on the Florentine political scene after the overthrow
of the Medici regime in 1494, had preached in the church of San
Marco. To Machiavelli, Savonarola's prophecies of a glorious future
if the Florentines followed his advice and his vehement denunciations
of his enemies as criminals and sinners, seemed to be nothing but the
lies of a man desperately striving to keep his hold over the people. One
year later, in 1498, Savonarola had been executed and Machiavelli
had been elected a member of the Florentine chancellery as the
candidate of the faction which had instigated the fall of the monk and
his party.

For fourteen years, until the return of the Medici in 1512, Machiavelli had a brilliant political career, which was astounding because he
was neither rich nor a member of one of the great Florentine families.
This career was made possible by what in the terms of the time would

Felix Gilbert is a Harvard University historian who has specialized in historiography. He is the author of several books dealing with the early Italian historians.

have been called a combination of *virtu* and *fortuna*. Machiavelli's quick and sharp intelligence, his gay and lively wit, his passionate political interest and untiring energy were powerful reasons for gaining the attention of the Florentine politicians. But Machiavelli was helped by a particular constellation of circumstances. In 1502 an important constitutional reform was effected in Florence. From early times the head of the Florentine Republic had been the *Gonfaloniere* who presided over the highest magistrate, the *Signoria*;* the *Gonfaloniere* and the eight members of the *Signoria* were restricted to a term of two months. In 1502 the Florentines, recognizing the need for greater steadiness and continuity in their government, decided to transform the Gonfalonierate into a lifetime position. Piero Soderini, who had been elected to this office, tried to steer a middle course in the bitter party struggle between the wealthy patricians and the middle classes, both of which were equally intent on exclusive political control. In order to carry through an independent policy Soderini needed people who were not tied to any of the opposing groups. Machiavelli, the able young chancellery official, seemed to Soderini a most suitable instrument for undertaking those tasks to which men involved in party strife might bring a biased outlook. The relationship between the Gonfaloniere and the secretary in the chancellery soon became close, and Machiavelli was entrusted with a number of diplomatic missions which brought him in contact with many of the rulers and tyrants of Italy, and led him beyond the Alps into France and Germany. He became aware of the differences in strength between Italy and the large territorial states of Western and Central Europe, and he drew the conclusion that the principle reason for Italian impotence in the face of the foreign invasions was the Italian form of warfare: the reliance of the Italian governments on mercenary soldiers. After persuading Soderini to introduce a militia system which would provide Florence with soldiers recruited from her own countryside, Machiavelli was put in charge of the organization and training of this Florentine conscript army. During this period, although Machiavelli never became a man of great standing and independent influence, he had his hand in all the important affairs of Florentine politics.

*The chief executive branch and deliberative body in Florence, instituted in 1282. Only the Signoria had the right to initiate legislation. It could issue ordinances on its own authority and it could deal with criminal cases involving the state. It also had wide powers over foreign affairs. Throughout the republican period, a combination of direct election by lot (from names placed in purses) was practiced.

The active political role which Machiavelli had been able to play under Soderini was his misfortune when the republican regime collapsed and the Medici returned as rulers to Florence in 1512. Machiavelli had not been an apolitical civil servant like some of his colleagues in the chancellery whom the Medici left in their positions. And after Soderini's disgrace and exile, he was deprived of any powerful political support, for to many of the aristocrats who rallied around the Medici rulers, he had always been an interloper. Unfortunately, when a conspiracy against the Medici failed, Machiavelli's name was found on a document in which the conspirators had listed possible supporters of an anti-Medicean regime. With no patrician allies to intervene for him, Machiavelli was not only dismissed from his office, but tortured and exiled. His exile did not last long, nor was it very severe. From his small estate at Sant' Andrea in Percussina, the exile could still see Florence's eternal signposts, Brunelleschi's Dome and Giotto's Campanile, embedded in the soft hills of the Tuscan landscape.

To Machiavelli, the attractions of life in the country were a meager consolation for what he had lost. Almost every writer on Machiavelli quotes as the most revealing testimony of his state of mind the anguished outcry which he addressed to his friend Vettori after his dismissal: "Since Fortune has willed that I can't reason about the silk trade or the wool trade, nor about gains or losses, it is my way of life to reason about politics, and I must either make a vow of silence, or reason about these matters."

Machiavelli's life was politics. Thus he bent all his efforts towards changing the attitudes of the Medici so that they would re-employ him and once again allow him to be part of the "secrets and negotiations" of political life. For Guilano de' Medici, the amiable, elegant, but weak youngest son of Lorenzo the Magnificent . . . Machiavelli wrote a treatise which preached the need for single-minded energy and ruthlessness to a new ruler, and which has become world famous under the title of *The Prince*. Machiavelli pestered his friend Vettori, who was Florentine ambassador in Rome, to intervene in his behalf with Leo X until Vettori's replies to Machiavelli's letters became less and less frequent. Knowing the role which poets and writers played at the court of the Pope, Machiavelli became a writer of comedies, mixing into the traditional scheme of the classical comedy a strong ingredient of Florentine realism. Meaning and hope, however, returned to his life through the appreciation which he encountered among the younger generation of aristocrats who, under the watchful control of the Medici, guided Florentine politics. To these youths, Machiavelli talked about his hopes of renewing the power of Florence by infusing into the life of the city the spirit and the institutions which had made Rome great. On the urging of these younger men, he set down these ideas in *The Discourses on Livy* and *The Art of War*. Finally his friends and adherents succeeded in opening for Machiavelli the door to the Medici rulers. In November 1520 the Florentine University (*Studio*, as it was called), whose head was Cardinal Giulio de' Medici, the cousin of Leo X and the chief representative of the Medici interests in Florence, agreed to employ Machiavelli to write a history of Florence. In May 1525 when Machiavelli had arrived in his manuscript at the death of Lorenzo the Magnificent, he went to Rome and presented the completed part of his work to Giulio de' Medici, who by then had become Pope Clement VII. The Pope now began to use Machiavelli's talents in some minor political tasks into which Machiavelli threw himself with all his energy. There was no time for further work on the manuscript of the *Florentine History* before Machiavelli died rather suddenly in 1527. Thus the *Florentine History* remains Machiavelli's last important literary work.

Machiavelli's personal situation—his straitened circumstances and his longing for political activity—made him eager to undertake the job offered by the Florentine University. Whether the particular character of his commission was entirely congenial to his talents and inclinations is debatable, however. As an "official historian," Machiavelli had to fit his work into a traditional scheme and make it the vehicle for prescribed political tendency.

The Italians of the Renaissance had a definite conception of the nature and purpose of the work of an official historian. The clearest statement of these views can be found in a decree by which, five years before Machiavelli received his Florentine commission, the Venetian government had appointed an official historian to write the history of Venice. Reputation, it was said here, is an important factor in the political strength of a state and contributes to its power in peace and war; it must be maintained at all costs not only among contemporaries but also among future generations by means of "authentic, elegant and eloquent histories." Presented in an ornate and decorous form, these histories should magnify the accomplishments of the past and increase their fame without violating truth.

Although the official historian ought not to falsify the facts, he was not expected to undertake research which might uncover "new" facts or the "true" facts behind the appearances. "Truth" was not the primary concern; form was the central issue. The official historian ought to make the well-known facts more memorable through the art of his presentation. In an age in which humanism was the dominating intellectual force, "imitation," the adoption of the formal pattern of classical works to the discussion of modern issues, was regarded as an essential element in scholarly activity. Like the Roman historians who formed the image of Rome for all later times, the official historian of the Renaissance was to hand down to posterity an equally lasting and monumental image of the city for which he worked. He was to fit its history into a Livian dress. Like Livy, he was expected to organize his history in a number of books. Each would begin with a general reflection. Events needing emphasis were to be punctuated by carefully worked-out speeches placed in the mouths of the chief actors, and which could be read as if they were brief independent treatises. The purpose of the history was a moral one: it showed what a citizen ought to do and what he ought not to do. The work was to fulfill the aim expressed in the classical dictum that "history teaches by examples."

The official history of a city was considered to be one great continuing enterprise. There was only one official historian at a time, and a successor was expected to go on from the point where his predecessor had ended. Two famous humanists, Leonardo Bruni Aretino and Poggio Bracciolini, both of whom had been heads of the Florentine chancellery, had written officially approved histories of Florence. Their accounts had not gone beyond the first half of the fifteenth century. Machiavelli was expected therefore to take up the story of events where they had left off. This was the time when the Medici had come to power. An account of the period in which the Medici had played the leading role in Florence was naturally of particular interest to Cardinal Giulio de' Medici, through whose influence Machiavelli had received his commission. The political implications of his task placed Machiavelli in a serious conflict of conscience: although he was willing to serve the Medici in order to earn his livelihood and to be close to the centers of political power, his intellectual honesty and his convictions were so strong that he could not easily foreswear his republican sympathies and become a literary propagandist for the Medici tyranny. Machiavelli complained about his dilemma to the two men whom we now regard, next to Machiavelli himself, as the greatest political thinkers of the Italian Renaissance. To his young friend Donato Giannotti, who became the owner of the original manuscript of Machiavelli's *Florentine History*, he confessed that he could not write the history from Cosimo de' Medici's rise to power to the death of Lorenzo the Magnificent as he would write it if he were free from personal concerns and obligations. To Francesco Guicciardini, who was then governor of the Romagna, Machiavelli wrote that he would gladly pay ten soldi or even more if he could have him at his side and get his advice about how to handle the ticklish subject of the Medici rule without too much praise or too much denigration.

The traditional literary scheme into which Machiavelli had fit his work, and the political conditions under which he wrote it must be kept firmly in mind while reading Machiavelli's *Florentine History*. They explain Machiavelli's method, and they influenced the organization of the work.

Although modern scholarly standards should not be expected from a historical work of the sixteenth century, the beginnings of critical historical scholarship can be traced back to the historiography of the Italian Renaissance. Fifteen years after Machiavelli wrote his *Florentine History*, Francesco Guicciardini composed his *History of Italy*, which through his use of documentary sources and through his careful examination and evaluation of narrative reports, pointed the way towards the adoption of a critical method in historical writing. Machiavelli's *Florentine History* does not show such modern features. When previous historians gave divergent reports of the same event, Machiavelli, unlike some of his contemporaries and some earlier historians, did not mention these differing accounts and state what seemed to him to be the most plausible version of the actual happenings. Machiavelli followed one author at a time. Long stretches of his work are based on the universal history of the humanist Biondo, others on the Florentine chronicle of Villani, and still others on the Florentine histories of Bruni or Cavalcanti. Machiavelli was content to condense the material which these writers offered, and to present it in a stylistically elevated form. His attempts to depict the Italians of the fifteenth century in classical poses appear somewhat ridiculous; it can hardly be imagined that Venetian statesmen, renowned for their political coolness and wisdom, broke into tears after hearing a speech by a Florentine ambassador.

The organization of Machiavelli's *Florentine History* is rather artificial and complicated. The first book surveys Italian politics from the end of the Roman Empire to the beginning of the fifteenth century. Then follow three books describing Florentine domestic developments to the time of the rise of the Medici in 1434. The second half of the work, which also contains four books, is devoted to the period of the Medici rule in Florence; here foreign policy and domestic events are interwoven. Machiavelli justified this form of organization by saying that after reading the Florentine histories of Bruni and Poggio, he discovered that ''in the descriptions of the wars waged by the Florentines against foreign princes and peoples they had been most exact, but upon the subject of civil discord and internal strifes and their consequences they had been entirely silent, or had written far too briefly about them.'' Thus he decided to fill the gap which they had left and to give a narration of Florentine domestic events from the early times of the city. However, because Machiavelli was well aware that the course of domestic events was decisively influenced by wars and foreign policy, he thought it necessary to survey the latter in an introductory first book. Domestic history probably held a great fascination for Machiavelli because he believed that it could illustrate permanent political problems and instruct future generations. This form of organization also served another purpose. By going back to the foundations of the city in his account of Florentine history, he could reduce the space which he would have to give to the Medici regime; he was able to be less detailed about the issues which involved a clash between his personal convictions and his interest in gaining the favor of the Medici. The manner in which Machiavelli then dealt with the history of Florence in the Medici period was most ingenious. Although he had indicated that he would give equal attention to Florentine domestic and foreign policy, foreign policy and wars constitute the main substance of this part of Machiavelli's work, and through this shift of focus from domestic to foreign policy, Machiavelli's brevity about the Florentine domestic situation under the Medici appears less noticeable. To the limited extent that he wrote about domestic politics in Florence under the Medici, he concentrated on the various attempts to overthrow their regime. By ridiculing the weaknesses, stupidity, and vacillations of the conspirators, Machiavelli was able to present the Medici as being far superior to their enemies; but he refrained from making a directly positive statement about the Medicean system of government. Certainly, Cosimo and Lorenzo de' Medici had to be displayed in a favorable light. After Machiavelli narrated the deaths of Cosimo and Lorenzo, he emphasized their importance by lengthy characterizations. It should be noted, however, that these evaluations of Cosimo and Lorenzo are given in the form of an eulogy, praising their personal qualities rather than their system of ruling Florence. In this ingenious manner in which Machiavelli maintained a precarious balance between the flattery demanded by his patrons and his own intellectual convictions, one can see a truly Machiavellian mind at work.

The prescribed form to which Machiavelli had to adjust his work also had the effect of giving his *Florentine History* its unique value and of making it an expression of his political thought. Because Machiavelli's *Florentine History* was not intended to accomplish what we usually expect from a work of history—namely, to present a new picture of the past on the basis of original research—but rather to present the well-known facts in a new form, Machiavelli could not proceed selectively. The *Florentine History* does not provide an even coverage of the course of events. Certain events and periods are touched upon only lightly; others, which fascinated Machiavelli, are worked out in great detail; some take on the character of short historical essays in which Machiavelli set forth his own ideas. For instance, of fourteenth century events, Machiavelli wrote about the tyranny of the Duke of Athens and the revolt of the Ciompi with much care and elaboration; in modern terms these accounts might be called sociological studies on the rise of tyrannies and on the course of revolutions. In his description of the fifteenth century, Machiavelli reported the campaigns of the Italian *condottieri* with infinite detail; he exaggerated their cautiousness and the "bloodlessness" of their battles in order to prove his thesis of the inefficiency of Italian military organization. The classical custom of beginning the various books of an historical work with general reflections and of embellishing history with long speeches offered Machiavelli another opportunity for propounding his own political views. The *Florentine History* contains concise statements of some of Machiavelli's favorite ideas: the constitutional cycle, the vitalizing effects of party struggles, and the amoral character of successful political action. Some of these ideas are stated in the *Florentine History* more forcefully and bluntly than any other place in Machiavelli's writings. As an expression of Machiavelli's political thought, the *Florentine History* takes its place next to *The Prince* and *The Discourses*.

Interest in Machiavelli's political ideas should not prevent us from recognizing value in his treatment of the subject matter. By limiting himself to an account of the accepted facts of Florentine history, Machiavelli's presentation contained what the Florentines of the sixteenth century expected to hear about their history. Thus we learn what the Florentines regarded as the distinguishing features of their city and as its most outstanding achievements: about the institutions under which they lived and the manner in which these institutions were believed to have originated, and about the decisive steps and triumphs in the process of extending Florentine power over Tuscany. It is characteristic of the Florentine feeling for the inextricable connection between political power and cultural achievement that even in this book which is foremost a political history, Dante and Brunelleschi, Ficino and Pico della Mirandola are mentioned at the appropriate places, and that we are made continuously aware of the setting in which the actors lived: of the villas on the surrounding hills, of Florence's graceful churches and severe palaces, and at the end, in a flash of lightning, the structure dominating the entire city—the dome of the Cathedral.

It is significant, therefore, that the tone of Machiavelli's *Florentine History* is not one of praise and pride. It is permeated by a pessimistic mood, an almost tragic despair. To Machiavelli, the work of the Roman historians offered more than a formal pattern for imitation. It was the spirit of Rome which served Machiavelli as a measure for evaluating the story of Florence. Machiavelli never ceased to ask why his own city did not come up to the standard which Rome had set: a free republic of virtuous citizens competing for fame and glory in the service of their government. In the history of Florence Machiavelli found again and again private ambitions, egoism, and thirst for personal power. He had seen these vices at work when he had served the republic in the chancellery. It was in the light of the knowledge he had gained then that he saw the Florentine history of the preceding centuries. Although in form and method Machiavelli's *Florentine History* remains traditional, the spirit with which he approached his task was that of a modern historian: to find in the past an explanation for the present.

The Seeds of Civil Strife

Thomas A. Trollope

Everybody who has ever heard of the history of Florence knows, in a general way, that a very large portion of that history is occupied with the never-ending dissensions and party feuds of the citizens. And they have heard these spoken of by names taken from the party rallying cries, which have become as well known in history as they once were in the streets of Florence. Who has not heard of the enmities of Bianchi and Neri; of Guelphs and Ghibellines . . . ? And in reading the historians of the different ages of the Commonwealth, each outbreak of hostilities will be found attributed to some special event, which is stated to have led to all the mischief. But an examination of the entire course of that history will lead the student of a later day to conclude that such divisions must be attributed to some underlying cause, of larger and deeper significance than any to which they are attributed. . . . A careful consideration of the political bearing of that incessant partisan warfare will, it seems to me, lead us one step further than this and bring us to the conviction that the real underlying cause of the differently named party feuds which divided the republic were throughout the entire course of the history one and the same.

These dissensions were in fact, and at the bottom, phases of the great quarrel as old as humanity, as widely spread as the world, the quarrel between the few who have, and would keep, the high places and the good things of society and the many who would share them. It is a quarrel that suffers truce only in climes and ages in which mankind

THOMAS TROLLOPE (1810–1892), was the brother of the noted Victorian novelist Anthony Trollope. An associate of Charles Dickens's and an accomplished novelist and biographer, Trollope became an early expatriate. He settled in Florence in 1843.

are making no onward movement, and have fallen furthest from our highest ideal of human destinies. It is a quarrel that was waged more or less actively in every part of Europe, in the ages of which we are speaking, but which was inflamed into acute excess and violent eruption in Florence by certain circumstances peculiar to that social organization . . . in Florence it produced devastating lacerations of the body social, and ultimately its destruction and extinction.

The disaster is attributable, I think, to two causes. In the first place it was due to the illegitimate pretensions and immoderate violence of those who sought to rise, and especially to their conception of the nature of the advantages to be attained by such rising; to their having conceived liberty to consist not so much in escaping from the undue interference of others with their own volitions as in attaining the power to interfere with the volitions of their neighbors; not so much in being themselves free from tyrannical government as in being admitted to become sharers in the power of tyrannizing. If the acts and pretensions of the Florentine populace at the period of their most successful attempts to participate in the governing power be examined, it will be found that they made no demand to the effect that freedom should be increased, that the citizens should be less shackled by governmental interference, less hedged about by rules and regulations, less exposed to espionage. They only insisted that a larger number should have the right to impose the shackles, make the rules and regulations. . . . In a community, where such notions prevailed, even if every smallest governmental act had been voted by an assembly of the entire population, individual freedom would have gained nothing. This was the first cause.

This evil worked to a more direct, decisive, and complete ruin in Florence, by reasons of the second of the two causes. This was the smallness of the community, and the consequent directness and immediateness of the action exercised by individuals on the social organization; to which is to be added, as arising from the same circumstance, that element of personal hatred which played so large a part in Florentine history, and which cannot exist where men are not brought into close personal contact with each other. A revolution, a rebellion, a disturbance in Florence, had all the intensity and peril of a mutiny on board ship, the dangers of which are increased tenfold by the confinement of the explosive elements within a small space. And in reading of the results produced in Florence by the will of an individual, or of a small knot of individuals, it is always necessary to remember and make allowance for this fact.

It is sufficient for my present purpose, while noting that already . . . the poison of civil discord had shown itself, to have drawn attention to the law, which will be found to contain the true explanation of this large portion of Florentine history, and of the deplorable failure of one of the most noteworthy tentatives at social organization ever seen in the world.

The appointment of a *Podestà* as chief magistrate of the city in 1207, which marks the commencement of the second century of the life of the Commonwealth, is spoken of by several chroniclers as the first occasion on which an officer of that name was known in Florence. But it would seem that such was not the case. The title is met with in some of the Lombard cities at a much earlier date; and an officer with that name is unquestionably mentioned in authentic Florentine documents of a date previous to the thirteenth century. The explanation of the contradiction, however, seems to be found in the fact, that in 1207 a *foreign* Podestà was appointed for the first time in Florence.

And in truth, the whole interest and importance of the innovation lies in this, that the new chief magistrate was to be thenceforward necessarily a foreigner. The adoption of one title or another would have been a matter of small moment; but the opinion maturely adopted by a free community, that they could not venture to entrust judicial power over their persons and property to any man among themselves, is a very curious and suggestive circumstance. . . .

The chroniclers who record this innovation agree together completely in the motives to which they assign the change. It was found that no citizen of Florence could be trusted to withstand, in the administration of civil and criminal justice, the influences of fear or friendship or interest or pity. A Florentine judge would decide a suit unjustly in favor of his friend. Therefore it was determined to have a judge who had no friends among his suitors. A Florentine magistrate would be deterred from putting the laws in action against a criminal for fear of the subsequent vengence of that criminal or his friends. Therefore a stranger must be brought from a distance to do this odious duty, who, returning at the end of a year to his own distant home, would be safe from such danger, and therefore uninfluenced by such fears.

The measure has been praised as indicating a determination on the part of the community to secure purity of justice and equal administration of the law and as a wise and ingenious method to the attainment of this end. But I confess that the provision suggests to my mind reflections of a different kind. Doubtless the Florentines objected to leave their property at the mercy of a magistrate who could not be trusted to give a sentence at variance with his own or his friends' interest; or to entrust the protection of their lives and persons to a judge who feared to put the law in action against powerful or desperate evil-doers. But surely the remedy adopted—not to insist on the great probability that it would prove inefficacious—admits the existence of a very unsound condition in the body politic; while the disposition to acquiesce in that condition, and to accept it as a normal and inevitable incident of human society, betokens an exceedingly unsatisfactory tone in the public mind and conscience, and discloses ominously discouraging symptoms of the prevailing views respecting the objects to which a community should direct its efforts. A pack of hounds may obtain fairness in the distribution of their rations by submission to the huntsman; but they will nonetheless remain hounds to the end of the chapter. . . .

The events of these first years of the thirteenth century continue to be of the same kind as those which made up the history of the growing Commonwealth during the preceding period—fresh destructions of feudal castles, fresh encroachments on neighboring jurisdictions, and almost unceasing pushing back of the frontier. What mainly characterizes the new century, however, is an increased frequency of war with the neighboring rival cities. The course of continual aggrandizement on which the Commonwealth had been advancing for several generations past made it evident that such must before long be the case. The Florentine frontier had already . . . advanced more than halfway towards Siena. There it met the advanced posts of another vigorous and growing community, a rival of its own sort. And a series of struggles commenced with a far more equally matched adversary than any with whom Florence had yet contended. Henceforward, accordingly, the military career of the Commonwealth was by no means so unchequered by reverses as it had been while engaged in sweeping from the surface of the soil one after the other the castles of the feudal nobility.

Siena was no mouthful to be snatched, swallowed, and assimilated after the fashion in which Florence had disposed of the feudal tenures which had stood in her path. The enmity therefore, which was sure to arise between the two communes when brought face to face with each other, did not assume the form of an attack with the avowed object of conquest, but broke out on occasion of questions of frontier line and jealousies of the relations of either party with other smaller communes.

The small but strongly situated town of Montepulciano, perched on top of its lofty hill, after the fashion of the old Etruscan cities, the site of one of which it occupies, is much nearer to Siena than to Florence. It lies indeed on the other side of Siena away to the southeastward, towards Perugia, and is in fact little less than halfway from Florence to Rome. The surrounding powers therefore, of every kind, whether princes or cities, might well begin to ask where the aggressions and pretensions of this upstart Florence were likely to stop when that ambitious community announced its intention of taking Montepulciano "under its protection" and marched an army to prevent Siena from meddling with it in any way. Already, once before, a peace had been made with Siena on condition that she was in no way to interfere with Montepulciano. But in the first year of the new Podestà's rule, Siena broke the treaty by attacking her weaker neighbor. Whereupon Florence at once marched out against the Sienese forces and defeated them at Montalto, a fortress on the Sienese frontier to the eastward, about halfway between Siena and Arezzo, leaving many of the enemy dead on the field, and bringing back with them to Florence 1331 prisoners.

Siena sued for peace; and it was granted on condition that she should rebuild the walls of Montepulciano, and also those of Montalcino, another hill town about twenty miles to the south of Siena which Florence chose equally to protect and that she should promise not to make war on either of these two communities for the future. Both of these two little "protected" cities were but outposts of the Florentine power, which thus had already hemmed in Siena well-nigh on all sides.

Looked at from without, while she was thus victoriously and proudly dictating conditions of peace to neighboring cities, and pushing the limits of her power halfway towards Rome, all appearances testified to the wonderful vigor and prosperity of the young state and called the attention of Europe to the advent among the nations of a newcomer already evidently destined to occupy a place of primary importance among them. But within the walls our attention is called to events of a very different character and significance.

In the year 1215 it chanced that a quarrel occurred at a festival between some young nobles of Florence. It was an event of as frivolous, and apparently unimportant, a character as thousands of other such broils; but this obscure quarrel has been treated by the whole body of Florentine historians as the origin and starting point of that series of civil wars which shaped the entire future fortunes of the community and shook to its center the whole fabric of society throughout central Italy. The story of it has become memorable therefore in Florentine annals, and has been rendered famous not only by the writers of history, but by many generations of poets, painters, novelists, and sculptors.

Messer Mazzino Tegrini de' Mazzinghi had been admitted to the order of knighthood; and about the beginning of the year 1215, a festival was to be given to celebrate the occasion. . . . Among the guests was the young and remarkably handsome Buondelmonte de' Buondelmonti . . . considered one of the most desirable sons-in-law by the matchmaking mothers of Florence.

Young Buondelmonte had taken with him to the festival his friend Uberto degli Infangati—Hubert the Mudbedraggled, of that ilk. While they were sitting at table, "a jester," the chronicle says, snatched a plate of meat from before this Hubert, who was so much nettled at the impertinence that when Oddo Arringhi dei Fifanti, one of the guests, proceeded to banter him, he lost his temper completely, and in reply to something said by Oddo, gave him the lie direct. Whereupon Oddo seized a plate from the table and hurled it at Hubert's head.

Hitherto Buondelmonte had not been concerned in the quarrel in any wise, but he seems to have thought that it was incumbent on him to resent the insult thus publicly offered to his friend; and as soon as the "tables were withdrawn" he stabbed Oddo with his poniard. On this, the party broke up in anger and confusion; and the special friends and connections of the wounded man, returning to Florence together, took counsel respecting the satisfaction to be exacted from the assailant. . . . It was agreed that reconciliation would be effected by a marriage between Buondelmonte and the niece of the injured man, Oddo Arringhi; and it would seem that this arrangement was at once acceded to by Buondelmonte, inasmuch as it is recorded that the betrothal was fixed to take place on the next day but one.

But on that intervening day, while the bridegroom was riding through the city, as he passed by the mansion of the Donati family,

Monna Gualdrada, the wife of Donati, called to him from her window to alight and come up to speak with her. There was a marriageable daughter too in the house of the Donati, and Monna Gualdrada had long cherished the hope of obtaining the handsome scion of the Buondelmonti for a son-in-law. So she spoke after the manner of would-be mothers-in-law in all ages and climes—taunted him bitterly with taking a wife at the bidding and for fear of the Amidei and the Lamberti—contrasted the wife thus forced upon him with the bride she had, as she declared, long reserved for him, having with a view to his alliance already rejected many brilliant offers—and finished by throwing open the door of an inner chamber in which her daughter was sitting and telling him to look at the bride who might yet be his if he had but the courage to take her.

The lady of the Amidei family whom he had agreed to marry as a fine for having been too ready with his dagger was, we are told, not handsome; and the chroniclers all dwell on the matchless beauty of the young Donati. The result was that the young man thus sorely tempted, became, ''by the devil's assistance,'' as Villani says, desperately enamored of the beautiful girl thus offered for his acceptance; told Monna Gualdrada that he did dare to please himself, despite all the Amidei in Florence; and the next day, which was Thursday, the 10th of February, while all the parties to the other engagement were waiting at the house of the Amidei for the ceremony of the betrothal, went publicly and betrothed himself to the beautiful Donati.

It could hardly be supposed that such an insult as this would be allowed to pass without signal vengeance. All the friends of the Amidei assembled . . . Mosca de' Lamberti warned the meeting against . . . any half measures. ''Beat him, or mark him as you will,'' said he; ''but if you stop there you may as well take thought for your own graves. No! he deserves death. Let him die! *Che cosa fatta capo ha!*'' This counsel prevailed. . . . The faithless bridegroom was doomed to be slain on his return from the church with his newly wedded bride.

The wedding took place in the church of Santa Felicita, near the foot of the Ponte Vecchio, on the morning of Easter Sunday. After the ceremony, the wedding party, returning over the Ponte Vecchio, had to pass before the houses of the Amidei. The conspirators were all gathered there; and it could hardly be that Buondelmonte could have seen that knot of the men he had deceived and so grievously insulted standing there with their lowering faces and fancied that he was to ride by them in his gala triumph with his bride, unquestioned. Nevertheless, he came riding on in the pride of his beauty, "clad in jacket and mantle of white silk, with a garland on his head," till he came in front of the home of the lady he had jilted.

Then with a shout, Schiatta de'Lamberti sprung out into the street, and with one blow of an iron mace brought the gay rider from his saddle to the ground. In an instant he was surrounded by the rest of the band; and Oddo Arringhi, the man whom he had wounded, and whose niece he had wronged, cut his throat with his dagger.

The assassins retired to their fortress houses and left the bridal party to form itself as it might into a funeral procession. "Great was the uproar in the city. He was placed on a bier; and his wife took her station on the bier also, and held his head in her lap, violently weeping; and in that manner they carried him through the whole of the city; and on that day began the ruin of Florence."*

The last phrase of the above citation marks the significance which the Tuscan historians have attributed to this incident, and the important place that has always been assigned to it in Florentine history.
. . . From this quarrel began the great, fatal, and world-famous division of Florence into the parties of Guelph and Ghibelline. Dante goes so far as to consider the conduct of Buondelmonte in this affair so entirely the cause of the evils that arose from the Guelph and Ghibelline wars that, had that cause not existed, no such misfortunes would have arisen. He exclaims—

"O Buondelmonte, how ill thou didst in evading the alliance with the Amidei by listening to the counsels of another. Many would now be happy who are in sorrow, if God had given thee a victim to the river Ema, when first thou crossedst it to come to the city."

Yet the historians admit that the party names of Guelph and Ghibelline were known in Florence long before; but they say that not till then did the city divide itself into two hostile camps under those rallying cries . . . the Florentines understood that Ghibelline meant attachment to the Empire in opposition to the Church, and Guelph attachment to the Church in opposition to the Empire. But it would be a mistake tending to prevent a right understanding of the future course of Florentine politics to suppose that enthusiasm in favor of either of these two institutions, or hatred against either of them, had much to do with the party strife that divided Florence. The antagonism between

*All the historians relate the facts without any material discrepancy. But the above details have been taken from a little chronicle by a contemporary, or nearly contemporary, writer belonging to the Buondelmonti family.

the civil and the ecclesiastical power is in truth as old as ecclesiastical encroachment and must be as perennial as the existence of Church temporalities. But the quarrel of Guelph with Ghibelline in Florence was the expression of a still wider spread and more perennial conflict. It was the struggle of those who have, and would keep to themselves, wealth, power, station, and pre-eminence, with those who have not, and would acquire all these things. The Ghibellines were the old Imperial nobles, who, whether more anciently or more recently incorporated into the body of Florentine citizens, formed the aristocracy of the social body, and were naturally Imperialist in their sympathies. . . . The body of people were Guelphs, naming themselves after the party professing attachment to the Church only because the Papacy was in opposition to the Empire.

Assuredly all this would have happened in no very material circumstance differently from what did happen, even had the first Buondelmonte who ever came to Florence perished in the Ema on his way thither. It can hardly, I think, be doubted that the writers who have represented all this great series of social developments as arising from the fault of Buondelmonte, and the punishment of it, have fallen into the common error of mistaking for a cause that which was only a symptom or manifestation of a condition produced by causes of much wider operation.

It is very significant that the Buondelmonti family, which had previously been Ghilbelline in its politics and sympathies, as was naturally to be expected from its feudal origin, became at this time, and from henceforth remained, Guelph. The meaning of this is that, in order to obtain vengeance for murder of their kinsman by those who were, as we have seen, all Ghibellines, they found it necessary to take advantage of the passions of the opposite party. Had the division of the city taken its rise from the Buondelmonti quarrel, the citizens would have divided themselves differently, and no such change of political party would have been needed. Nobles and people alike would have espoused either side of the quarrel according to their personal sympathies and connections. But this change of party by the Buondelmonti proves clearly that the hatreds arising from the murder of their kinsman were but engrafted on pre-existing enmities. . . .

The Buondelmonte tragedy was a spark falling on open gunpowder —the scratch on the finger of the fevered and unhealthy body politic; and in that sense, but in no other, I think it may be called the cause of the civil wars which followed it in Florence.

Eulogy to
"The Laurell'd Dante:
Poet of Heaven and Hell"
(1265–1321)

Giovanni Villani

In the month of July, 1321, died the Poet Dante Alighieri of Florence,
in the city of Ravenna in Romagna, after his return from an embassy to
Venice for the Lords of Polenta with whom he resided; and in Ravenna
before the door of the principal church he was interred with high
honor, in the habit of a poet and great philosopher. He died in
banishment from the community of Florence, at the age of about
fifty-six. This Dante was an honorable and ancient citizen of Porta
San Piero at Florence, and our neighbor; and his exile from Florence
was on the occasion of Charles of Valois, of the house of France,
coming to Florence in 1301, and the expulsion of the White party. . . .
The said Dante was of the supreme governors of our city, and of that
party although a Guelph; and therefore without any other crime was
with the said White party expelled and banished from Florence; and he
went to the University of Bologna, and into many parts of the world.
This was a great and learned person in almost every science, although
a layman; he was a consummate poet and philosopher and rhetorician;
as perfect in prose and verse as he was in public speaking a most noble
orator; in rhyming excellent, with the most polished and beautiful
style that ever appeared in our language up to his time or since. He
wrote in his youth the book of *La Vita Nuova*, and afterwards when in
exile made twenty moral and amorous canzonets very excellent, and

GIOVANNI VILLANI (1275–1348), Florentine historian. Villani wrote a history of
Florence and was a participant in many of the events he describes. His *History*, written
in Italian prose, served to establish the Tuscan language as the standard of Italy.
Villani died in the plague recounted in Boccaccio's *Decameron*.

amongst other things three noble epistles: one he sent to the Florentine government, complaining of his undeserved exile; another to the Emperor Henry when he was at the siege of Brescia, reprehending him for his delay, and almost prophesying; the third to the Italian cardinals during the vacancy after the death of Pope Clement, urging them to agree in electing an Italian Pope; all in Latin, with noble precepts and excellent sentences and authorities, which were much commended by the wise and learned. And he wrote the *Commedia*, where, in polished verse and with great subtile arguments, moral, natural, astrological, philosophical, and theological, with new and beautiful figures, similes, and poetical graces, he composed and treated in a hundred chapters or cantos of the existence of hell, purgatory, and paradise; so loftily as may be said of it, that whoever is of subtile intellect may by his said treatise perceive and understand. He was well pleased in this poem to blame and cry out, in the manner of poets, in some places perhaps more than he ought to have done; but it may be that his exile made him do so. He also wrote the *Monarchia*, where he treats of the office of popes and emperors. And he began a comment on fourteen of the above-named moral canzonets in the vulgar tongue, which in consequence of his death is found imperfect except on three, which to judge from what is seen would have proved a lofty, beautiful, subtile, and most important work; because it is equally ornamented with noble opinions and fine philosophical and astrological reasoning. Besides these he composed a little book which he entitled *De Vulgari Eloquentia*, of which he promised to make four books, but only two are to be found, perhaps in consequence of his early death; where, in powerful and elegant Latin and good reasoning, he rejects all the vulgar tongues of Italy. This Dante, from his knowledge, was somewhat presumptuous, harsh, and disdainful, like an ungracious philosopher; he scarcely deigned to converse with laymen; but for his other virtues, science, and worth as a citizen, it seems but reasonable to give him perpetual remembrance in this our chronicle; nevertheless, his noble works, left to us in writing, bear true testimony of him, and honorable fame to our city.

Letter to a Friend in Florence, 1315

Dante Alighieri

From your letter, which I received with due respect and affection, and have diligently studied, I learn with gratitude how my recall to Florence has been the object of your care and concern; and I am the more beholden to you therefor, inasmuch as it rarely happens that an exile finds friends. My reply to what you have written, although perchance it be not of such tenor as certain faint hearts would desire, I earnestly beg may be carefully examined and considered by you before judgment be passed upon it.

I gather, then, from the letter of your nephew and mine, as well as from those of sundry other friends, that, by the terms of a decree lately promulgated in Florence touching the pardon of the exiles, I may receive pardon, and be permitted to return forthwith, on condition that I pay a certain sum of money, and submit to the stigma of the oblation—two propositions, my Father, which in sooth are as ridiculous as they are ill-advised—ill-advised, that is to say, on the part of those who have communicated them, for in your letter, which was more discreetly and cautiously formulated, no hint of such conditions was conveyed.

This, then, is the gracious recall of Dante Alighieri to his native city, after the miseries of well-nigh fifteen years of exile! This is the reward of innocence manifest to all the world, and of the sweat and toil of unremitting study! Far be from a familiar of philosophy such a senseless act of abasement as to submit himself to be presented as the oblation, like a felon in bonds, as . . . other infamous wretches have done! Far be it from the preacher of justice, after suffering wrong, to pay of his money to those that wronged him, as though they had deserved well of him!

No! my father, not by this path will I return to my native city. If some other can be found, in the first place by yourself and thereafter by others, which does not derogate from the fame and honor of Dante, that will I tread with no lagging steps. But if by no such path Florence may be entered, then will I enter Florence never. What! can I not anywhere gaze upon the face of the sun and the stars? can I not under any sky contemplate the most precious truths, without I first return to Florence, disgraced, nay dishonored, in the eyes of my fellow citizens? Assuredly bread will not fail me!

Account of the Discovery of the First Seven and Last Thirteen Cantos of *The Divine Comedy*

Giovanni Boccaccio

. . . Dante had a sister who was married to one of our citizens, Leon Poggi, by whom she had several children. Among these was one called Andrea, who wonderfully resembled Dante in the outline of his features, and in his height and figure; and he also walked rather stooping, as Dante is said to have done. He was a weak man, but with naturally good feelings, and his language and conduct were regular and praiseworthy. And I having become intimate with him, he often spoke to me of Dante's habits and ways; but among those things which I delight most in recollecting is what he told me relating to that of which we are now speaking. He said then that Dante belonged to the party of Viere de' Cerchi, and was one of its great leaders; and when Vieri and many of his followers left Florence, Dante left that city also and went to Verona. And on account of this departure, through the solicitation of the opposite party, Messer Vieri, and all who had left Florence, especially the principal persons, were considered as rebels, and had their persons condemned and their property confiscated. When the people heard this, they ran to the houses of those proscribed, and plundered all that was within them. It is true that Dante's wife, Madonna Gemma, fearing this, and by the advice of some of her friends and relations, had withdrawn from his house some chests containing certain precious things, and Dante's writings along with them, and had put them in a place of safety. And not satisfied with having plundered the houses of the proscribed, the most powerful partisans of the opposite faction occupied their possessions—some taking one and some another—and thus Dante's house was occupied.

But after five years or more had elapsed, and the city was more rationally governed, . . . persons began to question their rights, on different grounds, to what had been the property of the exiles, and they were heard. Therefore Madonna Gemma was advised to demand back Dante's property, on the ground that it was her dowry. She, to prepare this business, required certain writings and documents which were in one of the chests, which, in the violent plunder of the effects, she had sent away, nor had she ever since removed them from the place where she had deposited them. For this purpose, this Andrea said, she had sent for him, and, as Dante's nephew, had entrusted him with the keys of these chests, and had sent him with a lawyer to search for the required papers; while the lawyer searched for these, he, Andrea, among other of Dante's writings, found many sonnets, *canzoni*, and such similar pieces. But among them what pleased him the most was a sheet in which, in Dante's handwriting, seven cantos were written; and therefore he took it and carrried it off with him, and read it over and over again; and although he understood but little of it, still it appeared to him a very fine thing; and therefore he determined, in order to know what it was, to carry it to an esteemed man of our city, who in those times was a much celebrated reciter of verses, whose name was Dino.

It pleased Dino marvellously; and having made copies of it for several of his friends, and knowing that the composition was merely begun, and not completed, he thought that it would be best to send it to Dante, and at the same time to beg him to follow up his design, and to finish it; and having inquired, and ascertained that Dante was at this time in the Lunigiana, with a noble man of the family of Malaspina, . . . who was a man of understanding, and who had a singular friendship for him, he thought of sending it, not to Dante himself, but to the Marquis, in order that he should show it to him: and so Dino did, begging him that, as far as it lay in his power, he would exert his good offices to induce Dante to continue and finish his work.

The seven aforesaid cantos having reached the Marquis's hands, and having marvellously pleased him, he showed them to Dante; and having heard from him that they were his composition, he entreated him to continue to work. To this it is said that Dante answered: ''I really supposed that these, along with many of my other writings and effects, were lost when my house was plundered, and therefore I had given up all thoughts of them. But since it has pleased God that they should not be lost, and he has thus restored them to me, I shall endeavor, as far as I am able, to proceed with them according to my first design." And recalling his old thoughts, and resuming his interrupted work, he speaks thus in the beginning of the eighth canto: "My wondrous history I here renew."

Now precisely the same story, almost without any alteration, has been related to me by a Dino Perino, one of our citizens and an intelligent man, who, according to his own account, had been on the most friendly and familiar terms with Dante; but he so far alters the story, that he says, "It was not Andrea Leoni, but I myself, who was sent by the lady to the chests for the papers, and that found these seven cantos and took them to Dino, reciter of verses." I do not know to which of these I ought to give most credit, but whichever of them spoke the truth, still a doubt occurs to me in what they say, which I cannot in any manner solve to my satisfaction; and my doubt is this. The poet introduces Ciacco into the sixth canto, and makes him prophesy, that before three years had elapsed from the moment he was speaking, the party to which Dante belonged should fall, and so it happened. But we know the removal of the Bianchi from office, and their departure from Florence, all happened at once; and therefore, if the author departed at that time, how could he have written this,—and not only this, but another canto after it? . . .

And those friends he left behind him, his sons and his disciples, having searched at many times and for several months everything of his writing, to see whether he had left any conclusion to his work, could find in nowise any of the remaining cantos; his friends generally being much mortified that God had not at least lent him so long to the world, that he might have been able to complete the small remaining part of his work; and having sought so long and never found it, they remained in despair. Jacopo and Piero were sons of Dante, and each of them being rhymers, they were induced by the persuasions of their friends to endeavor to complete, as far as they were able, their father's work, in order that it should not remain imperfect; when to Jacopo, who was more eager about it than his brother, there appeared a wonderful vision, which not only induced him to abandon such presumptuous folly, but showed him where the thirteen cantos were which were wanting to the *Divina Commedia*, and which they had not been able to find . . .

A worthy man of Ravenna, whose name was Pier Giardino, and who had long been Dante's disciple, grave in his manner and worthy of credit, relates that, after the eighth month from the day of his master's death, there came to his house before dawn Jacopo di Dante, who told him that that night, while he was asleep, his father Dante had appeared to him, clothed in the whitest garments, and his face resplendent with extraordinary light; that he, Jacopo, asked him if he lived, and that Dante replied: "Yes, but in the true life, not our life." Then he, Jacopo, asked him if he had completed his work before passing into the true life, and, if he had done so, what had become of that part of it which was missing, which they none of them had been able to find. To this Dante seemed to answer, "Yes, I finished it"; and then took him, Jacopo, by the hand, and led him into that chamber in which he, Dante, had been accustomed to sleep when he lived in this life, and, touching one of the walls, he said, "What you have sought for so much, is here"; and at these words both Dante and sleep fled from Jacopo at once. For which reason Jacopo said he could not rest without coming to explain what he had seen to Pier Giardino, in order that they should go together and search out the place thus pointed out to him, which he had retained excellently in his memory, and to see whether this had been pointed out by a true spirit, or a false delusion. For which purpose, although it was still far in the night, they set off together, and went to the house in which Dante resided at the time of his death. Having called up its present owner, he admitted them, and they went to the place thus pointed out; there they found a blind fixed to the wall, as they had always been used to see it in the past days; they lifted it gently up, when they found a little window in the wall, never before seen by any of them, nor did they even know it was there, In it they found several writings, all mouldy from the dampness of the walls, and had they remained there longer, in a little while they would have crumbled away. Having thoroughly cleared away the mold, they found them to be the thirteen cantos that had been wanting to complete the *Commedia*.

The Divine Comedy
"Paradiso," Canto XV
(Abridged)

Dante Alighieri

"Florence, within the ancient boundary 97
   From which she taketh still her tierce and nones,
   Abode in quiet, temperate and chaste.
No golden chain she had, nor coronal, 100
   Nor ladies shod with sandal shoon, nor girdle
   That caught the eye more than the person did.
Not yet the daughter at her birth struck fear
   Into the father, for the time and dower
   Did not o'errun this side or that the measure. 105
No houses had she void of families,
   Not yet had thither come Sardanapalus
   To show what in a chamber can be done;
Not yet surpassed had Montemalo been
   By your Uccellatoio, which surpassed 110
   Shall in its downfall be as in its rise.
Bellincion Berti saw I go begirt
   With leather and with bone, and from the mirror
   His dame depart without a painted face;
And him of Nerli saw, and him of Vecchio 115
   Contented with their simple suits of buff,
   And with the spindle and the flax their dames.
O fortunate women! and each one was certain
   Of her own burial place, and none as yet
   For sake of France was in her bed deserted. 120
One o'er the cradle kept her studious watch,
   And in her lullaby the language used
   That first delights the fathers and the mothers;

Another, drawing tresses from her distaff,
    Told o'er among her family the tales   125
    Of Trojans and of Fiesole and Rome.
As great a marvel then would have been held
    A Lapo Salterello, a Cianghella,
    As Cincinnatus or Cornelia now.
To such a quiet, such a beautiful   130
    Life of the citizen, to such a safe
    Community, and to so sweet an inn,
Did Mary give me, with loud cries invoked,
    And in your ancient Baptistery at once
    Christian and Cacciaguida I became.   135
Moronto was my brother, and Eliseo;
    From Val di Pado came to me my wife,
    And from that place thy surname was derived.
I followed afterward the Emperor Conrad,
    And he begirt me of his chivalry,   140
    So much I pleased him with my noble deeds.
I followed in his train against that law's
    Iniquity, whose people doth usurp
    Your just possession, through your Pastor's fault.
There by that execrable race was I   145
    Released from bonds of the fallacious world,
    The love of which defileth many souls,
And came from martydom unto this peace."

Footnotes

97. "The ancient boundary": the old city walls, beside which stood the ancient Abbey, whose bell marked the hours ("tierce and nones") for the Florentines.

99. "Quiet, temperate and chaste": "The simplicity of Florentine manners in 1260, described by Villani and Malespini, justifies a similar picture as drawn by their great poet. 'Then,' say these writers, 'the Florentines lived soberly on the simplest food at little expense; many of their customs were rough and rude, and both men and women went coarsely clad; many even wearing plain leather garments without fur or lining: they wore boots on their feet and caps on their head: the women used unornamented buskins, and even the most distinguished were content with a close gown of scarlet serge or camlet, confined by a leather waist-belt of the ancient fashion, and a hooded cloak lined with miniver; and the poorer classes wore a coarse green cloth dress of the same form. A hundred lire was the common dowry of a girl, and two and three hundred were then considered splendid fortunes: most young women waited until they were twenty years old and upwards before they married. And such was the dress, and such the manners and simple habits of the Florentines of that day; but loyal in heart,

faithful to each other, zealous and honest in the execution of public duties; and with their coarse and homely mode of life they gained more virtue and honor for themselves and their country than they who now live so delicately are able to accomplish.' "

What Florence had become in Dante's time may be seen from the following extract from Frate Francesco Pippino, who wrote in 1313: "Now indeed, in the present luxurious age, many shameful practices are introduced instead of the former customs; many indeed to the injury of people's minds, because frugality is exchanged for magnificence; the clothing being now remarkable for its exquisite materials, workmanship, and superfluous ornaments of silver, gold, and pearls; admirable fabrics; wide-spreading embroidery; silk for vests, painted or variously colored, and lined with divers precious furs from foreign countries. Excitement to gluttony is not wanting; foreign wines are much esteemed, and almost all the people drink in public. The viands are sumptuous; the chief cooks are held in great honor; provacatives of the palate are eagerly sought after; ostentation increases; moneymakers exert themselves to supply these tastes; hence usuries, frauds, rapine, extortion, pillage, and contentions in the commonwealth: also unlawful taxes; oppression of the innocent; banishment of citizens, and the combinations of rich men. Our true god is our belly; we adhere to the pomps which were renounced at our baptism, and thus desert to the great enemy of our race. Well indeed does Seneca, the instructor of morals, in his book of orations, curse our times in the following words: 'Daily, things grow worse because the whole contest is for dishonorable matters. Behold! the indolent senses of youth are numbed, nor are they active in the pursuit of any one honest thing. Sleep, languor, and a carefulness for bad things, worse than sleep and languor, have seized upon their minds; the love of singing, dancing, and other unworthy occupations possesses them: they are effeminate: to soften the hair, to lower the tone of their voice to female compliments; to vie with women in effeminacy of person, and adorn themselves with unbecoming delicacy, is the object of our youth.' "

107. "Sardanapalus," king of Assyria, was notorious for his luxury.

109-110. "Montemalo": the hill from which the traveler coming from Viterbo first catches sight of Rome. "Uccellatoio": the hill from which the traveler coming from Bologna first catches sight of Florence. Here the two hills are used to signify what is seen from them, namely, the two cities; and Dante means to say that Florence had not yet surpassed Rome in the splendor of its buildings, but as Rome would one day be surpassed in its rise, so would it be in its downfall.

112. "Berti": a worthy citizen.

128. "Cianghella" and "Lapo" were notorious for their immodesty. Monna Cianghella della Tosa was a gay widow who led such a life of pleasure that her name passed into proverb as a dissolute woman.

135. "Cacciaguida": of this ancestor of Dante, nothing is known but what the poet here tells us.

137. "Wife": Cacciaguida's wife came from Ferrara in the Val di Pado, or Val di Po, the Valley of the Po. She was of the Aldighieri or Alighieri family, and from her Dante derived his surname.

139. "Conrad" III, of Swabia, leader of the crusade of 1147.

The Plague, 1348
The Decameron

Giovanni Boccaccio
(1313–1375)

THE FIRST DAY

Here begins the first day of the *Decameron*, wherein, after the author has showed the reasons why certain persons gathered to tell tales, they treat of any subject pleasing to them, under the rule of Pampinea.

Most gracious ladies, knowing that you are all by nature pitiful, I know that in your judgment this work will seem to have a painful and sad origin. For it brings to mind the unhappy recollection of that late dreadful plague, so pernicious to all who saw or heard of it. But I would not have this frighten you from reading further, as though you were to pass through nothing but sighs and tears in your reading. This dreary opening will be like climbing a steep mountain side to a most beautiful and delightful valley, which appears the more pleasant in proportion to the difficulty of the ascent. The end of happiness is pain, and in like manner misery ends in unexpected happiness.

This brief fatigue (I say brief, because it occupies only a few words) is quickly followed by pleasantness and delight, as I promised you above; which, if I had not promised, you would not expect perhaps from this opening. Indeed, if I could have taken you by any other way than this, which I know to be rough, I would gladly have done so; but since I cannot otherwise tell you how the tales you are about to read came to be told, I am forced by necessity to write in this manner.

In the year 1348 after the fruitful incarnation of the Son of God, that most beautiful of Italian cities, noble Florence, was attacked by deadly plague. It started in the East either through the influence of the heavenly bodies or because God's just anger with our wicked deeds sent it as a punishment to mortal men; and in a few years killed an innumerable quantity of people. Ceaselessly passing from place to place, it extended its miserable length over the West. Against this plague all human wisdom and foresight were vain. Orders had been given to cleanse the city of filth, the entry of any sick person was forbidden, much advice was given for keeping healthy; at the same time humble supplications were made to God by pious persons in processions and otherwise. And yet, in the beginning of the spring of the year mentioned, its horrible results began to appear, and in a miraculous manner. The symptoms were not the same as in the East, where a gush of blood from the nose was the plain sign of inevitable death; but it began both in men and women with certain swellings in the groin or under the armpit. They grew to the size of a small apple or an egg, more or less, and were vulgarly called tumors. In a short space of time these tumors spread from the two parts named all over the body. Soon after this the symptoms changed and black or purple spots appeared on the arms or thighs or any other part of the body, some-times a few large ones, sometimes many little ones. These spots were a certain sign of death, just as the original tumor had been and still remained.

No doctor's advice, no medicine could overcome or alleviate this disease. An enormous number of ignorant men and women set up as doctors in addition to those who were trained. Either the disease was such that no treatment was possible or the doctors were so ignorant that they did not know what caused it, and consequently could not administer the proper remedy. In any case very few recovered; most people died within about three days of the appearance of the tumors described above, most of them without any fever or other symptoms.

The violence of this disease was such that the sick communicated it to the healthy who came near them, just as a fire catches anything dry or oily near it. And it even went further. To speak to or go near the sick brought infection and a common death to the living; and moreover, to touch the clothes or anything else the sick had touched or worn gave the disease to the person touching.

What I am about to tell now is a marvelous thing to hear; and if I and others had not seen it with our own eyes I would not dare to write it, however much I was willing to believe and whatever the good faith of the person from whom I heard it. So violent was the malignancy of this plague that it was communicated, not only from one man to another, but from the garments of a sick or dead man to animals of another species, which caught the disease in that way and very quickly died of it. One day among other occasions I saw with my own eyes (as I said just now) the rags left lying in the street of a poor man who had died of the plague; two pigs came along and, as their habit is, turned the clothes over with their snouts and then munched at them, with the result that they both fell dead almost at once on the rags, as if they had been poisoned.

From these and similar or greater occurrences, such fear and fanciful notions took possession of the living that almost all of them adopted the same cruel policy, which was entirely to avoid the sick and everything belonging to them. By so doing, each one thought he would secure his own safety.

Some thought that moderate living and the avoidance of all superfluity would preserve them from the epidemic. They formed small communities, living entirely separate from everybody else. They shut themselves up in houses where there were no sick, eating the finest food and drinking the best wine very temperately, avoiding all excess, allowing no news or discussion of death and sickness, and passing the time in music and suchlike pleasures. Others thought just the opposite. They thought the sure cure for the plague was to drink and be merry, to go about singing and amusing themselves, satisfying every appetite they could, laughing and jesting at what happened. They put their words into practice, spent day and night going from tavern to tavern, drinking immoderately, or went into other people's houses, doing only those things which pleased them. This they could easily do because everyone felt doomed and had abandoned his property, so that most houses became common property and any stranger who went in made use of them as if he had owned them. And with all this bestial behavior, they avoided the sick as much as possible.

In this suffering and misery of our city, the authority of human and divine laws almost disappeared, for, like other men, the ministers and the executors of the laws were all dead or sick or shut up with their families, so that no duties were carried out. Every man was therefore able to do as he pleased.

Many others adopted a course of life midway between the two just described. They did not restrict their victuals so much as the former, nor allow themselves to be drunken and dissolute like the latter, but satisfied their appetites moderately. They did not shut themselves up, but went about, carrying flowers or scented herbs or perfumes in their hands, in the belief that it was an excellent thing to comfort the brain with such odors; for the whole air was infected with the smell of dead bodies, of sick persons and medicines.

Others again held a still more cruel opinion, which they thought would keep them safe. They said that the only medicine against the plague-stricken was to go right away from them. Men and women, convinced of this and caring about nothing but themselves, abandoned their own city, their own houses, their dwellings, their relatives, their property, and went abroad or at least to the country round Florence, as if God's wrath in punishing men's wickedness with this plague would not follow them but strike only those who remained within the walls of the city, or as if they thought nobody in the city would remain alive and that its last hour had come.

Not everyone who adopted any of these various opinions died, nor did all escape. Some when they were still healthy had set the example of avoiding the sick, and, falling ill themselves, died untended.

One citizen avoided another, hardly any neighbor troubled about others, relatives never or hardly ever visited each other. Moreover, such terror was struck into the hearts of men and women by this calamity, that brother abandoned brother, and the uncle his nephew, and the sister her brother, and very often the wife her husband. What is even worse and nearly incredible is that fathers and mothers refused to see and tend their children, as if they had not been theirs.

Thus, a multitude of sick men and women were left without any care except from the charity of friends (but these were few), or the greed of servants, though not many of these could be had even for high wages. Moreover, most of them were coarse-minded men and women, who did little more than bring the sick what they asked for or watch over them when they were dying. And very often these servants lost their lives and their earnings. Since the sick were thus abandoned by neighbors, relatives and friends, while servants were scarce, a habit sprang up which had never been heard of before. Beautiful and noble women, when they fell sick, did not scruple to take a young or old man-servant, whoever he might be, and with no sort of shame, expose every part of their bodies to these men as if they had been women, for they were compelled by the necessity of their sickness to do so. This, perhaps, was a cause of looser morals in those women who survived.

In this way many people died who might have been saved if they had been looked after. Owing to the lack of attendants for the sick and the violence of the plague, such a multitude of people in the city died day and night that it was stupifying to hear of, let alone to see. From sheer necessity, then, several ancient customs were quite altered among the survivors.

The custom had been (as we still see it today), that women relatives and neighbors should gather at the house of the deceased, and there lament with the family. At the same time the men would gather at the door with the male neighbors and other citizens. Then came the clergy, few or many according to the dead person's rank; the coffin was placed on the shoulders of his friends and carried with funeral pomp of lighted candles and dirges to the church which the deceased had chosen before dying. But as the fury of the plague increased, this custom wholly or nearly disappeared, and new customs arose. Thus, people died, not only without having a number of women near them, but without a single witness. Very few indeed were honored with the piteous laments and bitter tears of their relatives, who, on the contrary, spent their time in mirth, feasting and jesting. Even the women abandoned womanly pity and adopted this custom for their own safety. Few were they whose bodies were accompanied to church by more than ten or a dozen neighbors. Nor were these grave and honorable citizens but grave-diggers from the lowest of the people who got themselves called sextons, and performed the task for money. They took up the bier and hurried it off, not to the church chosen by the deceased but to the church nearest, preceded by four or six of the clergy with few candles and often none at all. With the aid of the grave-diggers, the clergy huddled the bodies away in any grave they could find, without giving themselves the trouble of a long or solemn burial service.

The plight of the lower and most of the middle classes was even more pitiful to behold. Most of them remained in their houses, either through poverty or in hopes of safety, and fell sick by thousands. Since they received no care and attention, almost all of them died. Many ended their lives in the streets both at night and during the day; and many others who died in their houses were only known to be dead because the neighbors smelled their decaying bodies. Dead bodies filled every corner. Most of them were treated in the same manner by the survivors, who were more concerned to get rid of their rotting bodies than moved by charity towards the dead. With the aid of porters, if they could get them, they carried the bodies out of the houses and laid them at the doors, where every morning quantities of the dead might be seen. They then were laid on biers or, as these were often lacking, on tables.

Often a single bier carried two or three bodies, and it happened frequently that a husband and wife, two or three brothers, or father and son were taken off on the same bier. It frequently happened that two priests, each carrying a cross, would go out followed by three or four biers carried by porters; and where the priests thought there was one person to bury, there would be six or eight, and often, even more. Nor were these dead honored by tears and lighted candles and mourners, for things had reached such a pass that people cared no more for dead men then we care for dead goats. Thus it plainly appeared that what the wise had not learned to endure with patience through the few calamities of ordinary life, became a matter of indifference even to the most ignorant people through the greatness of this misfortune.

Such was the multitude of corpses brought to the churches every day and almost every hour that there was not enough consecrated ground to give them burial, especially since they wanted to bury each person in the family grave, according to the old custom. Although the cemeteries were full they were forced to dig huge trenches, where they buried the bodies by hundreds. Here they stowed them away like bales in the hold of a ship and covered them with a little earth, until the whole trench was full.

Not to pry any further into all the details of the miseries which afflicted our city, I shall add that the surrounding country was spared nothing of what befell Florence. The villages on a smaller scale were like the city; in the fields and isolated farms the poor wretched peasants and their families were without doctors and any assistance, and perished in the highways, in their fields and houses, night and day, more like beasts than men. Just as the townmen became dissolute and indifferent to their work and property, so the peasants, when they saw the death was upon them, entirely neglected the future fruits of their past labors both from the earth and from cattle, and thought only of enjoying what they had. Thus it happened that cows, asses, sheep, goats, pigs, fowls and even dogs, those faithful companions of man, left the farms and wandered at their will through the fields, where the wheat crops stood abandoned, unreaped and ungarnered. Many of these animals seemed endowed with reason, for, after they had pastured all day, they returned to the farms for the night of their own free will, without being driven.

Returning from the country to the city, it may be said that such was the cruelty of Heaven, and perhaps in part of men, that between March and July more than one hundred thousand persons died within the walls of Florence, what between the violence of the plague and the abandonment in which the sick were left by the cowardice of the healthy. And before the plague it was not thought that the whole city held so many people.

Oh, what great palaces, how many fair houses and noble dwellings, once filled with attendants and nobles and ladies, were emptied to the meanest servant! How many famous names and vast possessions and renowned estates were left without an heir! How many gallant men and fair ladies and handsome youths, whom Galen, Hippocrates and Aesculapius themselves would have said were in perfect health, at noon dined with their relatives and friends, and at night supped with their ancestors in the next world!

But it fills me with sorrow to go over so many miseries. Therefore, since I want to pass over all I can leave out, I shall go on to say that when our city was in this condition and almost emptied of inhabitants, one Tuesday morning the venerable church of Santa Maria Novella had scarcely any congregation for divine service except (as I have heard from a person worthy of belief) seven young women in the mourning garments suitable to the times, who were all related by ties of blood, friendship or neighborship. None of them was older than twenty-eight or younger than eighteen; all were educated and of noble blood, fair to look upon, well-mannered and of graceful modesty.

I should tell you their real names if I had not a good reason for not doing so, which is that I would not have any of them blush in the future for things they say and hearken to in the following pages. The laws are now strict again, whereas then, for the reasons already shown, they were very lax, not only for persons of their age but for those much older. Nor would I give an opportunity to the envious (already ready to sneer at every praiseworthy life) to attack the virtue of these modest ladies with vulgar speech. But so that you may understand without confusion what each one says, I intend to give them names wholly or partly suitable to the qualities of each.

The first and eldest I shall call Pampinea, the second Fiammetta, the third Filomena, the fourth Emilia, the fifth Lauretta, the sixth Neifile, and the last Elisa (or "the virgin") for a very good reason. They met, not by arrangement, but by chance, in the same part of the church, and sat down in a circle. After many sighs they ceased to pray and began to talk about the state of affairs and other things. After a short space of silence, Pampinea said:

"Dear ladies, you must often have heard, as I have, that to make a sensible use of one's reasons harms nobody. It is natural for everybody to aid, preserve and defend his life as far as possible. And this is so far admitted that to save their own lives men often kill others who have done no harm. If this is permitted by the laws which are concerned with the general good, it must certainly be lawful for us to take any reasonable means for the preservation of our lives. When I think of what we have been doing this morning and still more on former days, when I remember what we have been saying, I perceive and you must perceive that each of us goes in fear of her life. I do not wonder at this, but, since each of us has a woman's judgment, I do wonder that we do not seek some remedy against what we dread.

"In my opinion we remain here for no other purpose than to witness how many bodies are buried, or listen whether the friars here (themselves reduced almost to nothing) sing their offices at the canonical hours, or to display by our clothes the quantity and quality of our miseries to anyone who comes here. If we leave this church we see the bodies of the dead and the sick being carried about. Or we see those who had been exiled from the city by the authority of the laws for their crimes, deriding this authority because they know the guardians of the law are sick or dead, and running loose about the place. Or we see the dregs of the city battening on our blood and calling themselves sextons, riding about on horseback in every direction and insulting our calamities with vile songs. On every side we hear nothing but So-and so is dead or So-and-so is dying. And if there were anyone left to weep we should hear nothing but piteous lamentations. I do not know if it is the same in your homes as in mine. But if I go home there is nobody left there but one of my maids, which fills me with such horror that the hair stands upon my head. Wherever I go or sit at home I seem to see the ghosts of the departed, not with the faces as I knew them but with dreadful looks which terrify me.

"I am ill at ease here and outside of here and at home; the more so since nobody who has the strength and ability to go away (as we have) now remains here, except ourselves. The few that remain (if there are any), according to what I see and hear, do anything which gives them pleasure or pleases their appetites, both by day and night, whether they are alone or in company, making no distinctions between right and wrong. Not only laymen, but those cloistered in convents have broken their oaths and given themselves up to the delights of the flesh, and thus in trying to escape the plague by doing what they please, they have become lascivious and dissolute.

"If this is so (and we may plainly see it is) what are we doing here? What are we waiting for? What are we dreaming about? Are we less eager and active than other citizens in saving our lives? Are they less dear to us than to others? Or do we think that our lives are bound to our bodies with stronger chains than other people's, and so believe that we need fear nothing which might harm us? We were and are deceived. How stupid we should be to believe such a thing! We may see the plainest proofs from the number of young men and women who have died of this cruel plague.

"I do not know if you think as I do, but in my opinion if we, through carelessness, do not want to fall into this calamity when we can escape it, I think we should do well to leave this town, just as many others have done and are doing. Let us avoid the wicked examples of others like death itself, and go and live virtuously in our country houses, of which each of us possess several. There let us take what happiness and pleasures we can, without ever breaking the rules of reason in any manner.

"There we shall hear the birds sing, we shall see the green hills and valleys, the wheat-fields rolling like a sea, and all kinds of trees. We shall see the open Heavens which, although now angered against man, do not withhold from us their eternal beauties that are so much fairer to look upon than the empty walls of our city. The air will be fresher there, we shall find a greater plenty of those things necessary to life at this time, and fewer troubles. Although the peasants are dying like the townsmen, still, since the houses and inhabitants are fewer, we shall see less of them and feel less misery. On the other hand I believe we are not abandoning anybody here. Indeed we can truthfully say that we are abandoned, since our relatives have either died or fled from death and have left us alone in this calamity as if we were nothing to them.

"If we do what I suggest, no blame can fall upon us; if we fail to do it, the result may be pain, trouble and perhaps death. Therefore I think that we should do well to take our servants and all things necessary, and go from one house to another, enjoying whatever merriment and pleasure these times allow. Let us live in this way (unless death comes upon us) until we see what end Heaven decrees to this plague. And remember that going away virtuously will not harm us so much as staying here in wickedness will harm others."

The other ladies listened to what Pampinea said, praised her advice, and in their eagerness to follow it began to discuss details, as if they were going to leave at once. . . .

While the ladies were thus arguing, three young men came into the church, the youngest of whom was not less then twenty-five. They were lovers whose love could not be quenched or even cooled by the horror of the times, the loss of relatives and friends, or even fear for themselves. The first was named Pamfile, the second Filostrato, and third Dioneo. They were pleasant, well-mannered men, and in this public calamity they sought the consolation of looking upon the ladies they loved. These ladies happened to be among our seven, while some of the others were related to one or other of the three men. . . . They agreed by common consent that the men should be spoken to, told their plan, and asked if they would accompany the ladies on their expedition. Without more ado, Pampinea, who was related to one of them, arose and went towards them where they stood looking at the ladies, saluted them cheerfully, told them the plan, and begged them in the name of all the ladies to accompany them out of pure and fraternal affection.

At first the young men thought this was a jest. But when they saw the lady was speaking seriously, they said they were willing to go. And in order to start without delay they at once gave the orders necessary for departure. Everything necessary was made ready, and word was sent on ahead to the place they were going. At dawn next morning, which was Wednesday, the ladies with some of their servants, and the young men with a man servant each, left the city and set out. They had not gone more than two miles when they came to the first place where they were to stay.

This estate was on slightly raised ground, at some distance from any main road, with many trees and plants, fair to look upon. At the top of the rise was a country mansion with a large inner courtyard. It had open colonnades, galleries and rooms, all beautiful in themselves and ornamented with gay paintings. Roundabout were lawns and marvelous gardens and wells of cool water. There were cellars of fine wines, more suitable to wine connoisseurs than to sober and virtuous ladies. The whole house had been cleaned, the beds were prepared in the rooms, and every corner was strewn with flowers of the season and fresh rushes. All of which the company beheld with no little pleasure.

They all sat down to discuss plans, and Dioneo, who was a most amusing young man and full of witticisms, remarked:

"Ladies, your good sense, rather than our foresight, has brought us here. I do not know what you are thinking of doing with your troubles here, but I dropped mine inside the gates of the city when I left it with you a little time ago. Therefore, either you must make up your minds to laugh and sing and amuse yourselves with me (that is, to the extent your dignity allows), or you must let me go back to my troubles and stay in the afflicted city."

Pampinea, who had driven away her woes in the same way, cheerfully replied:

"Dioneo, you speak well, let us amuse ourselves, for that was the reason why we fled from our sorrows. But when things are not organized they cannot long continue. And, since I began the discussion which brought this fair company together and since I wish our happiness to continue, I think it necessary that one of us should be made chief, whom the others will honor and obey, and whose duty shall be to regulate our pleasures. Now, so that everyone—both man and woman—may experience the cares as well as the pleasures of ruling and no one feel any envy at not sharing them, I think the weight and honor should be given to each of us in turn for one day. The first shall be elected by all of us. At vespers he or she shall choose the ruler for the next day, and so on. While their reigns last these rulers shall arrange where and how we are to spend our time."

These words pleased them all and they unanimously elected her for the first day. Filomena ran to a laurel bush, whose leaves she had always heard were most honorable in themselves and did great honor to anyone crowned with them, plucked off a few branches and wove them into a fair garland of honor. When this was placed on the head of any one of them, it was a symbol of rule and authority over the rest so long as the party remained together. . . .

The company of gay young men and women, thus given the queen's permission, went off together slowly through the gardens, talking of pleasant matters, weaving garlands of different leaves, and singing love songs. After the time allotted by the queen had elapsed they returned to the house and found that Parmeno, the steward, had carefully carried out the duties of his office. Entering a ground floor room decorated everywhere with broom blossoms, they found tables covered with white cloths and set with glasses which shone like silver. They washed their hands and, at the queen's command, all sat down in the places alloted them by Parmeno. Delicately cooked food was brought, exquisite wines were at hand, and the three men servants waited at table. Everyone was delighted to see things so handsome and well arranged, and they ate merrily with much happy talk.

All the ladies and young men could dance and many of them could play and sing; so, when the tables were cleared, the queen called for musical instruments. At her command Dioneo took a lute and

Fiammetta a viol, and began to play a dance tune. The queen sent the servants to their meal, and then with slow steps danced with the two young men and the other ladies. After that, they began to sing gay and charming songs.

In this way they amused themselves until the queen thought it was time for the siesta. So, at the queen's bidding, the three young men went off to their rooms (which were separated from the ladies') and found them filled with flowers as the dining hall had been. And similarly with the women. So they all undressed and went to sleep.

Not long after the hour of Nones the queen rose and made the other women and the young men also get up, saying that it was harmful to sleep too long during the daytime. Then they went out to a lawn of thick green grass entirely shaded from the sun. A soft breeze came to them there. The queen made them sit down in a circle on the grass, and said:

"As you see, the sun is high and the heat great, and nothing can be heard but the cicadas in the olive trees. To walk about at this hour would be foolish. Here it is cool and lovely, and, as you see, there are games of chess and draughts which everyone can amuse himself with, as he chooses. But, if my opinion is followed, we shall not play games, because in games the mind of one of the players must necessarily be distressed without any great pleasure to the other player or the onlookers. Let us rather spend this hot part of the day in telling tales, for thus one person can give pleasure to the whole company. When each of us has told a story, the sun will be going down and the heat less, and we can then go walking anywhere we choose for our amusement. If this pleases you (for here I am ready to follow your pleasure) let us do it. If it does not please you, let everyone do as he likes until evening."

The women and men all favored the telling of stories.

"Then if it pleases you," said the queen, "on this first day I order that everyone shall tell his tale about any subject he likes."

She then turned to Pamfilo, who was seated on her right, and ordered him to begin with a tale. Hearing this command, Pamfilo at once began as follows, while all listened.

The Decameron's Singular Destiny

Ugo Foscolo

Boccaccio died not only without the hope, but without the desire, that his *Decameron* should outlive him. His autograph copy has never been found, and from what we shall presently have occasion to observe, . . . we derive very strong presumptive evidence that he destroyed it himself. A young friend of his, Francesco Mannelli, eight or ten years after his death, transcribed it with the most scrupulous exactness, frankly confessing that the copy he used was full of errors After the introduction of printing, copies and editions were multiplied with mistakes, which, it was clear, were partly accumulated by the negligence of printers, while their art was yet in its infancy. But from the age of Boccaccio to that of Lorenzo de' Medici and the pontificate of Leo X, the Italian language was so barbarized that it seemed lost to the learned men of Italy; for more than a century they wrote in Latin, which had fixed rules and was common to all Europe. The critics of that illustrious epoch strove by every means to form the language spoken by Italians into a literary language, well adapted for written composition and for being understood by the whole nation, and in the penury of authors who could furnish observations, and examples, and principles, from which a right method might be derived, they had recourse, with common consent, to the tales of Boccaccio; they found words at once vernacular and perfectly elegant, distinct and expressive; skillful construction, musical periods, and diversity of style; nor perhaps could any expedient at that time have been found better adapted for obviating numerous difficulties which presented themselves. But the maxims and the practice of the literary men of that age

UGO FOSCOLO (1778–1827), Italian lyric poet. An ardent patriot, Foscolo fought on the side of Napoleon against the Austrians. He died in exile in London.

consisted not so much in constructing rules from observations as in imitating punctually, servilely, and childishly the most admired writers. . . .

This system of servilely imitating excellent authors did not prevent some men of genius, particularly historians, from attempting to relate in a style at once original, dignified, and energetic, the events of their country. But they were living writers, nor had long celebrity and prescriptive authority yet stamped them as models. To this reason, which holds good of every age and country, was added, that the liberty of the numerous republics of Italy which had sprung up in the barbarism of the Middle Ages, declined in the most fertile and splendid period of her literature, and the historians who were witnesses of the misfortunes and degradation of their country, wrote in a manner which was not agreeable to her tyrants. Hence Machiavelli, Guicciardini, Segni, and others who are now studied as masters of style, were not then read, except by a few; their works were hardly known in manuscript, and if published they were mutilated; nor were any complete editions of their histories printed until two centuries after they were written. Thus the *Novelle* of Boccaccio held the field, and their popularity was greatly increased by the abhorrence and contempt which they inspired against the wickedness of the monks.

Certain young men of Florence conspired against Duke Alexander, bastard of Clement VII, with the design of driving him from their country, and re-establishing the republic. They held meetings under the color of amending the text of Boccaccio by the collation of manuscripts, and by critical examination. Such was the source, and such the authors, of the celebrated edition of Giunti, in 1527, now regarded as one of the rarest curiosities of bibliography, and preserved from that time as a record of the Florentine republic, almost all these young men having fought against the house of Medici, and died at the siege of Florence or in exile. The work subsequently became more scarce, because it was constantly exposed to the danger of being mutilated or prohibited through the interest of the monks. . . . When the *Decameron*, which had already been translated into several languages, was quoted by the Anti-Papists, the Church ceased to confine herself to threats, and began actually to prohibit the reprinting and the reading of Boccaccio's tales; nor could anyone have a copy in his possession without a licence from his confessor. . . .

The Spanish domination in Italy, the long reign of Philip II (the most tyrannical of the tyrants), and the Council of Trent, had imposed silence upon genius. Cosimo I, Grand Duke of Tuscany, kept in his pay one or two historians of the house of Medici; he caused all books of a less servile character to be collected together from every part and burnt. The *Decameron* was, therefore, by an absolute political necessity, resorted to by literary men as a sole rule and standard of written prose language. To cancel every memorial of freedom, Cosimo I suppressed all the academies instituted in Tuscany during the republican government of its cities. . . .

Nevertheless the academicians found that the *Decameron* had never been printed in a genuine and correct form, fitted to serve as the groundwork of language. After many years spent in consulting, correcting and collating manuscripts, they prepared an edition which they hoped to consecrate as the oracle in all grammatical questions: but the Holy Office interposed in the most furious manner, and did not allow it to be printed. They therefore consented, as they could do no better, to publish a mutilated edition. . . .

At length an Italian Dominican, of a more facile character, . . . having been confessor to Pius V . . . prevailed on Gregory XIII to allow the *Decameron* to be printed without any other alteration than what was necessary for the good fame of the ecclesiastics. Thus, abbesses and nuns in love with their gardeners were transformed into matrons and young ladies; friars who got up impostures and miracles into necromancers; and priests who intrigued with their parishioners' wives into soldiers; and by dint of a hundred other inevitable transformations and mutilations, the academy, after four years' labor, succeeded in publishing the *Decameron* in Florence, illustrated by their researches. . . .

The singular destiny of a work composed as a mere pastime, threw into comparative oblivion its other literary merits, which were more useful to the civilization of Europe, and stamped upon the name of its author an infamous celebrity, which has always hidden from the world the true character of his mind . . .

The injury which Petrarch did to his native tongue, by his ambition of writing in Latin, was compensated by his indefatigable and generous perseverance in restoring to Europe the most noble remains of human intellect. No monument of antiquity, no series of medals, or manuscript of Roman literature was neglected by him wherever he had the least hope of rescuing the one from oblivion, or of multiplying copies of the other. He acquired a claim to the gratitude of all Europe, and is still deservedly called the first restorer of classical literature.

Boccaccio, however, is entitled not only to a share, but to an equal share, to say the least, of this honor. We are perfectly aware that our opinion on this subject will be at first regarded as a paradox put forth from a mere ambition of novelty; the proofs, however, which we shall briefly adduce, will convert the surprise of our readers at our temerity into wonder at the scanty recompense which Boccaccio has hitherto received, in spite of his gigantic and successful endeavors to dispel the ignorance of the Middle Ages.

The allegorical mythology, together with the theology and metaphysics of the ancients, the events of the history of ages less remote, and even geography, were illustrated by Boccaccio in his voluminous Latin Treatises, now little read, but at that time studied by all as the chiefest and best works of solid learning. Petrarch knew nothing of Greek; and whatever acquaintance, in Tuscany or Italy, they had with the writers of that language, they owed entirely to Boccaccio. He went to Sicily, where there were still some remains of a Greek dialect, and masters who taught the language; . . . he afterwards prevailed on the republic of Florence to establish a chair of Greek literature. . . . Had it not been for Boccaccio, the poems of Homer would have remained long undiscovered. The story of the Trojan War was read in the celebrated romance called the *History of Guido delle Colonne*, from which also were derived many wild inventions and apocryphal records of Homeric times, and various dramas, like Shakespeare's *Troilus and Cressida*, containing not a single circumstance to be met with in the *Iliad* or *Odyssey*. Nor should it be forgotten, that undertakings like these demanded affluence, which Petrarch possessed; while Boccaccio's whole life was passed in the midst of difficulties and privations. He compensated for the want of pecuniary resources by indefatigable industry; he submitted to mechanical labors, wholly unsuited to the bent of his character and genius, and copied manuscripts with his own hand. . . . A disciple of Boccaccio relates a curious anecdote on this subject, which as we do not recollect that it is anywhere to be met with, except in the great collection of the writers of the Middle Ages, . . . we shall insert. Going once to the abbey of Monte Cassino, celebrated for the number of manuscripts which lay there, unknown and neglected, Boccaccio humbly requested to be shown into the library of the monastery. A monk dryly replied, "Go, it stands open," and pointed to a very high staircase. The good Boccaccio found every book he opened torn and mutilated; lamenting that all these fruits of the labors of the great men of antiquity had fallen into the hands of such masters, he went away weeping. Coming down the staircase he met another monk, and asked him "How could those books possibly have been so mutilated?" "We make covers for little Prayer-books out of the parchment leaves of those volumes," said he, coolly, "and sell them for twopence, threepence and sometimes fivepence each." "And now go," concludes the pupil of Boccaccio, "go, you unfortunate author, and distract your brain in composing more books." Such were the obstacles [imposed] by the imperfect civilization of his age which this admirable man, together with Petrarch, had to surmount; and it is an act of tardy religious justice to show that the tribute of grateful recollection which they were both entitled to receive from posterity was almost [only] awarded to his more fortunate contemporary. We cannot conclude our remarks, without paying another debt to the memory of Boccaccio. The indecency of the *Novelle*, and their immoral tendency, can neither be justified nor extenuated; but from the herd of writers in England, who confidently repeat this merited censure of Boccaccio, year after year, it appears but too much as if the study of the language and of the style had been made a pretext for feeding the imaginations of the readers with ideas which all are prone to indulge, but compelled to conceal; and that the tales of Boccaccio would not have predominated so much over all other literature, if they had been more chaste. The art of suggesting thoughts, at once desired and forbidden, flatters while it irritates the passions, and is an efficacious instrument for governing the consciences of boys, and of the most discreet old men. The Jesuits, therefore, no sooner made themselves masters of the schools of Italy, than they adopted this book, mutilated in the same manner as some of the licentious Latin poets, well knowing that the expunged passages are the most coveted, precisely because they *are* expunged, and that the imaginations of youth supply ideas worse than they would have formed had the books been left entire.

Before Baccaccio died he had atoned for his want of respect for decorum; he felt that men thought him culpable, and he expiated his tales by a punishment heavier, perhaps, than the offence. There is some reason to believe that he wrote them when under the influence of a lady whom he abjured just before, and whom he defames in his *Laberinto d'Amore.* However this may be, he conjured fathers of families not to suffer the *Decameron* to go into the hands of any who had not already lost the modesty of youth. "Do not let that book be read; and if it is true that you love me, and weep for my afflictions, have pity, were it only for my honor's sake."

With remorse of conscience which does more honor to the excellence of his intentions than to the strength of his mind, he even tried to atone for the ridicule he had poured upon the priests and their infamous superstitions. No writer, perhaps, since Aristophanes, has so bitterly satirized the effrontery of ignorant preachers, and the credulity of their ignorant hearers, as Boccaccio in the *Novelle*, which are written in a spirit of implacable hostility to monks.... [Still] he bequeathed all his books and manuscripts to his confessor and to the convent of Santo Spirito, in order that the monks might pray to God for his soul, and that his fellow citizens might read and copy them for their instruction. It is therefore more than probable that there was among these books no copy of the *Decameron*; and from the following anecdote, which being found in books which are read by very few is little known, it appears that the original manuscript of the *Novelle* was destroyed long before by the author; it is, in fact, as we have already remarked, impossible to find it.

Toward the end of his life, poverty, which is rendered more grievous by old age, and the turbulent state of Florence, made social life a burden to him, so that he fled to solitude; but his generous and amiable soul was debased and depressed by religious terrors.... The blessed Petroni, at his death, which happened about the year 1360, charged a monk to advise Boccaccio to desist from his studies and to prepare for death. Boccaccio wrote in terror to Petrarch, who replied: "My brother, your letter filled my mind with horrible fantasies, and I read it assailed by great wonder and great affliction. And how could I, without fearful eyes, behold you weeping and calling to mind your near-approaching death; whilst I, not well informed of the fact, most anxiously explored the meaning of your words? But now that I have discovered the cause of your terrors, and have reflected somewhat upon them, I have no longer either sadness or surprise. You write that a—I know not what—Pietro di Siena, celebrated for his piety, and also for his miracles, predicted to us two, many future occurrences; and in the witness of the truth of them, sent to signify to us certain past things which you and I have kept secret from all men, and which he, who never knew us, nor was known by us, knew as if he had seen them with his mind's eye. This is a great thing, if indeed it be true. But the art of covering and adorning impostures with the veil of religion and of sanctity, is most common and old. Those who use it explore the age, the countenance, the eyes, the manners of the man; his daily customs, his motions, his standing, his sitting, his voice, his speech, and above all, his intentions and affections; and draw predictions which they ascribe to divine inspiration. Now if he, dying, foretold your death, so also did Hector in former times to Achilles; . . . and Posidonius, the illustrious philosopher, when dying, named six of his contemporaries who were soon to follow him, and told who should die first, and who afterwards. It matters not to dispute now concerning the truth or the origin of such-like predictions; nor to you, if even this your alarmer had told the truth, would it avail anything to afflict yourself. How then? If this man had not sent to let you know, would you have been ignorant that there remains not to you a long space of life? and even if you were young, is death any respecter of age?'' But neither of these, nor all the other arguments in Petrarch's letter, which is very long, nor the eloquence with which he combines the consolations of the Christian religion with the manly philosophy of the ancients, could deliver his friend from superstitious terrors.

Boccaccio survived the prediction more than twelve years, and the older he grew the more did he feel the seeds scattered in his mind by his grandmother and his nurse, spring up like thorns. He died in 1375, aged sixty-two, and not more than twelve or fourteen months after Petrarch. Nor did Petrarch himself always contemplate death with a steadfast eye. Such was the character of those times; and such, under varied appearances, will always be the nature of man.

Lorenzo de' Medici
(1449–1492)

William Dean Howells

The name of Lorenzo de' Medici is the next name of unrivaled greatness to which one comes in Florence after Dante's. The Medici, however one may be principled against them, do possess the imagination there, and I could not have helped going for their sake to the Piazza of the Mercato Vecchio, even if I have not wished to see again and again one of the most picturesque and characteristic places in the city. As I think of it, the pale, delicate sky of a fair winter's day in Florence spreads over me, and I seem to stand in the midst of the old square, with its moldering colonnade on one side, and on the other its low, irregular roofs, their brown tiles thinly tinted with a growth of spindling grass and weeds, green the whole year round. In front of me a vast, white old palace springs seven stories into the sunshine, disreputably shabby from basement to attic, but beautiful, with the rags of a plebeian washday caught across it from balcony to balcony, as if it had fancied trying to hide its forlornness in them. Around me are peasants and donkey carts and Florentines of all sizes and ages; my ears are filled with the sharp din of an Italian crowd, and my nose with the smell of immemorial, innumerable market days, and the rank, cutting savor of frying fish and cakes from a score of neighboring cook-shops; but I am happy, happier than I should probably be if I were actually there. Through an archway in the street behind me, not far from an admirably tumble-down shop full of bric-a-brac of low degree, all huddled—old bureaus and bedsteads, crockery, classic lamps, assorted saints, shovels, flatirons, and big-eyed madonnas— under a sagging roof, I enter a large court, Piazza Donati. Here the Medici, among other great citizens, had their first houses; and in the narrow street opening out of this court stands the little church which was then the family chapel of the Medici, after the fashion of that time, where all their marriages, christenings, and funerals took place. In time this highly respectable quarter suffered the sort of social decay which so frequently and so capriciously affects highly respectable quarters in all cities; and it had at last fallen so low, in the reign of Cosimo I, that when that grim tyrant wished cheaply to please the Florentines by making it a little harder for the Jews than for the Christians under him, he shut them up in the old court. They had been let into Florence to counteract the extortion of the Christian usurers, and upon the condition that they would not ask more than twenty per cent interest. How much more had been taken by the Christians one can hardly imagine; but if this was a low rate to Florentines, one easily understands how the bankers of the city grew rich by lending to the necessitous world outside. Now and then they did not get back their principal, and Edward III of England has still an outstanding debt to the house of Peruzzi, which he bankrupted in the fourteenth century. . . .

The ancient home of the Medici has none of the feudal dignity, the baronial pride, of the quarter of the Lamberti and the Buondelmonti; and, disliking them as I did, I was glad to see it in the possession of that squalor, so different from the cheerful and industrious thrift of Piazza Donati and the neighborhood of Dante's house. No touch of sympathetic poetry relieves the history of that race of demagogues and tyrants, who, in their rise, had no thought but to aggrandize themselves, and whose only greatness was an apotheosis of egotism. It is hard to understand through what law of development, from lower to higher, the Providence which rules the affairs of men permitted them supremacy; and it is easy to understand how the better men whom they supplanted and dominated should abhor them. They were especially a bitter dose to the proud-stomached aristocracy of citizens which had succeeded the extinct Ghibelline nobility in Florence; but, indeed, the three pills which they adopted from the arms of their guild of physicians, together with the only appellation by which history knows their lineage, were agreeable to none who wished their country well. From the first Medici to the last, they were nearly all hypocrites or ruffians, bigots or imbeciles; and Lorenzo, who was a scholar and a poet, and the friend of scholars and poets, had the genius and science of tyranny in supreme degree, though he wore no princely title and assumed to be only the chosen head of the commonwealth.

"Under his rule," says Villari, in his *Life of Savonarola*, that almost incomparable biography, "all wore a prosperous and contented aspect; the parties that had so long disquieted the city were at peace; imprisoned, or banished, or dead, those who would not submit to the Medicean domination; tranquility and calm were everywhere. Feasting, dancing, public shows, and games amused the Florentine people, who, once so jealous of their rights, seemed to have forgotten even the name of liberty. Lorenzo, who took part in all these pleasures, invented new ones every day. But among all his inventions, the most famous was that of the carnival songs, of which he composed the first, and which were meant to be sung in the masquerades of carnival, when the youthful nobility, disguised to represent the Triumph of Death, or a crew of demons, or some other caprice of fancy, wandered through the city, filling it with their riot. The reading of these songs will paint the corruption of the town far better than any other description. Today, not only the youthful nobility, but the basest of the populace, would hold them in loathing, and to go singing them through the city would be an offense to public decency which could not fail to be punished. These things were the favorite recreation of a prince lauded by all the world and held up as a model to every sovereign, a prodigy of wisdom, a political and literary genius. . . . "They would forgive him the blood spilt to maintain a dominion unjustly acquired by him and his; the disorder wrought in the commonwealth; the theft of the public treasure to supply his profligate waste; the shameless vices to which in spite of his feeble health he abandoned himself; and even that rapid and infernal corruption of the people, which he perpetually studied with all the force and capacity of his soul. And all because he was the protector of letters and the fine arts!

"In the social condition of Florence at that time there was indeed a strange contrast. Culture was universally diffused; everybody knew Latin and Greek, everybody admired the classics; many ladies were noted for the elegance of their Greek and Latin verses. The arts, which had languished since the time of Giotto, revived, and on all sides rose exquisite palaces and churches. But artists, scholars, politicians, nobles, and plebeians were rotten at heart, lacking in every public and private virtue, every moral sentiment. Religion was the tool of the government or vile hypocrisy; they had neither civil, nor religious, nor moral, nor philosophic faith; even doubt feebly asserted itself in their souls. A cold indifference to every principle prevailed, and those visages full of guile and subtlety wore a smile of chilly superiority and compassion at any sign of enthusiasm for noble and generous ideas. They did not oppose these or question them, as a philosophical skeptic would have done; they simply pitied them. . . . But Lorenzo had an exquisite taste for poetry and the arts. . . . Having set himself up to protect artists and scholars, his house became the resort of the most illustrious wits of his time, . . . and whether in the meetings under his own roof, or in those of the famous Platonic Academy, his own genius shone brilliantly in that elect circle. . . . A strange life indeed was Lorenzo's. After giving his whole mind and soul to the destruction, by some new law, of some last remnant of liberty, after pronouncing some fresh sentence of ruin or death, he entered the Platonic Academy, and ardently discussed virtue and the immortality of the soul; then sallying forth to mingle with the dissolute youth of the city, he sang his carnival songs, and abandoned himself to debauchery; returning home with Pulci and Politian, he recited verses and talked of poetry; and to each of these occupations he gave himself up as wholly as if it were the sole occupation of his life. But the strangest thing of all is that in all that variety of life they cannot cite a solitary act of real generosity toward his people, his friends, or his kinsmen; for surely if there had been such an act, his indefatigable flatterers would not have forgotten it. . . . He had inherited from Cosimo all that subtlety by which, without being a great statesman, he was prompt in cunning subterfuges, full of prudence and acuteness, skillful in dealing with ambassadors, most skillful in extinguishing his enemies, bold and cruel when he believed the occasion permitted. . . . His face revealed his character; there was something sinister and hateful in it; the complexion was greenish, the mouth very large, the nose flat, and the voice nasal; but his eye was quick and keen, his forehead was high, and his manner had all of gentleness that can be imagined of an age so refined and elegant as that; his conversation was full of vivacity, of wit and learning; those who were admitted to his familiarity were always fascinated by him. He seconded his age in all its tendencies; corrupt as it was, he left it corrupter still in every way; he gave himself up to pleasure, and he taught his people to give themselves up to it, to its intoxication and its delirium.'' . . .

There is, to my thinking, no such mirror of the spirit of that time as the story of [the Pazzi] conspiracy. A pope was at the head of it, and an archbishop was there in Florence to share actively in it. Having failed to find Lorenzo and Giuliano de' Medici together at Lorenzo's villa, the conspirators transfer the scene to the cathedral; the moment chosen for striking the blow is that supremely sacred moment when the very body of Christ is elevated for the adoration of the kneeling worshippers. What a contempt they all have for the place and the office! In this you read one effect of that study of antiquity which was among the means Lorenzo used to corrupt the souls of men; the Florentines are half repaganized. Yet at the bottom of the heart of one conspirator lingers a medieval compunction, and though not unwilling to kill a man, this soldier does not know about killing one in a church. Very well, then, give up your dagger, you simple soldier; give it to this priest; *he* knows what a church is, and how little sacred!

The cathedral is packed with people, and Lorenzo is there, but Giuliano is not come yet. Are we to be fooled a second time? Malediction! Send someone to fetch that Medicean beast, who is so slow coming to the slaughter! I am one of the conspiracy, for I hate the Medici; but these muttered blasphemies, hissed and ground through the teeth, this frenzy for murder—it is getting to be little better than that—make me sick. Two of us go for Giuliano to his house, and being acquaintances of his, we laugh and joke familiarly with him; we put our arms caressingly about him, and feel if he has a shirt of mail on, as we walk him between us through the crowd at the corner of the cafe there, invisibly, past all the cabmen ranked near the cathedral and the baptistery, not one of whom shall snatch his horse's oat-bag from his nose to invite us phantoms to a turn in the city. We have our friend safe in the cathedral at last—hapless, kindly youth, whom we have nothing against except that he is of that cursed race of the Medici—and now at last the priest elevates the host and it is time to strike; the little bell tinkles, the multitude holds its breath and falls upon its knees; Lorenzo and Giuliano kneel with the rest. A moment, and Bernardo Bandini plunges his short dagger through the boy, who drops dead upon his face, and Francesco Pazzi flings himself upon the body, and blindly striking to make sure of his death, gives himself a wound in the leg that disables him for the rest of the work. And now we see the folly of entrusting Lorenzo to the unpracticed hand of a priest, who would have been neat enough, no doubt, at mixing a dose of poison. The bungler has only cut his man a little in the neck! Lorenzo's sword is out and making desperate play for his life; his friends close about him, and while the sacred vessels are tumbled from the altar and trampled under foot in the melee, and the cathedral rings with yells and shrieks and curses and the clash of weapons, they have hurried him into the sacristy and barred the doors, against which we shall beat ourselves in vain. Fury! Infamy! Malediction! Pick yourself up, Francesco Pazzi, and get home as you may! There is no mounting to horse and crying liberty through the streets for you! All is over! The wretched populace, the servile signory, side with the Medici; in a few hours the Archbishop of Pisa is swinging by the neck from a window of the Palazzo Vecchio; and while he is yet alive you are dragged, bleeding and naked, from your bed through the streets and hung beside him, so close that in his dying agony he sets his teeth in your breast with convulsive frenzy that leaves you fast in the death-clutch of his jaws till they cut the ropes and you ruin hideously down to the pavement below. . . .

I walked out one pleasant Sunday afternoon to the Villa Careggi, where Lorenzo made a dramatic end fourteen years after the tragedy in the cathedral. It is some two miles from the city; I could not say in just what direction; but it does not matter, since if you do not come to Villa Careggi when you go to look for it, you come to something else equally memorable, by ways as beautiful and through landscapes as picturesque. I remember that there was hanging from a crevice of one of the stone walls which we sauntered between, one of those great purple anemones of Florence, tilting and swaying in the sunny air of February, and that there was a tender presentiment of spring in the atmosphere, and people were out languidly enjoying the warmth about their doors, as if the winter had been some malady of theirs, and they were now slowly convalescent. The mountains were white with snow beyond Fiesole, but that was perhaps to set off to better advantage the nearer hillsides, studded with villas gleaming white through the black plumes of cypress, and blurred with long gray stretches of olive orchard; it is impossible to escape some such crazy impression of intention in the spectacular prospect of Italy, though that is probably less the fault of the prospect than of the people who have painted and printed so much about it. There were vineyards, of course, as well as olive orchards on all those broken and irregular slopes, over which wandered a tangle of the high walls which everywhere shut you out from intimate approach to the fields about Florence; you may look up at them, afar off, or you may look down at them, but you cannot look into them on the same level. . . .

As to the interior of the villa, everyone may go there and observe its facts; its vast, cold dim salons, its floors of polished cement, like ice to the foot, and its walls covered with painted histories and anecdotes and portraits of the Medici. The outside warmth had not got into the house, and I shivered in the sepulchral gloom, and could get no sense of the gay, voluptuous, living past there, not even in the prettily painted loggia where Lorenzo used to sit with his friends overlooking Val d' Arno, and glimpsing the tower of Giotto and the dome of Brunelleschi. But there is one room, next to the last of the long suite fronting on the lovely garden, where the event which makes the place memorable has an incomparable actuality. It is the room where Lorenzo died, and his dying eyes could look from its windows out over the lovely garden, and across the vast stretches of villa and village, olive and cypress, to the tops of Florence swimming against the horizon. He was a long time dying, of the gout of his ancestors and his own debauchery, he drew near his end cheerfully enough, and very much as he had always lived, now reasoning high of philosophy and poetry with Pico della Mirandola and Politian, and now laughing at the pranks of the jesters and buffoons whom they brought in to amuse him, till the very last, when he sickened of all those delights, fine or gross, and turned his thoughts to the mercy despised so long. But, as he kept saying, none had ever dared give him a resolute No, save one; and dreading in his final hours the mockery of flattering priests, he sent for this one fearless soul; and Savonarola, who had never yielded to his threats or caresses, came at the prayer of the dying man, and took his place beside the bed we still see there—high, broad, richly carved in dark wood, with a picture of Perugino's on the wall at the left beside it. Piero, Lorenzo's son, from whom he has just parted, must be in the next room yet, and the gentle Pico della Mirandola, whom Lorenzo was so glad to see that he smiled and jested with him in the old way, has closed the door on the preacher and the sinner. Lorenzo confesses that he has heavy on his soul three crimes: the cruel sack of Volterra, the theft of the public dower of young girls, by which many were driven to a wicked life, and the blood shed after the conspiracy of the Pazzi. ''He was greatly agitated, and Savonarola to quiet him kept repeating 'God is good; God is merciful. But,' he added, when Lorenzo had ceased to speak, 'there is need of three things.' 'And what are they, father?' 'First, you must have a great and living faith in the mercy of God.' 'This I have—the greatest.' 'Second, you must restore that which you have wrongfully taken, or require your children to restore it for you.' Lorenzo looked surprised and troubled; but he forced himself to compliance, and nodded his head in sign of assent.

Then Savonarola rose to his feet, and stood over the dying prince. 'Last, you must give back their liberty to the people of Florence.' Lorenzo, summoning all his remaining strength, disdainfully turned his back; and, without uttering a word, Savonarola departed without giving him absolution.''

It was as if I saw and heard it all, as I stood there in the room where the scene had been enacted; it still remains to me the vividest event in Florentine history, and Villari has no need, for me at least, to summon all the witnesses he calls to establish the verity of the story. There are some disputed things that establish themselves in our credence through the nature of the men and the times of which they are told, and this is one of them. Lorenzo and Savonarola were equally matched in courage, and the Italian soul of the one was as subtle for good as the Italian soul of the other was subtle for evil. In that encounter, the preacher knew that it was not the sack of a city or the blood of conspirators for which the sinner really desired absolution, however artfully and naturally they were advanced in his appeal; and Lorenzo knew when he sent for him that the monk would touch the sore spot in his guilty heart unerringly. It was a profound drama, searching the depths of character on either side, and on either side it was played with matchless magnanimity.

Fra Girolamo Savonarola
Prophet and Apostle
(1452–1498)

Jacob Burckhardt

The greatest of prophets and apostles—Fra Girolamo Savonarola of Ferrara had been burnt in Florence in the year 1498.

The instrument by means of which he transformed and ruled the city of Florence (1494–98) was his eloquence. Of this the meager reports that are left to us, which were taken down mostly on the spot, give us evidently a very imperfect notion. It was not that he possessed any striking outward advantages, for voice, accent, and rhetorical skill constituted precisely his weakest side; and those who required the preacher to be a stylist, went to his rival Fra Mariano da Genazzano. The eloquence of Savonarola was the expression of a lofty and commanding personality, the like of which was not seen again till the time of Luther. He himself held his own influence to be the result of a divine illumination, and could therefore, without presumption, assign a very high place to the office of the preacher, who, in the great hierarchy of spirits, occupies, according to him, the next place below the angels.

This man, whose nature seemed made of fire, worked another and greater miracle than any of his oratorical triumphs. His own Dominican monastery of San Marco, and then all the Dominican monasteries of Tuscany, became like-minded with himself, and undertook voluntarily the work of inward reform. When we reflect what the monasteries then were, and what measureless difficulty attends the least change where monks are concerned, we are doubly astonished at so complete a revolution. While the reform was still in progress large numbers of Savonarola's followers entered the Order, and thereby greatly facilitated his plans. Sons of the first houses in Florence entered San Marco as novices.

This reform of the Order in a particular province was the first step to a national Church, in which, had the reformer himself lived longer, it must infallibly have ended. Savonarola, indeed, desired the regeneration of the whole Church, and near the end of his career sent pressing exhortations to the great potentates urging them to call together a Council. But in Tuscany his Order and party were the only organs of his spirit—the salt of the earth—while the neighboring provinces remained in their old condition. Fancy and asceticism tended more and more to produce in him a state of mind to which Florence appeared as the scene of the kingdom of God upon earth.

His prophecies, whose partial fulfilment conferred on Savonarola a supernatural credit, were the means by which the ever-active Italian imagination seized control of the soundest and most cautious natures. At first the Franciscans, trusting in the reputation which had been bequeathed to them by St. Bernardino of Siena, fancied that they could compete with the great Dominican. They put one of their own men into the Cathedral pulpit, and outbid the Jeremiads of Savonarola by still more terrible warnings, till Piero de' Medici, who then still ruled over Florence, forced them both to be silent. Soon after, when Charles VIII came to Italy and the Medici were expelled, as Savonarola had clearly foretold, he alone was believed in. . . .

He only undertook the reorganization of the State for the reason that otherwise his enemies would have got the government into their own hands. It is unfair to judge him by the semidemocratic constitution of the beginning of the year 1495, which was neither better nor worse than other Florentine constitutions.

He was at bottom the most unsuitable man who could be found for such a work. His idea was a theocracy, in which all men were to bow in blessed humility before the Unseen, and all conflicts of passion were not even to be able to arise. His whole mind is written in that inscription on the Palazzo della Signoria, the substance of which was his maxim as early as 1495, and which was solemnly renewed by his partisans in 1527: "Jesus Christus Rex populi Florentini S.P.Q. decreto creatus." He stood in no more relation to mundane affairs and their actual conditions than any other inhabitant of a monastery. Man, according to him, has only to attend to those things which make directly for his salvation.

This temper comes out clearly in his opinions on ancient literature: "The only good thing which we owe to Plato and Aristotle is that they brought forward many arguments which we can use against the heretics. Yet they and other philosophers are now in Hell. An old woman

knows more about the Faith than Plato. It would be good for religion if
many books that seem useful were destroyed. When there were not so
many books and not so many arguments and disputes, religion grew
more quickly than it has done since.'' He wished to limit the classical
instruction of the schools to Homer, Virgil and Cicero, and to supply
the rest from Jerome and Augustine. Not only Ovid and Catullus, but
Terence and Tibullus, were to be banished. This may be no more than
the expressions of a nervous morality, but elsewhere in a special work
he admits that science as a whole is harmful. He holds that only a few
people should have to do with it, in order that the tradition of human
knowledge may not perish, and particularly that there may be no want
of intellectual athletes to confute the sophisms of the heretics. For all
others, grammar, morals, and religious teachings suffice. Culture and
education would thus return wholly into the charge of the monks, and
as, in his opinion, the ''most learned and the most pious'' are to rule
over the States and empires, these rulers would also be monks.
Whether he really foresaw this conclusion, we need not inquire.

A more childish method of reasoning cannot be imagined. The
simple reflection that the newborn antiquity and the boundless enlargement of human thought and knowledge which was due to it,
might give splendid confirmation to a religion able to adapt itself
thereto, seems never even to have occurred to the good man. He
wanted to forbid what he could not deal with by any other means. In
fact, he was anything but liberal, and was ready, for example, to send
the astrologers to the same stake at which he afterwards himself died.

How mighty must have been the soul which dwelt side by side with
this narrow intellect! And what a flame must have glowed within him
before he could constrain the Florentines, possessed as they were by
the passion for knowledge and culture, to surrender themselves to a
man who could thus reason! . . .

All this could not, however, be effected without the agency of a
tyrannical police. He did not shrink from the most vexatious inter-
ferences with the much-prized freedom of Italian private life, using
the espionage of servants on their masters as a means of carrying out
his moral reforms. That transformation of public and private life
which the Iron Calvin was but just able to effect at Geneva with the aid
of a permanent state of seige necessarily proved impossible at Florence, and the attempt only served to drive the enemies of Savonarola
into a more implacable hostility. Among his most unpopular measures
may be mentioned those organized parties of boys, who forced their

way into the houses and laid violent hands on any objects which seemed suitable for the bonfire. . . .

On the last day of the Carnival in the year 1497, and on the same day the year after, the great Auto da Fé took place on the Piazza della Signoria. In the center of it rose a high pyramid of several tiers. . . . On the lowest tier were arranged false beards, masks, and carnival disguises; above came volumes of the Latin and Italian poets, among others Boccaccio, . . . and Petrarch, partly in the form of valuable printed parchments and illuminated manuscripts; then women's ornaments and toilet articles, scents, mirrors, veils and false hair; higher up, lutes, harps, chessboards, playing cards; and finally, on the two uppermost tiers, paintings only, especially of female beauties. . . . On the first occasion a Venetian merchant who happened to be present offered the Signoria 22,000 gold florins for the objects on the pyramid; but the only answer he received was that his portrait, too, was painted, and burned along with the rest. When the pile was lighted, the Signoria appeared on the balcony, and the air echoed with song, the sound of trumpets, and the pealing of bells. The people then adjourned to the Piazza San Marco, where they danced round in three concentric circles. The innermost was composed of monks of the monastery, alternating with boys, dressed as angels; then came young layment and ecclesiastics; and on the outside, old men, citizens, and priests, the latter crowned with wreaths of olive.

All the ridicule of his victorious enemies, who in truth had no lack of justification or of talent for ridicule, was unable to discredit the memory of Savonarola. The more tragic the fortunes of Italy became, the brighter grew the halo which in the recollection of the survivors surrounded the figure of the great monk and prophet. Though his predictions may not have been confirmed in detail, the great and general calamity which he foretold was fulfilled with appalling truth.

Great, however, as the influence of all these preachers may have been, and brilliantly as Savonarola justified the claim of the monks to this office, nevertheless the order as a whole could not escape the contempt and condemnation of the people. Italy showed that she could give her enthusiasm only to individuals.

Persecution and Execution
of Savonarola

Francesco Guicciardini

The year 1498 was full of many grave and varied events which opened
with the downfall of Fra Girolamo. He had stopped preaching on the
orders of the Signoria, and just when the violent persecution he
suffered from both clerics and laymen seemed to have died down, a
small incident gave rise to a complete reversal of his fortunes. About
two years before, when preaching in Santa Liperata, Fra Domenico da
Pescia, his companion in the Order of San Marco, who was a simple
man with a reputation for living a saintly life and who followed Fra
Girolamo's style in predicting future events in his sermons, had said
that if it were necessary to prove the truth of what they foretold, they
would revive a corpse and walk through fire unharmed through God's
grace; and Fra Girolamo had later repeated this. Nothing had been said
about this since, until one Fra Francesco of the Franciscan Order, who
preached in Santa Croce and loathed Fra Girolamo and all his works,
began to say in his sermons that to prove how false these were he was
willing to walk through fire in the Piazza de' Signori if Fra Girolamo
would do so too. He added that he was sure he would burn, but so
would Fra Girolamo, and this would prove that there was no truth in
him, as he had so often boasted that he would issue unhurt from the
fire. Fra Domenico was told of this while he was preaching instead of

FRANCESCO GUICCIARDINI (1483–1540) was a Florentine historian and statesman and a
disciple of Machiavelli. A contemporary of Savonarola, he wrote a history of Florence
in his youth, and, later, a history of Italy. The latter is regarded as the masterpiece of
Italian historical literature of the Renaissance.

Fra Girolamo; and so he accepted the challenge in the pulpit, offering not Fra Girolamo but himself for this experiment.

This pleased many citizens of both parties who wished these divisions to end and all the uncertainties to be settled once and for all. They began to negotiate with the two preachers about putting the trial into effect. Finally after much argument all the friars agreed that a fire should be lit, and for Fra Girolamo a friar of his Order should enter it, the choice of the representative being left to him. Likewise for the other side a Franciscan friar should be nominated by his superiors. Having decided also on the date, Fra Girolamo had permission from the Signoria to preach; and preaching in San Marco he showed the great importance of miracles and said that they should not be used except in dire necessity when reasoning and experience proved insufficient; as the Christian faith had been proved in infinitely varied ways, and the truth of the things he had predicted had been shown with such effect and reason that anyone who was not hardened in wickedness could understand them, he had not had recourse to miracles so as not to tempt God. Nevertheless, since they had now been challenged, they willingly accepted, and all could be sure that on entering the fire the result would be that their friar would come out alive and unharmed while the other would be burned. If the opposite happened, they might freely say that he had preached lies. He added that not only his friars but anyone who entered the fire in defense of this truth would have the same experience. And then he asked them whether, if need be, they would go through fire to support the cause of so great a work ordered by God. With a great cry nearly everyone present answered that they would. An amazing thing to think of, because without any doubt, if Fra Girolamo had told them to, very many would indeed have gone through fire. Finally on the appointed day, . . . the Saturday before Palm Sunday, a platform was set up in the middle of Piazza de' Signori with a great bonfire of faggots. The Franciscans came at the appointed time and went into the loggia of the Signoria; and then the Dominican friars arrived, . . . and with them Fra Girolamo bearing the Host, in honor of which some friars and many lay-followers carried lighted torches. Their procession was so devout and showed so clearly that they came to the trial with the highest courage, that it not only reassured their own followers but even made their enemies flinch.

When they had entered the loggia, separated however from Franciscans by a wooden partition, some difficulty arose about the clothes Fra Domenico da Pescia was to wear to walk through the fire. The

Franciscans were afraid they might be enchanted. As they could not agree, the Signoria repeatedly sent two citizens from each party to discuss their differences. . . . When they had so arranged matters that agreement was near, they took the leaders of the friars into the palace and here resolved their difficulties and agreed on terms. But when they were about to start the ordeal, it came to the knowledge of the Franciscans that Fra Domenico was to enter the fire bearing the Host. They began vehemently to reject this proposal, arguing that if the Host were burned it would be a scandal and a grave danger to the whole Christian faith. On the other side, Fra Girolamo continued to insist that he should carry it, and in the end after much argument, with both sides persisting in their own views and there being no way of reconciling them, they all went home without even lighting the bonfire. And although Fra Girolamo went at once into the pulpit and showed how the failure of the ordeal was due to the Franciscans and that the victory was his, many people thought that the question of the Host was a quibble rather than a genuine reason; he lost many of his friends that day and public opinion became very hostile to him. In consequence, on the following day his supporters were disillusioned, and were insulted in the streets by the populace, while his adversaries were much emboldened by popular support, and by having the backing of the Compagnacci under arms and a sympathetic Signoria in the palace. A friar of San Marco was to preach in Santa Liperata after dinner that day, when a great tumult arose as if by chance, spreading rapidly throughout the city as happens when people are excited and minds are full of doubt and suspicion. The enemies of the friar and the Compagnacci took up arms and began to drive the mob toward San Marco. Many of the friar's followers were at vespers, and they began to defend the convent with weapons and stones although it was not besieged. The fury of the mob then turned toward the house of Francesco Valori, which they attacked while it was defended by those within. Francesco's wife . . . appeared at a window and was struck in the head by a spear which killed her instantly. Then the mob broke into the house and found Francesco in an attic; he begged to be taken alive to the palace and was brought outside. As he was accompanied on his way by a guard, he had gone only a few steps when he was attacked and killed. . . .

Thus was shown in Francesco Valori a great example of the reversal of fate. But a short time before he had been undoubtedly the city's most important figure in authority, following and popularity: then suddenly all was changed. In the same day his house was sacked, his wife killed before his eyes, and he himself almost at the same moment basely murdered by his enemies. . . .

When Francesco Valori had been killed and his house sacked, the fury of the mob turned toward the house of Paolantonio Soderini, who after Francesco was . . . the leader of that party. . . . Then the mob returned to San Marco, where a spirited defense was put up. . . . At last, after many hours of fighting, they forced their way into San Marco and took as prisoners to the palace Fra Girolamo, Fra Domenico, and Fra Silvestro. . . . who, although he did not preach, was one of Fra Girolamo's intimates and was believed to know all his secrets. . . .

About twenty citizens were then entrusted with the task of examining Fra Girolamo and his companions—all of them his direst enemies. Eventually after they had given him a few drops on the *strappado*, without the Pope's permission, a few days later they drew up a document and published in the great council what they said they had extracted from him. This was signed by the vicars of Florence and Fiesole and by some of the principal friars of San Marco in whose presence the document had been read to Fra Girolamo; and when he was asked if it were true, he agreed that what was written down was true. The most important conclusions were to this effect: the things he had predicted he had not had from God or from revelation or any other divine means—they had been his own invention without the participation or knowledge of any other person lay or cleric; he had acted out of pride and ambition, and his purpose had been to provoke a general council of the Christian princes which should depose the Pope and reform the Church, and if he had been elected Pope he would have accepted; nevertheless he was much more desirous that the great reform should be carried out by his agency than that he should become Pope, because any man may be Pope—even one of little worth—but only a great man could be author and leader of such an endeavor. . . . He had not proposed the ordeal by fire, but Fra Domenico had done so without his knowledge, and he had consented as he could not honorably withdraw and hoping that the Franciscans would be frightened into giving way; and yet he was sure that, if the ordeal were carried out, the Host borne in his friar's hands would save him. These were the conclusions against him; the rest were rather in his favor, for they showed that apart from pride there had been no vice of any kind in him, and that he was absolutely innocent of lust, avarice, and such sins. And further, that he had not had any political dealings either with princes abroad or citizens within.

When these proceedings had been published, his punishment was delayed for a few days because the Pope, having heard of his arrest and confession, which were most pleasing to him, had sent his absolution not only to the citizens who had examined him without ecclesiastical license, but to those who had attended his sermons in defiance of the apostolic order. He had then asked that Fra Girolamo should be sent to Rome. This was refused, as it seemed dishonorable that our city should serve as a gaol. In the end he sent . . . apostolic commissioners to Florence to examine Fra Girolamo and his companions. . . . The commissioners from Rome arrived, and having re-examined Fra Girolamo and the others, all three were condemned to be burned at the stake. On the [23rd] day of May they were first degraded in the Piazza de' Signori and then hanged and burned before a greater crowd than used to come to their sermons. It was thought an astonishing thing that none of them, particularly Fra Girolamo, should have said anything publicly on that occasion to accuse or excuse themselves.

Thus Girolamo Savonarola came to a shameful end; and perhaps it will not be out of place here to speak at greater length about his qualities, for we have not seen in our times—nor did our fathers and grandfathers in theirs—a monk so full of many virtues or with so much credit and authority as he enjoyed. Even his enemies admit that he was extremely learned in several branches of knowledge, especially philosophy, which he possessed so thoroughly and could use so aptly for all his own purposes as if he had invented it himself—but more particularly in Holy Scripture in which it is believed there had not been anyone to compare with him for several centuries. He had wonderfully sound judgment not only in scholarship but also in worldly affairs, in the principles of which he had great understanding, as in my opinion his sermons show. . . .

But doubt and difference remain regarding the saintliness of his life. All that one can say about this is that if there was any vice in him it was simply that of inventing things out of pride and ambition. Those who long observed his life and habits found in them not the slightest trace of avarice or lust or any other sort of greed or weakness; on the contrary they saw in him a most religious life, full of charity and prayer and strict observance not of the outward forms of religion but of its very essence. And so, although in his trials his calumniators made every effort to discover faults in him, not the least trace of that kind of thing could be found. His endeavors in securing decent behavior were most holy and wonderfully successful; and there was never in Florence so much virtue and religion as in his time. After his death manners decayed to such an extent that it proved that what good was done had been brought in by and depended upon him. There was no public gambling, and only with restraint in private houses. The taverns, where all the vicious and ill-conducted youths tend to gather, were closed. Sodomy was suppressed and punished severely. Women to a great extent gave up indecent and lascivious dress. Boys were almost all reformed from many wicked ways and led to a decent and God-fearing life. They were gathered together in companies under the care of Fra Domenico, attended church, wore their hair short, and pursued with stones and insults wicked men and gamblers and immodestly dressed women. . . . Through his preaching a great number of friars entered his order—of every age and class, many noble youths from the leading families of the city, many men of advanced years and great reputation. . . . The result was that there was no convent like it in Italy; and he so directed the young men in their studies—not only of Greek and Latin but also of Hebrew—that they gave promise of being the very ornaments of religion. While he thus made a great contribution to spiritual affairs, he did no less good to the affairs of the city and to the public weal. . . .

Without any doubt Savonarola's actions saved Florence; and as he very truly said, they benefited those who now ruled the city, as well as those who had ruled in the past. Indeed his works were so good, while in particular some of his prophecies turned out to be true, that many have continued for long to believe that he was really sent by God and a true prophet in spite of the excommunication, his trial and death. I am doubtful and I have not been able to make up my mind at all; I must wait—if I live long enough—for time to reveal the truth. But I draw this conclusion: if he were really a good man, then we have seen in our days a great prophet; if he were wicked, then we have seen a great man, because, apart from his learning, if he were able to feign in public for so many years so great a mission without ever being caught out in a falsehood, one must admit that he had a most remarkable judgment, talent, and power of invention.

PART 2

''HERE CIVILIZATION OF MANKIND WAS BORN ANEW''

FLORENCE: WORKS OF ART

Florence, father of Michelangelo,
Dante, da Vinci, Fra Angelico,
Cellini, Botticelli, Brunelleschi,
Giotto, Donatello, Masaccio!

We shall not see their like, or yours, again.
Painters depart, and patrons. You remain,
Your bridges blown, your glory catalogued,
A norm for scholars and for gentlemen.

Reverend city; sober, unperplexed,
Turning your page to genius annexed
I breathe the mint and myrrh of Tuscan hills,
The tart aroma of some classic text.

Shields and medallions; overshadowing eaves
Like studious brows; the light that interleaves
Your past with amber: all's definitive, all
In changeless chiaroscuro one conceives.

I sometimes think the heart is ne'er so dead
As where some vanished era overspread
The soil with Titian foliage, scattering down
Eternal rubies when its bloom was shed.

Where rode Lorenzo, panoplied and plumed,
Where Savonarola burned, and Ruskin fumed,
The lady artist sets her easel up,
The tourist with mild wonder is consumed.

Yet still the Arno navigably flows
And saunterers past the Ponte Vecchio's
Jewel shops cast a shadow: here is still
A taste for life, a market for the rose.

Cecil Day Lewis

The Renaissance

John Addington Symonds

The word "Renaissance" has of late years received a more extended significance than that which is implied in our English equivalent—the Revival of Learning. We use it to denote the whole transition from the Middle Ages to the Modern World; and though it is possible to assign certain limits to the period during which this transition took place, we cannot fix on any dates so positively as to say—between this year and that the movement was accomplished. To do so would be like trying to name the days on which spring in any particular season began and ended. . . .

In like manner we cannot refer the whole phenomena of the Renaissance to any one cause or circumstance, or limit them within the field of any one department of human knowledge. If we ask the students of art what they mean by the Renaissance, they will reply that it was the revolution effected in architecture, painting, and sculpture by the recovery of antique monuments. Students of literature, philosophy, and theology see in the Renaissance that discovery of manuscripts, that passion for antiquity, that progress in philology and criticism, which led to a correct knowledge of the classics, to a fresh taste in poetry, to new systems of thought, to more accurate analysis, and finally to the Lutheran schism and the emancipation of the conscience. Men of science will discourse about the discovery of the solar system by Copernicus and Galileo, the anatomy of Vesalius, and Harvey's theory of the circulation of the blood. The origination of a truly scientific method is the point which interests them most in the Renaissance. The political historian, again, has his own answer to the question. The extinction of feudalism, the development of the great nationalities of Europe, the growth of monarchy, the limitation of the ecclesiastical authority and the erection of the Papacy into an Italian kingdom, and in the last place the gradual emergence of that sense of popular freedom which exploded in the Revolution; these are the aspects of the movement which engross his attention. . . . Men whose attention has been turned to the history of discoveries and inventions will relate the exploration of America and the East, or will point to the benefits conferred upon the world by the arts of printing and engraving, by the compass and the telescope, by paper and by gunpowder; and will insist that at the moment of the Renaissance all these instruments of mechanical utility started into existence, to aid the dissolution of what was rotten and must perish, to strengthen and perpetuate the new and useful and life-giving. Yet neither any one of these answers taken separately, nor indeed all of them together, will offer a solution of the problem. By the term Renaissance, or new birth, is indicated a natural movement, not to be explained by this or that characteristic, but to be accepted as an effort of humanity for which at length the time had come. . . . The history of the Renaissance . . .is the history of the attainment of self-conscious freedom by the human spirit manifested in the European races. It is no mere political mutation, no new fashion of art, no restoration of classical standards of taste. The arts and the inventions, the knowledge and the books, which suddenly became vital at the time of the Renaissance, had long lain neglected on the shores of the Dead Sea which we call the Middle Ages. It was not their discovery which caused the Renaissance. But it was the intellectual energy, the spontaneous outburst of intelligence, which enabled mankind at that moment to make use of them. . . .

Dante's [*Divine Comedy*], a work of conscious art, conceived in a modern spirit and written in a modern tongue, was the first true sign that Italy, the leader of the nations of the West, had shaken off her sleep. Petrarch followed. His ideal of antique culture as the everlasting solace and the universal education of the human race, his lifelong effort to recover the classical harmony of thought and speech, gave a direct impulse to one of the chief movements of the Renaissance—its passionate outgoing toward the ancient world. After Petrarch, Boccaccio opened yet another channel for the stream of freedom. His conception of human existence as joy to be accepted with thanksgiving, not as a gloomy error to be rectified by suffering, familiarized the fourteenth century with that form of semipagan gladness which marked the real Renaissance.

In Dante, Petrarch, and Boccaccio Italy recovered the consciousness of intellectual liberty. What we call the Renaissance had not yet arrived; but their achievement rendered its appearance in due season certain. With Dante the genius of the modern world dared to stand alone and to create confidently after its own fashion. With Petrarch the same genius reached forth across the gulf of darkness, resuming the tradition of a splendid past. With Boccaccio the same genius proclaimed the beauty of the world, the goodliness of youth and strength and love and life, unterrified by hell, unappalled by the shadow of impending death.

It was now, at the beginning of the fourteenth century, when Italy had lost indeed the heroic spirit which we admire in her Communes of the thirteenth, but had gained instead ease, wealth, magnificence, and that repose which springs from long prosperity, that the new age at last began. Europe was, as it were, a fallow field, beneath which lay buried the civilization of the old world. Behind stretched the centuries of medievalism, intellectually barren and inert. Of the future there were as yet but faint foreshadowings. Meanwhile, the force of the nations who were destined to achieve the coming transformation was unexhausted; their physical and mental faculties were unimpaired. No ages of enervating luxury, of intellectual endeavor, of life artificially preserved or ingeniously prolonged, had sapped the fiber of the men who were about to inaugurate the modern world. Severely nurtured, unused to delicate living, these giants of the Renaissance were like boys in their capacity for endurance, their inordinate appetite for enjoyment. No generations, hungry, sickly, effete, critical, disillusioned, trod them down. Ennui and the fatigue that springs from skepticism, the despair of thwarted effort, were unknown. Their fresh and unperverted senses rendered them keenly alive to what was beautiful and natural. They yearned for magnificence, and instinctively comprehended splendor. At the same time the period of satiety was still far off. Everything seemed possible to their young energy; nor had a single pleasure palled upon their appetite. Born, as it were, at the moment when desires and faculties are evenly balanced, when the perceptions are not blunted nor the senses cloyed, opening their eyes for the first time on a world of wonder, these men of the Renaissance enjoyed what we may term the first transcendent springtide of the modern world. Nothing is more remarkable than the fullness of the life that throbbed in them. . . .

The great achievements of the Renaissance were the discovery of the world and the discovery of man. . . .The discovery of the world divides itself into two branches—the exploration of the globe, and that systematic exploration of the universe which is in fact what we call Science. Columbus made known America in 1492; the Portuguese rounded the Cape in 1497; Copernicus explained the solar system in 1507. It is not necessary to add anything to this plain statement; for, in contact with fact of such momentous import, to avoid what seems like commonplace reflection would be difficult. Yet it is only when we contrast the ten centuries which preceded these dates with the four centuries which have ensued that we can estimate the magnitude of that Renaissance movement by means of which a new hemisphere had been added to civilization. In like manner, it is worth while to pause a moment and consider what is implied in the substitution of the Copernican for the Ptolemaic system. The world, regarded in old times as the center of all things, the apple of God's eye, for the sake of which were created sun and moon and stars, suddenly was found to be one of the many balls that roll round a giant sphere of light and heat, which is itself but one among innumerable suns attended each by a cortege of planets, and scattered, how we know not, through infinity. What has become of that brazen seat of the old gods, that Paradise to which an ascending Deity might be caught up through clouds, and hidden for a moment from the eyes of his disciples? The demonstration of the simplest truths of astronomy destroyed at a blow the legends that were most significant to the early Christians by annihilating their symbolism. Well might the Church persecute Galileo for his proof of the world's mobility. Instinctively she perceived that in this one proposition was involved the principle of hostility to her most cherished conceptions, to the very core of her mythology. Science was born, and the warfare between scientific positivism and religious metaphysic was declared. . . .

Thus by the discovery of the world is meant on the one hand the appropriation by civilized humanity of all corners of the habitable globe, and on the other the conquest by Science of all that we now know about the nature of the universe. In the discovery of man, again, it is possible to trace a twofold process. Man in his temporal relations, illustrated by pagan antiquity, and man in his spiritual relations, illustrated by biblical antiquity; these are the two regions, at first apparently distinct, afterwards found to be interpenetrative, which the critical and inquisitive genius of the Renaissance opened for investigation. In the former of these regions we find two agencies at work, art and scholarship. During the Middle Ages the plastic arts, like philosophy, had degenerated into barren and meaningless scholasticism—a frigid reproduction of lifeless forms copied technically and without inspiration from debased patterns. Pictures became symbolically connected with the religious feelings of the people, formulas from which to deviate would be impious in the artist and confusing to the worshipper. Superstitious reverence bound the painter to copy the almond eyes and stiff joints of the saints whom he had adored from infancy; and, even had it been otherwise, he lacked the skill to imitate the natural forms he saw around him. But with the dawning of the Renaissance a new spirit in the arts arose. Men began to conceive that the human body is noble in itself and worthy of patient study. The object of the artist then became to unite devotional feeling and respect for the sacred legend with the utmost beauty and the utmost fidelity of delineation. He studied from the nude; he drew the body in every posture; he composed drapery, invented attitudes, and adapted the action of his figures and the expression of his faces to the subject he had chosen. In a word, he humanized the altar pieces and the cloister-frescoes upon which he worked. In this way the painters rose above the ancient symbols, and brought heaven down to earth. By drawing Madonna and her son like living human beings, by dramatizing the Christian history, they silently substituted the love of beauty and the interests of actual life for the principles of the Church. The saint or angel became an occasion for the display of physical perfection, and to introduce "*un bel corpo ignudo*" into the composition was of more moment to them than to represent the macerations of the Magdalen. Men thus learned to look beyond the relic and the host, and to forget the dogma in the lovely forms which gave it expression. Finally, when the classics came to aid this work of progress, a new world of thought and fancy, divinely charming, wholly human, was revealed to their astonished eyes. Thus art, which had begun by humanizing the legends of the Church, diverted the attention of its students from the legend to the work of beauty, and lastly, severing itself from the religious tradition, became the exponent of the majesty and splendor of the human body. This final emancipation of art from ecclesiastical trammels culminated in the great age of Italian painting. . . .

The transition at this point in the discovery of man, the revelation to the consciousness of its own spiritual freedom, is natural. Not only did scholarship restore the classics and encourage literary criticism; it also restored the text of the Bible, and encouraged theological criticism. In the wake of theological freedom followed a free philosophy, no longer subject to the dogmas of the Church. To purge the Christian faith from false conceptions, to liberate the conscience from the tyranny of priests, and to interpret religion to the reason, has been the work of the last centuries; nor is this work as yet by any means accomplished. On the one side Descartes and Bacon, Spinoza and Locke, are sons of the Renaissance, champions of new-found philosophical freedom; on the other side, Luther is a son of the Renaissance, the herald of new-found religious freedom. The whole movement of the Reformation is a phase in that accelerated action of the modern mind which at its commencement we call the Renaissance. . . .

Thus what the word Renaissance really means is new birth to liberty—the spirit of mankind recovering consciousness and the power of self–determination, recognizing the beauty of the outer world, and of the body through art, liberating the reason in science and the conscience in religion, restoring culture to the intelligence, and establishing the principle of political freedom. The Church was the schoolmaster of the Middle Ages. Culture was the humanizing and refining influence of the Renaissance. The problem for the present and the future is how through education to render knowledge accessible to all—to break down that barrier which in the Middle Ages was set between clerk and layman, and which in the intermediate period has arisen between the intelligent and ignorant classes. Whether the Utopia of a modern world, in which all men shall enjoy the same social, political, and intellectual advantages, be realized or not, we cannot doubt that the whole movement of humanity from the Renaissance onward has tended in this direction. To destroy the distinctions, mental and physical, which nature raises between individuals, and which constitute an actual hierarchy, will always be impossible. Yet it may happen that in the future no civilized man will lack the opportunity of being physically and mentally the best that God has made him. . . .

In the work of the Renaissance all the great nations of Europe shared. But it must never be forgotten that as a matter of history the true Renaissance began in Italy. It was there that the essential qualities which distinguish the modern from the ancient and the medieval world were developed. Italy created that new spiritual atmosphere of culture and of intellectual freedom which has been the life—breath of the European races. As the Jews are called the chosen and peculiar people of divine revelation, so may the Italians be called the chosen and peculiar vessels of the prophecy of the Renaissance. In art, in scholarship, in science, in the mediation between antique culture and the modern intellect, they took the lead, handing to Germany and France and England the restored humanities complete. . . . Spain and England have since done more for the exploration and colonization of the world. Germany achieved the labor of the Reformation almost single—handed. France has collected, centralized, and diffused intelligence with irresistible energy. But if we return to the first origins of the Renaissance, we find that, at a time when the rest of Europe was inert, Italy had already begun to organize the various elements of the modern spirit, and to set the fashion whereby the other great nations should learn and live.

Giotto: Herald of the Renaissance

Bernard Berenson

Florentine painting between Giotto [1266–1337] and Michelangelo contains the names of such artists as Orcagna, Masaccio, Fra Filippo, Pollaiolo, Verrocchio, Leonardo, and Botticelli. Put beside these the greatest names in Venetian art, the Vivarini, the Bellini, Giorgione, Titian, and Tintoretto. The difference is striking. The significance of the Venetian names is exhausted with their significance as painters. Not so with the Florentines. Forget that they were painters, they remain great sculptors, forget that they were sculptors, and still they remain architects, poets, and even men of science. They left no form of expression untried, and to none could they say, "This will perfectly convey my meaning." Painting, therefore, offers but a partial and not always the most adequate manifestation of their personality, and we feel the artist as greater than his work, and the man as soaring above the artist.

The immense superiority of the artist even to his greatest achievement in any one art form means that his personality was but slightly determined by the particular art in question, that he tended to mold it rather than let it shape him. It would be absurd, therefore, to treat the Florentine painter as a mere link between two points in a necessary evolution. The history of the art of Florence can never be, as that of Venice, the study of a placid development. Each man of genius brought to bear upon his art a great intellect, which, never condescending merely to please, was tirelessly striving to reincarnate what it comprehended of life in forms that would fitly convey it to others; and in this endeavor each man of genius was necessarily compelled to create forms essentially his own. But because Florentine painting was pre-eminently an art formed by great personalities, it grappled with problems of the highest interest, and offered solutions that can never lose their value. . . .

The first of the great personalities in Florentine painting was Giotto. Although he affords no exception to the rule that the great Florentines exploited all the arts in the endeavor to express themselves, he, Giotto, renowned as architect and sculptor, reputed as wit and versifier, differed from most of his Tuscan successors in having peculiar aptitude for the essential in painting *as an art*.

Before we can appreciate his real value, we must come to an agreement as to what in the art of figure painting—the craft has its own altogether diverse laws—*is* the essential; for figure painting, we may say at once, was not only the one preoccupation of Giotto, but the dominant interest of the entire Florentine school.

Psychology has ascertained that sight alone gives us no accurate sense of the third dimension. In our infancy, long before we are conscious of the process, the sense of touch, helped on by muscular sensations of movement, teaches us to appreciate depth, the third dimension, both in objects and in space.

In the same unconscious years we learn to make of touch, of the third dimension, the test of reality. The child is still dimly aware of the intimate connection between touch and the third dimension. He cannot persuade himself of the unreality of Looking-Glass Land until he has touched the back of the mirror. Later, we entirely forget the connection, although it remains true, that every time our eyes recognize reality, we are, as a matter of fact, giving tactile values to retinal impressions.

Now, painting is an art which aims at giving an abiding impression of artistic reality with only two dimensions. The painter must, therefore, do consciously what we all do unconsciously—construct his third dimension. And he can accomplish his task only as we accomplish ours, by giving tactile values to retinal impressions. His first business, therefore, is to rouse the tactile sense, for I must have the illusion of being able to touch a figure, I must have the illusion of varying muscular sensations inside my palm and fingers corresponding to the various projections of this figure, before I shall take it for granted as real, and let it affect me lastingly.

It follows that the essential in the art of painting—as distinguished from the art of coloring, I beg the reader to observe—is somehow to stimulate our consciousness of tactile values, so that the picture shall have at least as much power as the object represented, to appeal to our tactile imagination.

Well, it was of the power to stimulate the tactile consciousness—of the essential, as I have ventured to call it, in the art of painting—that Giotto was supreme master. This is his everlasting claim to greatness, and it is this which will make him a source of highest aesthetic delight for a period at least as long as decipherable traces of his handiwork remain on moldering panel or crumbling wall. For great though he was as a poet, enthralling as a storyteller, splendid and majestic as a composer, he was in these qualities superior in degree only to many of the masters who painted in various parts of Europe during the thousand years that intervened between the decline of antique, and the birth, in his own person, of modern painting. But none of these masters had the power to stimulate the tactile imagination, and, consequently, they never painted a figure which has artistic existence. Their works have value, if at all, as highly elaborate, very intelligible symbols, capable, indeed, of communicating something, but losing all higher value the moment the message is delivered.

Giotto's paintings, on the contrary, have not only as much power of appealing to the tactile imagination as is possessed by the objects represented—human figures in particular—but actually more; with the necessary result that to his contemporaries they conveyed a *keener* sense of reality, of lifelikeness than the objects themselves! We whose current knowledge of anatomy is greater, who expect more articulation and suppleness in the human figure, who, in short, see much less naively now than Giotto's contemporaries, no longer find his paintings more than lifelike; but we still feel them to be intensely real in the sense that they powerfully appeal to our tactile imagination, thereby compelling us, as do all things that stimulate our sense of touch while they present themselves to our eyes, to take their existence for granted. And it is only when we can take for granted the existence of the object painted that it can begin to give us pleasure that is genuinely artistic, as separated from the interest we feel in symbols. . . .

Furthermore, the stimulation of our tactile imagination awakens our consciousness of the importance of the tactile sense in our physical and mental functioning, and thus, again, by making us feel better provided for life than we were aware of being, gives us a heightened sense of capacity. And this brings us back once more to the statement that the chief business of the figure painter, as an artist, is to stimulate the tactile imagination. . . .

Let us now . . . see in what way Giotto fulfills the first condition of painting as an art, which condition, as we agreed, is somehow to stimulate our tactile imagination. We shall understand this without difficulty if we cover with the same glance two pictures of nearly the same subject that hang side by side in the Uffizi at Florence, one by Cimabue, and the other by Giotto. The difference is striking, but it does not consist so much in a difference of pattern and types, as of realization. In the Cimabue we patiently decipher the lines and colors, and we conclude at last that they were intended to represent a woman seated, men and angels standing by or kneeling. To recognize these representations we have had to make many times the effort that the actual objects would have required, and in consequence our feeling of capacity has not only not been confirmed, but actually put in question. With what sense of relief, of rapidly rising vitality, we turn to the Giotto! Our eyes scarcely have had time to light on it before we realize it completely—the throne occupying a real space, the Virgin satisfactorily seated upon it, the angels grouped in rows about it. Our tactile imagination is put to play immediately. Our palms and fingers accompany our eyes much more quickly than in presence of real objects, the sensations varying constantly with the various projections represented, as of face, torso, knees; confirming in every way our feeling of capacity for coping with things—for life, in short. I care little that the picture endowed with the gift of evoking such feelings has faults, that the types represented do not correspond to my ideal of beauty, that the figures are too massive, and almost unarticulated; I forgive them all, because I have much better to do than to dwell upon faults.

But how does Giotto accomplish this miracle? With the simplest means, with almost rudimentary light and shade, and functional line, he contrives to render, out of all the possible outlines, out of all the possible variations of light and shade that a given figure may have, only those that we must isolate for special attention when we are actually realizing it. This determines his types, his schemes of color, even his compositions. He aims at types which both in face and figure are simple, large-boned, and massive—types, that is to say, which in actual life would furnish the most powerful stimulus to the tactile imagination. Obliged to get the utmost out of his rudimentary light and shade, he makes his scheme of color of the lightest that his contrasts may be of the strongest. In his compositions he aims at clearness of grouping, so that each important figure may have its desired tactile value. Note in the *Madonna* we have been looking at, how the shadows compel us to realize every concavity, and the lights every convexity, and how, with the play of the two, under the guidance of line, we realize the significant parts of each figure, whether draped or undraped. Nothing here but has its architectonic reason. Above all, every line is functional; that is to say, charged with purpose. Its existence, its direction, is absolutely determined by the need of rendering the tactile values. Follow any line here, say in the figure of the angel kneeling to the left, and see how it outlines and models, how it enables you to realize the head, the torso, the hips, the legs, the feet, and how its direction, its tension, is always determined by the action. There is not a genuine fragment of Giotto in existence but has these qualities, and to such a degree that the worst treatment has not been able to spoil them. Witness the resurrected frescoes in Santa Croce at Florence!

The rendering of tactile values once recognized as the most important specifically artistic quality of Giotto's work, and as his personal contribution to the art of painting, we are all the better fitted to appreciate his more obvious though less peculiar merits—merits, I must add, which would seem far less extraordinary if it were not for the high plane of reality on which Giotto keeps us. Now what is behind this power of raising us to a higher plane of reality but a genius for grasping and communicating real significance? What is it to render the tactile values of an object but to communicate its material significance? A painter who, after generations of mere manufacturers of symbols, illustrations, and allegories, had the power to render the material significance of the objects he painted, must, as a man, have had a profound sense of the significant. No matter, then, what his theme, Giotto feels its real significance and communicates as much of it as the general limitations of his art and of his own skill permit. When the theme is sacred story, it is scarcely necessary to point out with what processional gravity, with what hieratic dignity, with what sacramental intentness he endows it; the eloquence of the greatest critics has here found a darling subject. But let us look a moment at certain of his symbols in the Scrovegni Chapel at Padua, at the Inconstancy, the Injustice, and Avarice, for instance. "What are the significant traits," he seems to have asked himself, "in the appearance and action of a person under the exclusive domination of one of these vices? Let me paint the person with these traits, and I shall have a figure that perforce must call up the vice in question." So he paints Inconstancy as a woman with a blank face, her arms held out aimlessly, her torso falling backwards, her feet on the side of a wheel. It makes one giddy to look at her. Injustice is a powerfully built man in the vigor of his years dressed in the costume of a judge, with his left hand clenching the hilt of his sword, and his clawed right hand grasping a double-hooked lance. His cruel eye is sternly on the watch, and his attitude is one of alert readiness to spring in all his giant force upon his prey. He sits enthroned on a rock, overtowering the tall waving trees, and below him his underlings are stripping and murdering a wayfarer. Avarice is a horned hag with ears like trumpets. A snake issuing from her mouth curls back and bites her forehead. Her left hand clutches her moneybag, as she moves forward stealthily, her right hand ready to shut down on whatever it can grasp. No need to label them: as long as these vices exist, for so long has Giotto extracted and presented their visible significance.

Still another exemplification of his sense for the significant is furnished by his treatment of action and movement. The grouping, the gestures, never fail to be just such as will most rapidly convey the meaning. So with the significant line, the significant light and shade, the significant look up or down, and the significant gesture, with means technically of the simplest, and, be it remembered, with no knowledge of anatomy, Giotto conveys a complete sense of motion such as we get in his Paduan frescoes of the *Resurrection of the Blessed*, of the *Ascension of our Lord*, of the God the Father in the *Baptism*, or the angel in *Zaccarias' Dream*.

This, then, is Giotto's claim to everlasting appreciation as an artist: that his thoroughgoing sense for the significant in the visible world enabled him so to represent things that we realize his representations more quickly and more completely than we should realize the things themselves, thus giving us that confirmation of our sense of capacity which is so great a source of pleasure.

"The Finest Church in Christendom," Santa Maria del Fiore: The Duomo of Arnolfo di Cambio and the Dome of Filippo Brunelleschi

Mary McCarthy

The position of frank rivalry and competition taken by the Florentines toward the ancient world was established remarkably early. When the Duomo was ordered, in 1296, from Arnolfo di Cambio [c. 1232–1310] to replace the old church of Santa Reparata, a proclamation explained the citizens' requirements. "The Florentine Republic, soaring ever above the conception of the most competent judges, desires that an edifice shall be constructed so magnificent in its height and beauty that it shall surpass anything of its kind produced in the times of their greatest power by the Greeks and the Romans." The intention of surpassing standards held to be fixed and eternal amounted almost to blasphemy or *hubris*; to modern ears, this very tall order has an "American" twang: so a millionaire might command his architect to build him something bigger and better than the Parthenon. . . .

Arnolfo's Duomo does not surpass the Parthenon; nevertheless, it is a very remarkable building. Bigness has always been one of the forms that beauty can take, and the Renaissance was more simply conscious of this than sophisticated people are today. "Let me tell you how beautiful the Duomo is," writes Vasari, and what follows is an account of its measurements. The scale of an effort was the measure of its sublimity; the public, running its eye over the sum of measurements, contemplated a feat of daring. In daring, the Florentines excelled; that is why their architecture and their sculpture and much of their painting have such a virile character.

The Duomo, outside, still astonishes by its bulk, which is altogether out of proportion with the narrow streets that lead up to it. It sits in the center of Florence like a great hump of a snowy mountain deposited by some natural force, and it is, in fact, a kind of man-made mountain rising from the plain of the city and vying with the mountain of Fiesole, which can be seen in the distance. Unlike St. Peter's in Rome, which is cleverly prepared for by colonnades, fountains, and an obelisk, the Duomo of Florence is stumbled on like an irreducible fact in the midst of shops, *pasticcerie*, and a wild cat's cradle of motor traffic. It startles by its size and also by its gaiety—the spread of its flouncing apse and tribune in the Tuscan marble dress, dark green from Prato, pure white from Carrara, pink from the Maremma. It is like a mountain but it is also like a bellying circus tent or festive marquee. Together with the Baptistery and Giotto's pretty bell tower, it constitutes a joyous surprise in the severe, dun, civic city, and indeed, throughout Tuscany there is always that characteristic contrast between the stone dread of politics and the marbled gaiety of churches.

Inside, Arnolfo's Duomo is very noble—sturdy, tall, grave, with great stone pillars rising like oaks from the floor to uphold massive arches so full they can hardly be called pointed. This splendid stone hall does not soar, like a Gothic cathedral; the upward thrust is broken by a strict, narrow iron gallery running around the whole interior, outlining the form. A few memorial busts; Uccello's clock; the two caparisoned knights on horseback in *trompe l'oeil*; round, deep eyes of windows, set with large-paned stained glass, high in the thick walls; a small, sculptured bishop, blessing; a few faded images on gold backgrounds; a worn fresco of Dante; two statues of the prophet Isaiah; a holy-water stoup—that is almost all there is in this quiet, long room until it swells out into the vast octagonal tribune, surrounded by dim, almost dark chapels and topped by Brunelleschi's dome. There is nothing here but the essentials of shelter and support and the essentials of worship: pillars, arches, ribbing, walls, light, holy water, remembrance of the dead, a clock that still tells time.

The daring of Arnolfo, who was the first of the great Florentine master builders, lay not only in the scale of his undertaking but in the resolute stressing of essentials—what the Italians call the *membratura*, or frame of the building, a term that is drawn from anatomy (i.e., from the human frame). Michelangelo, the last of the great builders in Arnolfo's tradition, considered architecture to be related to anatomy, and the Florentine Duomo, with its pronounced *membratura*, is like a building in the nude, showing its muscles and sinews and the structure of bone underneath. On the outside, it is a dazzling mountain, cased in the native marbles of Tuscany, and, inside, it is a man, erect. Arnolfo was a sculptor, too, and the sculptures he made for the old facade (now replaced by a Victorian facade) and interior of the Cathedral (they can be seen in the Museum of the Works of the Duomo) have an odd family resemblance to the interior of the Duomo itself, as though saints, Madonnas, bishops, and building were all one breed of frontiersman —tall, sturdy, impassive.

Arnolfo had got as far as the tribune, as far, some think, as the drum of the cupola, when he died. In the magnitude of his ambition, he left a problem for those who followed him that remained insoluble for more than a hundred years. The problem was how to put a roof over the enormous expanse of the tribune. No precedent existed, for no dome of comparable size had been raised since ancient times and the methods used by the ancients were a mystery. Experts were invited to contribute ideas. Someone proposed that a great mound of earth stuffed with small coins (*quattrini*) should be piled up in the tribune; the dome could be constructed on this base. When it was finished, the people of Florence should be called in to hunt for the *quattrini* in the mound of earth, which in this way would be quickly demolished, leaving the dome standing. The principal merit of this bizarre plan was that it promised a supply of almost free labor – ant labor, one might say. The Republic, ever soaring but ever mindful of expenses, had got round the problem of paying Arnolfo by the expedient of simply remitting his taxes in return for his work.

In the year 1418 a competition for the dome was announced to which masters from all over Italy were invited. Such competitions for public works were a regular feature of Florentine life, and the young Filippo Brunelleschi, [1377-1446], not long before, had lost a competition in sculpture to Lorenzo Ghiberti, whose model for the second set of bronze Baptistery doors had been accepted over his. Disappointed – so the story is told – he had gone off to Rome, with Donatello, and made himself an architect, knowing that in this field he could surpass everyone. He remained there several years, earning his living as a goldsmith, while he examined Roman buildings, with particular attention to the Pantheon and its dome. When the competition was announced, he came back to Florence, announcing that he had found a way of raising the dome of Santa Maria del Fiore without centering – a thing everyone believed to be impossible.

Faced, like Columbus, with an assembly of doubters, he anticipated Columbus with the egg trick. ''He proposed,'' says Vasari's version, "to all the masters, foreigners and compatriots, that he who could make an egg stand upright on a piece of smooth marble should be appointed to build the cupola, since, in doing that, his genius would be made manifest. They took an egg accordingly, and all those masters did their best to make it stand upright, but none discovered the method of doing so. Wherefore, Filippo, being told that he might make it stand himself, took it daintily into his hand, gave the end of it a blow on the plane of marble and made it stand upright." He vaulted the huge tribune by means of a double cupola, one shell resting on another inside it and thus distributing the weight – an idea he had probably got from the Pantheon.

This dome of Brunelleschi's, besides being a wonder, was extremely practical in all its details. It had gutters for rain, little ducts or openings to reduce wind pressure, iron hooks inside for scaffolding so that frescoes could be painted if they were ever wanted, light in the *ballatoio*, or gallery, that goes up to the top so that no one would stumble in the dark, and iron treads to give a footing in the steeper parts of the climb. While it was being built, it even had temporary restaurants and wineshops provided by Brunelleschi for the masons, so that they could work all day without having to make the long trip down and up again at lunch time. Brunelleschi had thought of everything.

In short, the dome was a marvel in every respect, and Michelangelo, when he was called on to do the dome of St. Peter's, paid his respects to Brunelleschi's in a rhyming couplet:

> *Io farò la sorella,*
> *Già più gran ma non più bella.*
> (I am going to make its sister,
> Bigger, yes, but not more beautiful.)

Vasari said that it dared competition with the heavens. "This structure rears itself to such an elevation that the hills around Florence do not appear to equal it." Lightning frequently struck it, and this was taken as a sign that the heavens were envious. When the people of Florence learned that a lantern, on Brunelleschi's design though not begun until after his death, was about to be loaded on to the cupola, they took alarm and called this "tempting God."

Michelangelo was right when he said that the dome of St. Peter's would not be more beautiful. Brunelleschi's, moreover was the *first*. Michelangelo could be blunt and sarcastic about his fellow-architects and sculptors. . . . But he was very much aware of real greatness (he called Ghiberti's second set of Baptistery doors the "Gates of Paradise," and to Donatello's *San Giorgio* he said "March"!), and his architecture is always conscious of Brunelleschi, long dead before he was born, whom he could not surpass but only exceed: bigger, yes, but not more beautiful. The portentous staging of the Medici Tombs, the staircase of the Laurentian Library, the dome of St. Peter's are Brunelleschi, only more so. The heavy consoles and corbels of the Laurentian Library vestibule and staircase, with their strong, deep indentations, contrast of light and shade, their *pietra serena* and white plaster, are Brunelleschi, underscored or played *fortissimo*. Brunelleschi, like Arnolfo, had stressed the *membratura* of a building; in Michelangelo, there appears a false *membratura*, a fictive ensemble of windows, supporting pillars, brackets, and so on – in short, a display of muscle.

In Brunelleschi himself, the Florentine tradition reached its highest point. Here – in Santo Spirito, for instance, or the Pazzi Chapel or the Old Sacristy of San Lorenzo or the Badia at San Domenico de Fiesole – are the grave purity, simplicity, and peacefulness of the early Florentine churches. The germ of Brunelleschi can be found not in classical Rome but in the little church of Santi Apostoli that legend attributes to Charlemagne. All gray and white, the dark-gray stone that is called justly "serene" against white *intonaco*; three long aisles, one of which forms a nave; two processions of pillars with lovely Corinthian capitals marching down the church and upholding a rhythmic train of round arches; vaults interlacing like fans opening and closing; decorative motifs, always in dark-gray stone, of leaves, egg-and-dart pattern, scallop shells, and sun rays – these, generally speaking, are the elements of Tuscan classicism that are found, over and over, in the great Brunelleschi churches, sometimes with friezes and roundels added in the more frivolous parts, like the sacristy, by Donatello or Desiderio or Luca della Robbia: cherubs with rays like flower petals round their necks or with crossed wings like starchy bibs, the four Evangelists, or scenes from the life of Saint John.

The big churches of Brunelleschi, particularly San Lorenzo, which was the parish church of the Medici family, have been somewhat botched by later additions. The Pazzi chapel, which was built for the Pazzi family as a kind of private oratory just outside the Franciscan church of Santa Croce, has not been tampered with, however, since the fifteenth century, and here you find the quintessential Brunelleschi. It is a small, square, yellowish, discreet temple, with projecting eaves, almost like a little mausoleum, from the outside, or like one of those little brown Etruscan funeral urns in the shape of a house, one of which can be seen in the Archaeological Museum. It has an atrium or pronaos supported by slender Corinthian columns, above which runs a frieze of cherubs' heads in little medallions, done by Desiderio. Under the eaves is an attic and above them a cupola with a very delicate tall lantern. A *tondo* in glazed terracotta by Luca della Robbia of Saint Andrew (the chapel was done for Andrea de' Pazzi) stands over the door.

The interior is a simple rectangle with four high narrow windows and bare white walls and at the end a small apse. In the four corners tall closed arches are drawn in dark-gray *pietra serena* on the white walls, like the memory of windows. Fluted pilasters with Corinthian capitals, also in *pietra serena*, are spaced along the walls, marking the points of support, and in the same way, the lunettes and supporting arches of the chapel are outlined in dark ribbons of stone against the white plaster, and the binding arches have stone rosettes enclosed in rectangles drawn on the white background. Arch repeats arch; curve repeats curve; rosette repeats rosette. The rectangles of the lower section are topped by the semicircles of the lunettes and arches, which, in turn, are topped by the hemisphere of the cupola. The continual play of these basic forms and their variations – of square against round, deep against flat – is like the greatest music: the music of the universe heard in a small space. . . .

The chapel is not large, but it seems to hold the four corners of the earth and all the winds securely in its binding of *pietra serena*. No more exquisite microcosm than the Pazzi Chapel could be imagined, for everything is here, in just proportion and in order, as on the Seventh Day of Creation, when God rested from His labors, having found them good. . . .

Brunelleschi was a very down-to-earth person – simple, short, bald, plain. He disliked imbalance and exaggeration, and the story is told that when his friend Donatello showed him the wooden Crucifix, of a peasantlike, harshly suffering Christ, he had made for Santa Croce, Brunelleschi said to him sharply: "You have put a clown on the Cross." Donatello then asked him whether he thought he could do better, and Brunelleschi made no reply but went away and secretly made a wooden crucifix of his own (it is in a chapel of Santa Maria Novella) which so astonished Donatello by its beauty, when he finally saw it in his friend's studio, that he dropped some eggs he was carrying, in an apron, for their lunch.

The homely lives led by these artists, in which aprons and eggs figure as in the daily lives of ordinary workmen, are reflected in the character of their art, which is an art of essentials, of the bread-and-wine staples of the human construct. The big Brunelleschi churches – San Lorenzo and Santo Spirito – are almost free of tourists . . . they belong, appropriately, to the people, and just outside them are the main Florentine markets, where the poor come to buy. Around Santo Spirito are the fruit and vegetable sellers of the Oltrarno quarter and old beggars, lame and halt, who sit in the sun, while across from San Lorenzo (the big covered market is just beyond) are the peddlers of cheap shoes, chiefly for men, hundreds and hundreds of rows of them, and displays of workmen's aprons and coveralls, hanging from clothes-hangers, like votive offerings, in brown, blue, and white – the colors of Saint Francis and the Madonna. Work and rest, weekday and Sunday, *pietra forte* and *pietra serena* make up the Florentine chiaroscuro, and the sense of their interplay, as of sphere and square, explains the unique ability of the Florentines to create cosmic myths in the space of a small chapel or a long poem. The unitary genius of the Florentines, that power of binding expressed in Brunelleschi's virile *membratura*, is evidently the product of a small world held in common and full of ''common'' referents. . . .

Simplicity of life Florence shared with Athens and the great Florentines of the *quattrocento*, Donatello and Brunelleschi, lived like barefoot philosophers. Socrates traced his descent from Daedalus, the cunning craftsman, whom Brunelleschi, too, might have claimed as a mythic ancestor. Brunelleschi's architecture, moreover, is a species of wisdom, like Socratic and Platonic philosophy, in which forms are realized in their absolute integrity and essence; the squareness of square, the slenderness of slender, the roundness of round. A window, say, cut out by Brunelleschi is, if that can be conceived, a platonic *idea* of a window: not any particular window or the sum of existing windows in the aggregate but the eternal model itself. This is something different from the so-called ''ideal forms'' of Michelangelo's sculptures, where ''ideal'' means ''mental,'' ''imaginary,'' ''not true to life,'' or, in other words, ''idealized,'' like the dukes on the Medici Tombs. Brunelleschi's windows are not idealized in this sense at all; they are a plain statement of the notion ''window,'' cut out of a wall with a terse finality that makes other windows appear haphazard accidents or bellicose rhetoric in comparison. These framed openings in space recall in their uncompromising depth the remark of Leonardo, which is both profound and simple, that the eyes are the windows of the body's prison. Florentine architecture became deep with Brunelleschi, deep in both senses; each object and kind of thing – corbels, capitals, arches, shafts, vaulting – is so intensely itself, so immersed in its own being, that it gives a sort of pain along with its joy, as though this being-itself were a memory stirring of something other, of the lost realm of perfect, changeless shapes. No better illustration of the old doctrine of universals and particulars and their mysterious consanguinity can be found than in the Pazzi Chapel or the Second Cloister of Santa Croce, with its poignant slender columns and its cruelly incised decorations of urns, wreaths, scallop shells, and strigil molding.

Italian critics speak of the "sincerity" of Brunelleschi's architecture; "*schietto*," or "frank," he is always called. "Truthful" might be better, for he has the philosopher's love of eternal, elemental truths. Brunelleschi's dome compels a curious kind of slow, surprised recognition; it is the way a dome "ought" to be, just as love, for a young person, is at once a surprise and the way he knew it should be, from books and hearsay.

All great Florentine art, from Giotto through the *quattrocento*, has the faculty of amazing with its unexpected and absolute truthfulness. This faculty was once called beauty. The immediate effect of a great Giotto or a Masaccio is to strike the beholder dumb. Coming into the first room of the Uffizi or the Brancacci Chapel of the Carmine, he is conscious of a sensation he may not even associate with what is today called beauty (a voluptuary's compound of allure and strangeness): the inadequacy of words to deal with what is in front of him. What is there to say? This art cannot be likened to anything but itself, and in this sense it resembles architecture – a solid fact obtruded into the world. It is easy enough to talk about a lovely Giorgione, a Titian, a Giovanni Bellini, even a Piero dello Francesca; these paintings are, as it were, already coated with legend and literature so that they play on the fancy like fairytales. If there is nothing to say before a Giotto or a Masaccio, this, of course, is the sign that it continues to be a revelation, an event still so untoward and brusque that it results in a loss of speech, like the announcement of the conception of the Baptist to the old priest Zachary that deprived him of the use of his tongue.

Donatello:
"A Most Rare Sculptor"

Giorgio Vasari

Donato [1386-1466], called Donatello by his friends, and who thus signed himself on some of his works, was born in Florence. Devoting himself to the art of design he became not only a most rare sculptor and marvellous statue-maker, but was skillful in stucco, versed in perspective and highly esteemed in architecture, while his works possessed such grace, design and excellence that they were held to resemble the excellent productions of the ancient Greeks and Romans more than those of any other. Thus he is deservedly placed in the front rank of those who first showed the beauty of bas-reliefs, which were executed by him with great facility and mastery, and a more than ordinary beauty showing that he thoroughly understood that work. Indeed no other artist surpassed him in this branch, and even in our own age no one has equaled him.

Donatello was reared from his childhood in the house of Ruberto Martelli, and earned the love of Ruberto and of all that noble family by his good qualities and by his ardor for work. In his youth he produced many things, which were not highly valued because they were so numerous. But the work that made his name and brought him into notice was an Annunciation in *macigno* stone,* placed at the altar and

Macigno: A hard gray stone used for the corners of buildings or for grindstones.

GIORGIO VASARI (1511–1574), painter and architect, is best known for his art history, *The Lives of the Most Eminent Italian Architects, Painters and Sculptors from Cimabue to the Present Day, Described in the Tuscan Language, Together with Vasari's Useful and Necessary Introduction to Their Art*, published in 1550 and considerably enriched in its second edition in 1568. The *Lives* spans three hundred years with over one hundred accounts of the artists, concluding with a seventy-page autobiography of Vasari himself. At thirteen the young painter became the protégé of chapel of the Cavalcanti in S. Croce, for which he made an ornament in the grotesque manner, the base varied and twisted and the pediment a quarter-circle, adding six infants bearing festoons, who seem to be afraid of the height, and to be reassuring themselves by embracing each other. But he showed especial genius and art in the figure of the Virgin, who, affrighted at the sudden appearance of the angel, moves her person timidly and sweetly to a modest reverence, turning with beautiful grace to the one who salutes her, so that her face displays the proper humility and gratitude due to the bestower of the unexpected gift. Besides this, Donato showed a mastery in the arrangement of the folds of the drapery of the Madonna and of the angel, and by a study of the nude he endeavored to discover the beauty of the ancients which had remained hidden for so many years. He gave evidence of so much facility and art in this work that design, judgment and skilled use of the chisel could produce nothing finer. . . .

In the church of S. Giovanni, Donato made the tomb of Pope Giovanni Costa. . . . This work was a commission from Cosimo de' Medici, the close friend of Costa, and in it Donato represented the dead man in gilt bronze, with Hope and Charity in marble, while his pupil Michelozzo did the Faith. In the same church, opposite this work, may be seen a St. Mary Magdalene in wood, a very beautiful penitential figure, finely executed, as she is consumed by fasting and abstinence, so that her body exhibits a most perfect knowledge of anatomy in every part. In the Mercato Vecchio there is a stone figure of Plenty by Donato, placed upon a granite column by itself, which has been much admired by artists and all good judges for its excellent workmanship. . . . The same artist, while still a youth, also made the prophet Daniel in marble for the facade of S. Maria del Fiore, and a St. John the Evangelist seated, . . . clothed in a simple habit, which has been much admired. At the same place, on the angle facing the via del Cocomero, is an old man between two columns, more like the antique manner than any extant work of Donato, the head exhibiting that thoughtfulness which comes with years in those who are wasted by age and labor. For the interior of the same church he made the

the Medici, and his fortunes were linked with theirs. During various periods of self-exile Vasari traveled throughout Italy, accumulating knowledge of Italian artists which might otherwise not have come down to the present day. As chief architect to the Medici, Vasari remodeled the Palazzo Vecchio as a ducal residence, designed the Uffizi, and some years later painted the cupola of the Duomo. Upon Michelangelo's death Vasari was made chief architect of St. Peter's Cathedral in Rome, and it contains his paintings. Vasari murals are in the Vatican. He is buried in his birthplace, at Arezzo.

ornamentation of the organ over the door of the old sacristy, the figures depicted on it seeming in truth to be endowed with life and motion. For this reason it may be said that Donato employed his judgment as much as his hands, seeing that he made many things which look beautiful in the places where they are situated; but when they have been removed, and put elsewhere in another light or higher up, their appearance is changed and they create an entirely different impression. Thus Donato made his figures in such fashion that in his studio they did not appear half so remarkable as when they were set up in the appointed places. In the new sacristy of the same church he designed the children who hold the festoons which turn about the frieze, and he also designed the figures for the round window beneath the cupola containing the Coronation of Our Lady. This design is clearly superior to those of the other round windows. At S. Michele in Orto in that city he made the statue of St. Peter for the art of the butchers, a suave and marvelous figure, and a St. Mark the Evangelist for the art of the linen drapers, which he had undertaken to do in conjunction with Filippo Brunelleschi, but afterwards finished by himself, an arrangement to which Filippo had consented. This figure was executed by Donatello with so much judgment that when it was on the ground its excellence was not recognized by unskilled persons, and the consuls of the art were not disposed to accept it; but Donato asked them to allow it to be set up, as after he had retouched it the figure would appear quite different. This was done, the figure was veiled for fifteen days, and then, without having done anything more to it, he uncovered it, and filled everyone with admiration.

For the art of the armorers he made a fine statue of St. George armed, the head exhibiting the saint's youthful beauty, valor and spirit with extraordinary realism and life for a piece of stone. Certainly no modern figures in marble display so much force and realism as Nature and art have produced in this by means of Donato's hand. On the marble pedestal which bears the niche he carved in bas-relief the slaying of the serpent, including a horse, which has been highly valued and praised. On the pediment he made a God the Father in bas-relief. . . . For the front of the campanile of S. Maria del Fiore he did four marble figures, . . . the two middle ones being portraits of Francesco Soderini as a youth and Giovanni di Borduccio Cherichini, now known as Il Zuccone. This being considered a most rare work, and finer than anything else which he did, Donato used to say, when he wished to take an unusually solemn oath, "By the faith which I bear to my Zuccone"; and while he was at work on it he would look at it, and repeat, "Speak, plague take you, speak." On the side facing the Canonry, over the door of the campanile, he made an Abraham sacrificing Isaac and another prophet which were placed between two other statues. For the Signoria of the city he made a metal cast which was placed in an arch of their loggia on the piazza, representing Judith cutting off the head of Holophernes, a work of great excellence and mastery, which displays to anyone who will consider the external simplicity of Judith in her dress and aspect the great spirit of that lady and the assistance of God, while the appearance of Holophernes exhibits the effects of wine and sleep, with death in his cold and drooping limbs. This work was so well carried out by Donato that the slender and beautiful cast excited the utmost admiration after he had polished it. The pedestal, which is a granite baluster of simple design, is full of grace and pleasing to the eye. He was so delighted with this work that he put his name on it, contrary to his usual custom, as we see by the words *Donatelli opus*. In the courtyard of the palace of the Signoria there is a nude David of life size, who has cut off Goliath's head and places his raised foot upon it, while his right hand holds a sword. This figure is so natural and possesses such beauty that it seems incredible to artists that it was not molded upon a living body. . . .

The esteem which Cosimo entertained for Donato's talent was such that he kept him constantly employed, and Donato had so much affection for Cosimo that from the slightest indication he divined all that he required and punctiliously obeyed him. It is said that a Genoese merchant once employed Donato to make a fine bronze head of life size and very light, so that it might be carried to a distance, and that the work was given to him through the intervention of Cosimo. When it was finished, and the merchant wished to pay for it, it seemed to him that Donato asked too much. The question was referred to Cosimo, who caused the head to be brought to the court of his palace, and placed among the pinnacles on the street front, that it might be the better seen. Cosimo then decided that the merchant's offer was in-adequate, saying that the price asked was too small. The merchant, who thought it too high, said that Donato had completed it in a month or a little more, which came to more than half a florin a day. Donato turned round angrily, much incensed at the remark, and exclaiming to the merchant that in an instant he was able to destroy the work and toil of a year, gave the head a push into the street where it was broken into many pieces, saying that the merchant was accustomed to bargain for haricot beans but not for statues. Then he repented, and offered Donato double if he would make another, but the sculptor refused, though Cosimo united his prayers to those of the merchant. . . .

It happened at this time that the Republic of Venice, hearing of Donatello's fame, sent for him to make a monument to Gattamelata in the city of Padua. He went there very willingly and made the bronze horse which stands in the piazzo of S. Antonio, displaying the chafing and foaming of the animal and the courage and pride of the figure who is riding him with great truth. He showed such skill in the size of the cast in its proportions and general excellence that it may be compared with any antique for movement, design, artistic qualities, proportion and diligence. Not only did it fill all the men of that day with amazement, but it astonishes everyone who sees it at the present time. For this cause the Paduans endeavored by every means to make him a fellow-citizen and to detain him there by all manner of favors. To keep him employed they allotted him the predella of the high altar of the church of the friars minors, to represent scenes in the life of St. Anthony of Padua. These bas-reliefs are executed with such judgment that masters in the art have been struck dumb with admiration in beholding them when they have considered their beautiful and varied composition, comprising such a number of remarkable figures placed in diminishing perspective. For the front of the altar he made the Marys weeping over the dead Christ. In the house of one of the Counts of Capodilista he made the skeleton of a horse of wood without glue, which may still be seen, in which the joints are so well made that he who reflects upon the method of such work may form an opinion of the capacity of the brain and the greatness of the spirit of the author. An extraordinary number of his works may be met with all over Padua. But being considered as a miracle there and praised by every intelligent man, he determined to return to Florence, saying that if he remained longer at Padua he would have forgotten all that he ever knew, as he was so highly praised by everyone, and he returned gladly to his native town because there he was always being blamed, and this blame induced him to study and was productive of more glory. Accordingly he left Padua and, returning to Venice, left there a St. John the Baptist in wood, as a gift for the Florentine nation, for their chapel in the Frari church, executed by him with the greatest diligence and care, as a memorial of his excellence. In the city of Faenza he carved a St. John and a St. Jerome in wood, which were not less highly esteemed than his other works. Returning next to Tuscany, he made a marble tomb in the Pieve of Montepulciano with a very fine scene. In the sacristy of S. Lorenzo in Florence he made a fine marble lavatory at which Andrea Verocchio also worked, and in the house of Lorenzo della Stufa he made some very lifelike heads and figures. Leaving Florence after this he went to Rome, to imitate and study the antique as much as possible. At that time he made a stone tabernacle of the Sacrament, which is now in S. Peter's. . . . On his return to Florence he did the sacristy of S. Lorenzo in stucco for Cosimo de' Medici, namely, four circles at the foot of the vaulting with stories of the Evangelists in perspective, partly painted and partly bas-relief. He made two very beautiful little bronze doors in bas-relief, with the Apostles, martyrs and confessors, and above these some flat niches, one containing a St. Laurence and St. Stephen, and the other SS. Cosmo and Damian. In the crossing of the church he did four saints in stucco . . . which are skillfully executed. He also designed the bronze pulpits, representing the Passion of Christ, which possess design, force, invention and an abundance of figures and buildings. As he could not work at them himself on account of his age, his pupil, Bertoldo, completed them and put the finishing touches. At S. Maria del Fiore he made two colossal figures of bricks and stucco, which were placed outside the church on the sides of the chapels as an ornament. Over the door of S. Croce may be seen to this day a bronze St. Louis . . ., finished by him. When he was blamed for making this clumsily, it being considered perhaps the worst thing he ever did, he replied that he had made it so of set purpose, as it was a foolish trick to leave a kingdom to make oneself a friar. He also made in bronze the head of the wife of Cosimo de' Medici, which is preserved in the wardrobe of Duke Cosimo, where many other things of Donato in bronze and marble are preserved, among others a Madonna and Child in marble, in shadow relief, of matchless beauty. . . . In bronze the duke has a most beautiful and wondrous crucifix by Donato's hand in his studio, which contains a number of rare antiquities and beautiful medals. In the same wardrobe is the Passion of Our Lord in relief in a bronze panel, with a large number of figures, and in another panel, also of metal, another crucifix. . . .

Whoever desired to write in full of the life and works of this artist would have to make a longer story of it than is contemplated in the plan of this work, because Donato put his hand not only to the great things, of which enough has been said, but also to the smallest things of his art, making coats of arms on the chimney pieces and fronts of houses of citizens, a very fine example of which may be seen on the house of the Sommai opposite the tower of the Vacca. For the family of the Martelli he made a chest in the form of a cradle, constructed of wickerwork, to serve as a tomb. But it is below the church of S. Lorenzo, as no tombs of any sort appear above except the epitaph of that of Cosimo de' Medici, which also has its opening beneath like the rest. . . . In short, Donato was so admirable in his every act that in skill, judgment and knowledge he may be said to have been among the first to illustrate the art of sculpture and the good design of the moderns. He deserves the greater commendation, because in his day antiquities had not been dug out, such as columns, sarcophagi and triumphal arches. It was chiefly by his influence that Cosimo de' Medici conceived the desire to introduce to Florence the antiquities which are and were in the Casa Medici, all of which were restored by his hand. He was free, affectionate and courteous, and more so to his friends than to himself. He thought nothing of money, keeping it in a basket suspended by a rope from the ceiling, so that all his workmen and friends took what they wanted without saying anything to him. He passed his old age very happily, and when he could work no longer he was assisted by Cosimo and other friends. It is said that when Cosimo was on his deathbed he recommended Donato to his son Piero, who diligently executed his father's wish and gave the artist a property . . . which brought in sufficient income to permit him to live in comfort. At this Donato was greatly rejoiced, thinking himself more than assured against the fear of dying of hunger. But he had not possessed it a year before he returned to Piero and publicly renounced it, declaring that he would not give up his peace of mind to think of household affairs and the troubles of the country, which bothered him one day out of three, as either the wind blew down his dovecote, or his beasts were seized by the commune for taxes, or a tempest destroyed his vine and fruits. He had had enough of this and would rather die of hunger than be obliged to think of such things. Piero laughed at his simplicity, and to relieve him from this vexation took back the estate and assigned to Donato a pension of the same value or more in money to be drawn from the bank weekly. This gave him the utmost satisfaction, and as the servant and friend of the house of the Medici he lived happily and carefree all the rest of his days. Having attained the age of eighty-three, he became so paralytic that he could no longer do the slightest work, and remained in bed in a poor little house which he had in the Via del Cocomero, near the nuns of S. Niccolo. Growing daily worse and gradually wasting away, he died on 13th December, 1466, and was buried in the church of S. Lorenzo, near the tomb of Cosimo, as the latter had himself ordained, so that the dead body should be near him in death, as they had always been near him in spirit when alive.

The citizens sorrowed greatly at his death, as well as the artists and all who knew him. Thus, in order to honor him more in death than they had done when he was alive, they gave him a stately funeral in that church, all the painters, architects, sculptors, goldsmiths, and indeed practically the whole population of the city, accompanying the cortège, while they used for a long time afterwards to compose in his praise various verses in divers languages. . . .

I have another matter to relate of him. When he was sick, shortly before his death, some of his relations went to see him, and after they had greeted him and offered their condolences, as was customary, they told him it was his duty to leave them an estate which he had at Prato, although it was a small one and brought in but little, and they earnestly besought him to do this. Donato listened patiently and then said, for he was just in everything, "I cannot gratify you, for I think it only right to leave it to the peasant who has always toiled there, and not to you who have never done any good to it or had any other thought than to possess it, which is the sole object of this visit. Go in peace." And in truth such relations, who only love their kin for the hopes which they have from them, ought to be treated after this fashion. Donato accordingly sent for the notary and left the estate to the peasant who had always worked there, and who had probably conducted himself better toward his master in his need than the relations had done. . . .

The world is so full of Donato's works that it may be truthfully affirmed that no artist ever produced more than he. He took delight in everything, and undertook all kinds of work without looking whether it was common or pretentious. However, this productiveness was very necessary to sculpture in some kinds of round figures, half- and bas-reliefs, because, just as in the days of the ancient Greeks and Romans, many combined to attain perfection, so he, single-handed, brought perfection and delight back to our age by the multitude of his works. Thus artists ought to recognize the greatness of his art more than that of any modern, for he, besides rendering the difficulties of art easy by the number of his works, united in himself that invention, design, skill, judgment, and every other faculty that can or ought to be expected in a man of genius. Donato was very determined and quick, completing his things with the utmost facility, always performing much more than he promised. All his work was left to his pupil Bertoldo, principally the bronze pulpits of S. Lorenzo, which were polished by him and brought to their present state of completion.

The Visions of Fra Angelico in the Convent of San Marco

Hippolyte Taine

What commotion and what travail in this fifteenth century! In the midst of this pagan tumultuous hive there stands the tranquil convent of San Marco wherein sweetly and piously dreams a mystic of ancient days, Fra Angelico da Fiesole [1387-1455].

This convent remains almost intact; two square courts in it expose their files of small columns surmounted by arcades, with their little old tile roofs. In one of the rooms is a sort of memorial or genealogical tree, bearing the names of the principal monks who have died in the odor of sanctity. Among these is that of Savonarola, and mention is made of his having perished through false accusation. Two cells are still shown which he inhabited. Fra Angelico lived in the convent before him, and paintings by his hand decorate the chapter hall, the corridors and the gray walls of the cells.

He had dwelt a stranger in the world, and maintained amidst fresh sensations and curiosities the innocent, ravished life in God. . . . He lived in a state of primitive simplicity and obedience; it is said of him that "one morning being invited to breakfast by Pope Nicholas V his conscience forbade him to eat meat without the permission of his prior, never reflecting that the Pope's authority was superior." He refused the dignities of his order, and concerned himself only with prayer and penitence. "When any work was required of him he would answer with singular goodness of heart that they must go and ask the prior, and if the prior wished it he would not fail them." He never desired to paint any but the saints, and it is narrated of him that "he never took up his brushes without kneeling in prayer, and never painted a Christ on the cross without his eyes being filled with tears." It was his custom not to retouch or recast any of his pictures, but to let them remain as they first left his hand, "believing that they were as they were through the will of God." We can well understand why such a man did not study anatomy or contemporary models. His art is primitive like his life. He began with missals and so continued on the walls; gold, vermilion, bright scarlet, brilliant greens, the illuminations of the Middle Ages display themselves on his canvases the same as on old parchments. He even sometimes applies them to the roofs; an infantile piety is eager to decorate its saint or idol and render it radiant to excess. When he abandons small figures and composes on a grand scale a scene of twenty personages, he falters;* his figures are bodiless. Their affecting devotional expression is inadequate to animate them; they remain hieratic and stiff; all he comprehended was their spirit. That which he paints understandingly, and which he has everywhere repeated, are visions and the visions of blessed and innocent spirits. . . .

Such adoration as this is never unaccompanied by inward images; with closed eyes they are persistently followed, and without effort, as in a dream. Like a mother who, on finding herself alone, sees floating in memory the features of a beloved son, like a chaste poet who, in midnight silence, imagines and again sees the downcast eyes of his beloved, so does the heart involuntarily summon up and contemplate the concourse of divine figures. No object disturbs him in this peaceable contemplation. Around him all actions are prescribed and all objects are colorless; day after day uniform hours bring before him the same white walls, the same dark lustre of the wainscoting, the same straight folds of cowls and frocks, the same rustling of steps passing to and fro between refectory and chapel. Delicate, indeterminate sensations vaguely arise in this monotony, while tender reverie, like a rose sheltered from life's rude blasts, blooms afar from the great highway clattering with human footsteps. There is displayed to the eye the magnificence of eternal day, and henceforth every effort of the painter centers on expressing it. Glittering staircases of jasper and amethyst rise above each other up to the throne on which sit celestial beings. Golden aureoles gleam around their brows; red, azure and green robes, fringed, bordered and striped with gold, flash like glories. Gold runs in threads over baldachins, accumulates in embroideries on copes, radiates like stars on tunics and gleams from tiaras, while

---

*A Christ and seventeen saints in the convent of San Marco.

topazes, rubies and diamonds sparkle in flaming constellations on jeweled diadems.* All is light; it is the outburst of mystic illumination. Through this prodigality of gold and azure one tint prevails, that of the sun and of paradise. This is not common daylight; it is too brilliant; it effaces the brightest hues, it envelops forms on all sides; it weakens and reduces them to mere shadows. In fact the soul is everything; ponderable matter becomes transfigured; its relief is no longer perceptible, its substance having evaporated; nothing remains but an ethereal form which swims in azure and in splendor. At other times the blessed approach paradise over luxuriant meadows strewn with red and white flowers, and under beautiful blooming trees; angels conduct them, and, hand in hand, they form fraternally a circle; the burden of the flesh no longer oppresses them; their heads starred with rays they glide through the air up to the flaming gate from which issues a golden illumination; Christ, aloft, within a triple row of angels pressed together like flowers, smiles upon them beneath his aureole. Such are the delights and the radiance that Dante has portrayed.

His personages are worthy of their situation. Although beautiful and ideal, his Christ, even in celestial triumph, is pale, pensive and slightly emaciated; he is the eternal friend, the somewhat melancholy consoler of The Imitation, the poetic merciful Lord as the saddened heart imagines him; he is not the overhealthy figure of the Renaissance painters. His long curling tresses and blond beard sweetly surround his features; sometimes he smiles faintly, while his gravity is never dissociated with affectionate benignity. At the day of judgment he does not curse; only on the side of the damned his hand falls, while on the right, toward the blessed, toward those whom he loves, his full regards are turned. Near him the Virgin, kneeling with downcast eyes, seems to be a young maiden that has just communed. Occasionally her head is too large as is common with the inspired; her shoulders are narrow and her hands too small; the spiritual, inward life, too highly developed, has reduced the other; the long blue mantle wrought in gold in which she is wholly enveloped, scarcely allows it to be supposed that she has a body. No one can imagine before having seen it such immaculate modesty, such virginal candor; by her side Raphael's virgins are merely vigorous peasant girls. And the other

*See *The Coronation of the Virgin* in the Louvre, and the twelve angels around the infant Jesus in the Uffizi.

figures are of the same order. Every expression is based on two sentiments, the innocence of the calm spirit preserved in the cloister, and the rapture of the blessed spirit that sees God. The saints are portraits, but refined and beatified; celestial transfiguration eliminates from the body as from the soul the ideal portion concealed and transformed by the grossness of terrestrial being. No wrinkles appear on the countenances of the aged; they bloom afresh under the touch of eternal youth. No traces of physical austerity are visible; they have entered into the realm of pure felicity. The features of the blessed are in repose, we feel that they rest passive suspended in ecstasy; to move, to disturb a fold of their drapery would endanger some part of the vision; they turn their eyes to the heights above without bending their bodies; they are wrapt in meditation in order the better to enjoy their beatitude . . . . A few, the disciples, seem to be juvenile choristers, monastic novices imbued with a spirit of veneration, and timid. On seeing the infant Jesus they give way to a movement of infantile sprightliness and then, fearful of having done something wrong, hesitate and draw back. There are no violent or eager emotions in this world; all is partially veiled or arrested midway by the tranquility or the obedience of the cloister. But the most charming figures are those of the angels. We see them kneel down in silent rows around thrones or press together in garlands in the azure. The youngest are amiable, candid children, with minds unruffled by a suspicion of evil; they do not think much; each head, in its golden circle, smiles and is happy; it will smile forever, and this is its entire life. Others with flamboyant wings, like birds of paradise, play on instruments or sing, and their countenances are radiant. One of them, raising his trumpet to put it to his lips, stops as if surprised by a resplendent vision. This one with a violincello to his shoulder seems to muse over the exquisite tones of his own instrument. Two others with joined hands seem to be contemplating and adoring. One, quite youthful, with the full figure of a young girl, bends forward, as if to listen before striking her cymbal. To the harmony of tones must be added the harmony of colors. Tints do not increase or decrease in strength and intermingle as in ordinary painting. Every vestment is of one color, a red alongside of blue, a bright green alongside of a pale purple, an embroidery of gold placed on a dark amaranth, like the simple, sustained strains of an angelic melody. The painter delights in this; he cannot find colors for his saints pure enough or ornaments for them of sufficient preciousness. He forgets that his figures are images; he bestows upon them the faithful care of a believer, of a worshipper; he embroiders their robes as if they were real; he covers their mantles with filagree as fine as the finest work of the goldsmith; he paints on their copes small and perfect pictures; he applies himself to delicately unfolding their beautiful light tresses, to arranging their curls, to the proper adjustment of the folds of their tunics, to an accurate delineation of the round monastic tonsure; he enters into heaven with them in order to love and to serve them. Fra Angelico is the last of the mystic flowers. The society that surrounded him and of which he knew nothing, ended in taking an opposite direction, and, after a short respite of enthusiasm, proceeded to burn his successor, a Dominican like himself and the last of the Christians, Savonarola.

Masaccio: Master of the Significant

Bernard Berenson

Giotto born again, starting where death had cut short his advance, instantly making his own all that had been gained during his absence, and profiting by the new conditions, the new demands—imagine such an avatar, and you will understand Masaccio.

Giotto we know already, but what were the new conditions, the new demands? The medieval skies had been torn asunder and a new heaven and a new earth had appeared, which the abler spirits were already inhabiting and enjoying. Here new interests and new values prevailed. The thing of sovereign price was the power to subdue and to create; of sovereign interest all that helped man to know the world he was living in and his power over it. To the artist the change offered a field of the freest activity. It is always his business to reveal to an age its ideals. But what room was there for sculpture and painting—arts whose first purpose it is to make us realize the material significance of things—in a period like the Middle Ages, when the human body was denied all intrinsic significance? In such an age the figure artist can thrive, as Giotto did, only in spite of it, and as an isolated phenomenon. In the Renaissance, on the contrary, the figure artist had a demand made on him such as had not been made since the great Greek days, to reveal to a generation believing in man's power to subdue and to possess the world, the physical types best fitted for the task. And as this demand was imperative and constant, not one, but a hundred Italian artists arose, able each in his own way to meet it—in their combined achievement, rivaling the art of the Greeks.

In sculpture Donatello had already given body to the new ideals when Masaccio began his brief career [1401-1428?], and in the education, the awakening, of the younger artist the example of the elder must have been of incalculable force. But a type gains vastly in significance by being presented in some action along with other individuals of the same type; and here Donatello was apt, rather than to draw his meed of profit, to incur loss by descending to the obvious —witness his bas-reliefs at Siena, Florence, and Padua. Masaccio was untouched by this taint. Types, in themselves of the manliest, he presents with a sense for the materially significant which makes us realize to the utmost their power and dignity; and the spiritual significance thus gained he uses to give the highest import to the event he is portraying; this import, in turn, gives a higher value to the types, and thus, whether we devote our attention to his types or to his action, Masaccio keeps us on a high plane of reality and significance. In later painting we shall easily find greater science, greater craft, and greater perfection of detail, but greater reality, greater significance, I venture to say, never. Dust-bitten and ruined though his Brancacci Chapel frescoes now are, I never see them without the strongest stimulation of my tactile consciousness. I feel that I could touch every figure, that it would yield a definite resistance to my touch, that I should have to expend thus much effort to displace it, that I could walk around it. In short, I scarcely could realize it more, and in real life I should scarcely realize it so well, the attention of each of us being too apt to concentrate itself upon some dynamic quality, before we have at all begun to realize the full material significance of the person before us. Then what strength to his young men, and what gravity and power to his old! How quickly a race like this would possess itself of the earth, and brook no rivals but the forces of nature! Whatever they do—simply because it is they—is impressive and important, and every movement, every gesture, is world-changing. Compared with his figures, those in the same chapel by his precursor, Masolino, are childish, and those by his follower, Filippino, unconvincing and without significance, because without tactile values. Even Michelangelo, where he comes in rivalry, has, for both reality and significance, to take a second place. Compare his *Expulsion from Paradise* (in the Sistine Chapel) with the one here by Masaccio. Michelangelo's figures are more correct, but far less tangible and less powerful; and while he represents nothing but a man warding off a blow dealt by a sword, and a woman cringing with ignoble fear, Masaccio's Adam and Eve stride away from Eden heart-broken with shame and grief, hearing, perhaps, but not seeing, the angel hovering high overhead who directs their exiled footsteps.

Masaccio, then, like Giotto a century earlier—himself the Giotto of an artistically more propitious world—was, as an artist, a great master of the significant, and, as a painter, endowed to the highest degree with a sense of tactile values, and with a skill in rendering them. In a career of but few years he gave to Florentine painting the direction it pursued to the end. In many ways he reminds us of the young Bellini. Who knows? Had he but lived as long, he might have laid the foundation for a painting not less delightful and far more profound than that of Venice. As it was, his frescoes at once become, and for as long as there were real artists among them remained, the training school of Florentine painters.

The Mona Lisa of Leonardo da Vinci

Kenneth Clark

Some of the greatest pictures ever painted have been portraits – we need think only of Titian, Rembrandt and Velasquez to accept that statement; and yet the aesthetic theory of the last seventy years runs entirely counter to the fact of experience that a truthful likeness of an individual can be a great work of art. . . . The *Mona Lisa*, this mysterious *objet de culte*, even though it may have originated in the contemplation of a real person, has none of the qualities that move us in the works of Velasquez and Rembrandt. It is one of the few works of man that may properly be described as unique. There is no good trying to laugh it off or to think that one can explain it by the usual processes of formal or philological analysis. To try to answer the riddle of the Sphinx has been a traditional form of self-destruction. . . . At least I can begin by summarizing the facts as they are revealed by documents, comparative material and scientific examination.

The first reference to a portrait of a woman by Leonardo is in the account written by Antonio de Beatis of the visit on 10th October 1517, by Cardinal Louis of Aragon to Leonardo when he was living in the Manor of Cloux, near Amboise. He says that "Leonardo showed the Cardinal three pictures, one of a certain Florentine lady, done from life at the instance of . . . Giuliano de' Medici, the other of St. John the Baptist as a young man, and also one of the Madonna and child who are placed in the lap of St. Anne, all of them most perfect." The rest of de Beatis's description is equally convincing, and he says "all this I have seen with my own eyes." As the *St. Anne* and the *St. John* and a portrait of a lady are known to have been in the collection of Francis I there is a strong presumption that the portrait described by de Beatis is the so-called *Mona Lisa*. The next mention of the picture is by Vasari in 1550, which I must quote at length:

> Leonardo undertook to paint, for Francesco del Giocondo, the portrait of Mona Lisa, his wife; and after he had lingered over it four years, left it unfinished: which work is now in the possession of King Francis of France, at Fontainbleau. In this head, whoever wished to see how nearly art is able to imitate nature, was readily able to comprehend it; since therein are counterfeited all those minutenesses that with subtlety are able to be painted: seeing that the eyes had that lustre and watery sheen which are always seen in the living creature, and around them were all those rosy and pearly tints, together with the eyelashes, that cannot be depicted except by the greatest subtlety.
>
> The eyebrows, also, by reason of his having represented the manner in which the hairs issue from the flesh, here more thick and here more scanty, and turn according to the pores of the flesh, could not be more natural. The nose with its beautiful nostrils, rosy and tender, seems to be alive. The mouth with its opening, and with its ends united by the red of the lips to the flesh tints of the face, appeared, indeed, to be not colors but flesh. Whoever intently observed the pit of the throat, saw the pulse beating in it. And, in truth, one could say that it was painted in a manner that made every able artificer, be he whom he may, tremble and lose courage.
>
> He employed, also, this device: Monna Lisa being very beautiful, while he drew her picture, he retained those who played or sang, and continually jested, that they might make her continue merry, in order to take away that melancholy that painters are often used to give to the portraits which they paint. And in this picture of Leonardo's, there was a smile so pleasing, that the sight of it was a thing more divine than human: and it was held to be a marvel, in that it was not other than alive.

Vasari had not been to Fontainebleau, and so had never seen the picture, as is evident from his description. He describes a realistic picture of a beautiful woman, with various additional touches which make it more like a Fragonard than the submarine goddess of the

Louvre. He mistakenly assumes that, like all Leonardo's work, it was unfinished. He had evidently been informed that the sitter was smiling, and provides an unconvincing explanation. Nothing could be less likely to produce the Mona Lisa's expression than a series of funny stories. I will return to the question of the eyebrows later as they provide interesting evidence of the picture's material condition. But what about his identification of the sitter with *Mona Lisa?* There is not a shred of evidence, either way, any more than there is evidence for de Beatis's identification of the sitter as a friend of Giuliano de' Medici. But we may record that the Anonimo Gaddiano, from whom Vasari drew much of his information about Leonardo, says that Leonardo painted a picture of Francesco del Giocondo, but does not mention his wife. This could conceivably be the side door through which the Gioconda crept into history.

The first unquestionable description of the picture is by that most industrious and reliable scholar, Cassiano dal Pozzo. It dates from 1625, when Cassiano was recording his impressions of the picture at Fontainebleau. He says "A life-size portrait, half-length of a certain Gioconda, in a carved walnut frame. This is the most finished work of the painter that one could see, and lacks only speech for all else is there. It represents a woman of between 24 and 26 years old, seen from in front, but not entirely full face, as Greek statues are. It has certain delicate passages around the lips and the eyes that are more exquisite than anyone could hope to achieve. The head is adorned by a very simple veil, but this is painted with great finish. The dress is black, or dark brown, but it has been treated with a varnish which has given it a dismal tone, so that one cannot make it out very well. The hands are extremely beautiful, and, in short, in spite of all the misfortunes that this picture has suffered, the face and the hands are so beautiful that whoever looks at it with admiration is bewitched. Note that this lady, in other respects beautiful, is almost without eyebrows, which the painter has not recorded, as if she did not have them." . . .

This is all the written evidence about the *Mona Lisa* that is worth recording, and I must now turn to the stylistic or internal evidence. I will begin by trying to decide when the picture was painted.

Leonardo's career may be divided into five fairly distinct periods. First the young man in Florence, the painter of grace and movement, of the Uffizi *Adoration* and the *Virgin with the Cat*, the miraculous eye undistracted by science or speculation; second the official painter to the Milanese Court, occupied with great commissions, like the Sforza

Monument, the *Last Supper*, and the reinforcement of the Cathedral, and also with small ones, stables for the Duke, hot water for the Duchess's bathroom; also, with jokes and paradoxes to amuse the guests. In this period there appeared Leonardo the scientist, but it was mechanical science that interested him—the structure of a skull, the construction of machines, the measurement of light passing over a sphere. Third, the return to Florence in 1500, and a renewed interest in arts of design, intensified, no doubt, by a short visit to Rome. These were the years when Leonardo's ideas came to him in visual form, and practically all the great motives that were to occupy him for the rest of his life, first appear in small sketches done between 1500 and 1506: the *Battle of Anghiari*, the *Leda*, the *St. John*, the *Virgin and St. Anne*. There is also an intensified interest in anatomy and the movement of water. The fourth period begins with his return to Milan, with much to-ing and fro-ing to Florence. He continued reluctantly to work out the pictorial ideas of the Florentine period, but his real interest had shifted from art to science. His approach to science was no longer mechanical, or arithmetical, but organic. His researches into anatomy, in particular the problems of generation and the action of the heart, began to influence his sense of form. His observation of the forces of nature, wind, water and geology, intensified his sense of the mystery of creation. Finally, after his move to Rome in 1513 to work for Giuliano de' Medici, he retreated more and more into a private world, both of thought and form. Vasari's much criticized description of his activities has a kind of symbolic truth, because in his growing distrust of the powers of the human intelligence, he did spend a good deal of time on futile exercises. However, he continued sporadically to draw and paint, and even after his first move to France he occupied his mind with problems of architecture.

Now to which of these five periods would we, on internal evidence, be disposed to attribute the *Mona Lisa*? Obviously not the first two. Three of the portraits painted at the Court of Milan have survived, and they are a long way from the *Mona Lisa*, both in style and sentiment. Indeed the so-called *Belle Férronnière* is so different that for a long time its authenticity was doubted, although nobody who has looked intensely at her eye can doubt that she is by Leonardo. The *Belle Férronnière*, on grounds of costume and its relation to Boltraffio, must date from the middle or late 1490s. One would have supposed that the *Mona Lisa* must have been painted at least a decade later than this decidedly *un*-mysterious commission.

On almost every ground the *Mona Lisa* looks as if it were the work of Leonardo's fourth period, the years after his return to Milan, when he was at work on the *Leda* and the second stage of the *St. Anne*. . . .

All Leonardo's projects were worked on for many years: the Sforza monument for over eighteen; the *Leda* for over ten, the *St. Anne* for over twelve, the *St. John* at least ten. It is therefore reasonable to suppose that the most finished of his paintings should have occupied him for several years. The design came to him when practically all his visual inspirations came to him, between 1500 and 1504. When was it executed? . . . The background of the *Mona Lisa* is usually compared to a red chalk drawing at Windsor which shows a storm breaking over the foothills of the Alps. And this drawing is related to a magnificent passage in one of Leonardo's notebooks. . . . "On one occasion above Milan, over in the direction of Lake Maggiore, I saw a cloud, shaped like a huge mountain, made up of banks of fire, because the rays of the sun, which was then settting red on the horizon, dyed it with their color. The great cloud drew to itself all the little clouds that were round about it. And the great cloud remained stationary, and retained the lights of the sun on its apex for an hour and a half after sunset."
. . . It does confirm, what is indeed evident from the drawing, that Leonardo's careful studies of the Alps were made in Milan, that is to say before 1499 or after 1506; and there can be no question that of the two periods the latter is the more probable. On the other hand, I find it much firmer and more detailed than the Alpine studies on red paper, that can be dated precisely in 1511. These record the observations that Leonardo had at the back of his mind when he created the lunar landscape of the *St. Anne*, and they show that in the years before his departure from Milan he had made expeditions beyond the foothills of the Alps into the regions of perpetual snow. Flying back from Venice . . . , I was struck by how one passed from the landscape of the *Mona Lisa* to that of the *St. Anne*, both of which represent quite accurately the forms of the terrain.

All this confirms my belief that the *Mona Lisa* was painted between 1506 and 1510; but of course she was based on a drawing or cartoon which had been executed in Florence about 1504, and may conceivably have represented the third wife of Francesco del Giocondo. After all, the *Mona Lisa* would have been only about seventy when Vasari was collecting the materials for the 1550 edition of the *Lives*. It was hard luck on her to have to give up her portrait drawing (but then so did Isabella d'Este) and she may well have made a point of asserting her identity. . . . She was wearing the ordinary costume of the time, and her hair was bound by a simple fillet, without a veil. Leonardo took his cartoon with him to Milan, and transferred it to a panel, retaining the pose, but gave the sitter a timeless costume and a widow's veil. He probably added the landscape. . . . And of course he recreated the face. Did he find another sitter? The close continuous modeling of the Mona Lisa's face can hardly have been done from memory. But we know, from two examples, the Angel in the *Vierge aux Rochers* and the head of the Louvre *St. Anne*, how completely Leonardo could transform a study from nature into an ideal head, and we can reasonably suppose that the same process took place, to an even greater degree, with the *Mona Lisa*.

In the end, was the sitter a real person? Or did Leonardo develop his first cartoon of 1504 by studies of the head of an anonymous lady whose mysterious expression had taken his fancy and allowed him to release certain obsessions? I doubt if we shall ever know. . . .

The *Mona Lisa* seems to have exerted her spell as soon as the picture was completed, for a number of accurate copies were made, most of which, for some obscure reason, seem to have found their way into the great houses of England. Some of these seem to have been done in Milan, which is another reason for dating the picture earlier than 1512, for Leonardo certainly took it with him to Rome. I suppose that if all the early copies were put in a row (a nightmarish prospect) one might make some sort of guess at which were painted in Milan and which (if any) in Rome. Every thirty years or so collectors claim that they own the original *Mona Lisa*: it is a sort of epidemic. People who own copies of famous pictures are exceptionally obstinate and ingenious, as every gallery director knows. They will discover the most bizarre evidence, they will work out theories of substitution, they will have books privately printed, and they will even go to the expense of lawsuits. I hope I shall not be taken to court if I say that the dark green object that hangs almost invisibly in the Louvre is the original picture painted by Leonardo. It has an impeccable pedigree. It was bought by Francis I for the French Royal Collection. Whereas all the other Leonardos in Francis I's Collection escaped from Fontainebleau, and returned to the Royal Collection later, through Richelieu, the *Mona Lisa* never left it. As we saw, the picture was described in detail by Cassiano dal Pozzo in 1625. The head and shoulders were engraved as an illustration to the French translation of Leonardo's *Treatise on Painting*, published in 1651, the same year as the first edition: it was the only *picture* by Leonardo to be included, the other illustrations being derived from diagrams or from reconstructions based on drawings by Poussin. It followed the French court from Fontainebleau to Versailles, and there remained, without attracting any notice, till after the Revolution, when it was taken, with the rest of the Royal Collection, to the newly opened gallery in the Louvre.

But apart from this circumstantial evidence, there is the extraordinary quality of the picture itself. One can see it a good deal better in an unretouched black-and-white photograph than on the walls of the Louvre, where, in addition to crowds and darkness, it is obscured by a thick, green, bullet-proof glass. But when one sees the original out of the frame and in strong daylight, the effect is overwhelming. The majesty and finality of the pose, the uncanny delicacy with which light passes over the smooth white eggshell face, one had anticipated. But the beautiful color is a surprise. The cloak is a rich and subtle gray, quite blue in certain places, gradated to a darker tone. . . . The sleeves are cinnamon or saffron, the warmest note in the picture. The background is blue and was once much bluer, as one can see in certain places where the varnish has worn thin. The picture is exceptionally well preserved. Of course some color has faded from the cheeks, and even from the mouth, although that is pink enough. But there are only two areas of restoration. One of these, obvious in reproduction, is the lower hand (the lady's right hand), which is entirely repainted; there is also a certain amount of restoration in the left hand, although some of its original beauty is still perceptible. The other areas of restoration are in two small oblong patches where the eyebrows should have been. This suggests most strongly that Vasari's information was correct. The eyebrows really were drawn hair by hair, put in when the paint surface was dry; and so, on the first cleaning, they vanished. The fine edge of the lady's veil nearly disappeared at the same time. This cleaning must have taken place after Vasari's informant had seen the picture, i.e. after 1550. . . .

Finally the head, with which one imagines oneself to have been fairly familiar, seems to produce a vibration of life which is really quite alarming. The old Vasarian phrase, "This is not art but life itself" comes back to one's mind; and although our next thought is "What kind of life?", the fact that any painter created such a disturbingly living presence is miraculous and goes some way to justify the old criteria. . . .

It could be argued that the fame of the *Mona Lisa* was a by-product of the romantic movement, in particular of the romantic addiction to the *femme fatale, La Belle Dame sans Merci,* whose longest and most confusing emanation is in Coleridge's *Christabel*. The *Mona Lisa* re-entered the popular consciousness on this ticket. From having been to all critics from Vasari to Félibien a masterpiece of realism and finish, she became an embodiment of the mysterious. The process took quite a long time. In fact it was not till 1859 that Théophile Gautier wrote the first romantic description of the *Mona Lisa*: "Beneath the form expressed one feels a thought that is vague, infinite, inexpressible. One is moved, troubled, images already seen pass before one's eyes, voices whose notes seem familiar whispers . . . repressed desires, hopes that drive one to despair stir painfully." There, for the first time, is our own, our very own, *Mona Lisa*: but Gautier was a thoroughbred romantic and he has not been able to escape from that favorite image of the romantic movement, the *femme fatale*. He speaks of desires, those overwhelming desires that drive men to despair. Well, the *Mona Lisa* certainly does not exert her fascination in this manner. I cannot believe that she has ever aroused desire in anyone, although she has often aroused repulsion. Only ten years later a far more perceptive description of her character appeared in Walter Pater's essay on Leonardo da Vinci. It was first published in 1869, and reprinted in 1873 in the volume entitled *The Renaissance*. The passage was once so famous that it would have been unnecessary for me to quote it to you. Fifty years ago we all knew it by heart. W. B. Yeats thought it the beginning of modern poetry in England, and quoted it, chopped up into short lines, as the first poem in his *Oxford Book of Modern Verse*, saying, "Only by printing it in *vers libres* can one show its revolutionary importance." I will read it to you not as if it were a prose poem but for what it is: a piece of criticism that is not only deeply imaginative, but remarkably precise. The allusions are not, as Yeats believed, the result of rhythmic necessity, but of an almost uncanny insight into Leonardo's picture. Pater, of course, accepts Vasari's statement that it is a portrait, but he immediately sees how inadequate this word is.

> From childhood we see this image defining itself on the fabric of his dreams; and but for express historical testimony, we might fancy that this was but his ideal lady, embodied and beheld at last.
>
> What was the relationship of a living Florentine to this creature of his thought? By what strange affinities had the dream and the person grown up thus apart, and yet so closely together?

Then comes the description:

> The presence that rose thus so strangely beside the waters,
> is expressive of what in the ways of a thousand years men
> had come to desire. Hers is the head upon which all the ends
> of the world are come, and the eyelids are a little weary.
>
> It is a beauty wrought out from within upon the flesh,
> the deposit, little cell by cell, of strange thoughts and
> fantastic reveries and exquisite passions. Set it for a
> moment beside one of those white Greek goddesses or
> beautiful women of antiquity, and how would they be
> troubled by this beauty, into which the soul with all its
> maladies had passed.
>
> All the thoughts and experience of the world have
> etched and molded there, in that which they have of power
> to refine and make expressive the outward form; the ani-
> malism of Greece, the lust of Rome, the mysticism of the
> middle age with its spiritual ambition and imaginative
> loves, the return of the Pagan world, the sins of the Borgias.
>
> She is older than the rocks among which she sits; like
> the vampire, she has been dead many times, and learned
> the secrets of the grave; and has been a diver in deep seas,
> and keeps their fallen day about her; and trafficked for
> strange webs with Eastern merchants; and, as Leda, was
> the mother of Helen of Troy, and, as Saint Anne, the
> mother of Mary; and all this has been to her but as the
> sound of lyres and flutes, and lives only in the delicacy
> with which it has molded the changing lineaments, and
> tinged the eyelids and the hands.

One could have done without the sins of the Borgias, which are
something left over from Victor Hugo, and shows less than Pater's
usual insight. But otherwise what marvelous precision. Did Pater
really know that the *Mona Lisa* was being painted at the same time as
the *Leda* and the *St. Anne*? Or was he simply thinking of the two
mothers, one of carnal, the other of spiritual perfection? Can one add a
word to "beauty wrought out from within upon the flesh, little cell by
cell"; or to such a phrase as "the soul, with all its maladies has
passed"? Well, there *is* one word that the conventions of 1869 would
not have admitted (if indeed the word existed, which apparently it did
not as it is not to be found in the Oxford Dictionary of 1901), but
which is really essential to an understanding of the *Mona Lisa*, the

word "homosexual." It is a word of large coverage. Byron had homosexual instincts which he sometimes indulged, but his poetry is emphatically not that of a homosexual. According to reliable contemporary evidence Donatello was a homosexual, and the David certainly confirms this tradition. But there is not another trace of homosexuality in the rest of Donatello's sculpture. . . . Michelangelo was a devout Christian, and, although he tried to sublimate his homosexuality through neo-Platonism, the struggle cost him dear, especially in the 1520's, when he felt that he had been defeated, and crouched beneath the physical splendor of a young Florentine. But Leonardo, as even Vasari admits, was not a Christian, and he gladly allowed his homosexuality to penetrate to the depth of his being. As everyone knows, he was formally accused of sodomy in 1476; the charge was dismissed, was repeated, but does not seem to have been followed up. Indeed, to have done so with any determination in *quattrocento* Florence would have decimated the ranks of the enlightenment. Round about the year 1480 he seems to have taken pleasure in the graceful movements of women and children, but this did not last long. There is only one mention of a woman in all the thousands of pages of his notebooks: "*Caterina, viso fantastico, sta al' ospedale.*" But there are plenty of references to Giacomo Salai. He came to live with Leonardo on 20th July 1490, and Leonardo writes a preliminary list of his numerous misbehaviors, adding in the margin *ladro buggiardo ghiotto*. No royal favorite has ever got into more mischief—breaking the glasses, lying, guzzling, stealing—so that Leonardo had difficulty in keeping him out of prison. Yet Leonardo kept him with him throughout his life, always included his name among those who accompanied him on journeys, and finally mentioned him in his will. He no doubt formed other attachments, including the rich and *convenable* Francesco Melzi, but his obsession with Salai was as strong and persistent as that of Proust with Albertine. Vasari could not omit it from his life of Leonardo, mentioning that Salai, whom he calls his *creato*, had thick curly hair, "in which Leonardo took much delight."

We know Salai only in profile. What would that smiling, self-satisfied face have looked like if it had turned toward us? Please do not think I am suggesting that the *Mona Lisa* was painted from Salai: quite the contrary. Femininity is an essential element in this disquieting image. But one must recognize that the strong sexual impulse in Leonardo that was concentrated on Salai, was present in all his work and contributed to the alternating repugnance and detached fascination with which he viewed the opposite sex.

But, as I have said, the point of the *Mona Lisa* is precisely that she is a woman. Leonardo's convictions did not blind him to the fact that the creative process, which came more and more to occupy his thoughts, was predominantly a female process. The male part in procreation was short, easy and beyond his powers of analysis. The female part was long, complex and a possible subject for investigation. It was also more closely connected with the other observable processes in nature. At the time when he was making a portrait drawing of a young Florentine lady, who for convenience we call Mona Lisa, he was also making studies for a picture illustrating the myth of Leda and the Swan. One of these, the figure kneeling, dates from the year of Anghiari; another tiny one, the figure standing, appears on a sheet of anatomical studies dealing with the process of digestion and generation. Leonardo leaves us in no doubt that he chose this curious myth because he could make it into an allegory of the irrepressible forces of generation. The plants and grasses that he drew with a devouring eye were certainly studied with the *Leda* in mind, and are graphic expressions of his feeling that grasses push their way upward with the force of floods and whirlwinds. Leda herself, as we see her in copies of the lost original, is intended to be a sexual symbol, with the same ingredients as a piece of Hindu sculpture—the high breasts, the *déhanchement*—but these are put together by an intellectual process without a spark of emotion. Even her hair, which we know, from a note on another drawing, to have been a wig, made, no doubt, by Leonardo himself, has the intricate coils of his anatomical drawings of the womb. . . .

I may seem to have chosen a long and devious path to return to the subject. How much simpler if I could have followed those earlier critics who saw in [the *Mona Lisa*] only a masterpiece of realism and of pictorial skill. But that would be to close one's mind to events. A masterpiece of realism does not dislocate the traffic in Fifth Avenue, or cause a riot in the National Gallery of Washington. Nobody feels compelled to paint a moustache on the upper lip of Helene Fourment. There are millions of people who know the name of only one picture—the *Mona Lisa*. This is not simply due to an accident of accumulated publicity. It means that this strange image strikes at the subconscious with a force that is extremely rare in an individual work of art. Ancient symbols come from the subconscious and continue to touch it. *Mona Lisa* is a new creation that has the magical power of a very ancient one. She is older than the rocks among which she sits. What has given her this power?

Leonardo had no physical attachment to women; but as part of the creative process they obsessed him. They horrified him; but so did nature. Rocks, which by their fossils proved that life had existed on the earth long before the appearance of man; water, logical in its structure, ruthless in its operation, capable of wiping out the human race. Air, rain, fire, plants: all equally irrepressible. And at the center of these forces of nature, partaking to some extent of their processes, their flux and reflux, their momentum, was the figure of woman. She became the symbol of all that was alien to him and yet had some magic power.

Leonardo the scientist cannot be separated from Leonardo the magician; in his notes, no less than in his drawings, the two are constantly melting into one another. He passes in a sentence from observation to fantasy; and as he grows less confident in science the magician is in the ascendant. The *Mona Lisa* is the magician's cat, a familiar, who is nonetheless perfectly detached, and whose smile is the smile of derision.

And yet this theory may be too simple. Leonardo was surely one of the most complex men who have ever lived. Combined with his curiosity about nature and his horror at nature's power, there was his extraordinary tenderness toward living things. The only record of his character to be printed in his lifetime says how he will not eat any meat nor hurt any living thing. Such tenderness in physical action can well be combined with intellectual detachment or even repulsion; and as his eye actually rested on the Mona Lisa's cheek, and his hand began to record the passage of light, it was the tenderness that prevailed.

Finally, we come back to the word used by the first man whose record of the *Mona Lisa* has come down to us: de Beatis. *Perfettissimo*. The *Mona Lisa* is indeed the supreme example of perfection. A belief in the concept of perfection is a kind of religion; philosophically it may be one of the few indisputable arguments that man has within him something of the divine. Since perfection is so far out of reach, men have sought to achieve it by exclusion, so that it has become associated, even in such a great artist as Polykleitos, with a rejection, or at least a narrowing of experience. In the *Mona Lisa* Leonardo has achieved perfection through inclusion. His insatiable curiosity, his restless leaps from one subject to another, have been harmonized in a single work. The science, the pictorial skill, the obsession with nature, the psychological insight are all there, and so perfectly balanced that at first we are hardly aware of them. As we watch this watchful predator, and inspect this being who so confidently inspects us, we forget all our misgivings in admiration of perfect mastery.

The Poetry of Michelangelo

Walter Pater

. . . Of the whole story of the creation [Michelangelo] painted only the creation of the first man and woman, and, for him at least, feebly, the creation of light. It belongs to the quality of his genius thus to concern itself almost exclusively with the making of man. For him it is not, as in the story itself, the last and crowning act of a series of developments, but the first and unique act, the creation of life itself in its supreme form, off-hand and immediately, in the cold and lifeless stone. With him the beginning of life has all the characteristics of resurrection; it is like the recovery of suspended health or animation, with its gratitude, its effusion, and eloquence. Fair as the young men of the Elgin marbles, the Adam of the Sistine Chapel is unlike them in a total absence of that balance and completeness which express so well the sentiment of a self-contained, independent life. In that languid figure there is something rude and satyrlike, something akin to the rugged hillside on which it lies. His whole form is gathered into an expression of mere expectancy and reception; he has hardly strength enough to lift his finger to touch the finger of the creator; yet a touch of the finger tips will suffice.

This creation of life—life coming always as relief or recovery, and always in strong contrast with the roughhewn mass in which it is kindled—is in various ways the motive of all his work, whether its immediate subject be Pagan or Christian, legend or allegory; and this, although at least one-half of his work was designed for the adornment of tombs—the tomb of Julius, the tombs of the Medici. Not the Judgment but the Resurrection is the real subject of his last work in the Sistine Chapel; and his favorite Pagan subject is the legend of Leda,

the delight of the world breaking from the egg of a bird. . . . He secures
that ideality of expression which in Greek sculpture depends on a
delicate system of abstraction, and in early Italian sculpture on low-
ness of relief, by an incompleteness, which is surely not always
undesigned, and which, as I think, no one regrets, and trusts to the
spectator to complete the half-emergent form. And as his persons have
something of the unwrought stone about them, so, as if to realize the
expression by which the old Florentine records describe a sculptor—
master of live stone—with him the very rocks seem to have life. They
have but to cast away the dust and scurf that they may rise and stand on
their feet. He loved the very quarries of Carrara, those strange gray
peaks which even at midday convey into any scene from which they
are visible something of the solemnity and stillness of evening, sometimes wandering among them month after month, till at last their pale
ashen colors seem to have passed into his painting; and on the crown
of the head of the *David* there still remains a morsel of uncut stone, as
if by one touch to maintain its connection with the place from which it
was hewn.

And it is in this penetrative suggestion of life that the secret of that
sweetness of his is to be found. He gives us indeed no lovely natural
objects like Leonardo or Titian, but only the coldest, most elementary
shadowing of rock or tree; no lovely draperies and comely gestures of
life, but only the austere truths of human nature; ''simple persons''—
as he replied in his rough way to the querulous criticism of Julius the
Second that there was no gold on the figures of the Sistine Chapel—
''simple persons, who wore no gold on their garments''; but he
penetrates us with a feeling of that power which we associate with all
the warmth and fullness of the world, the sense of which brings into
one's thoughts a swarm of birds and flowers and insects. The brooding
spirit of life itself is there; and the summer may burst out in a moment.

He was born in an interval of a rapid midnight journey in March, at a
place in the neighborhood of Arezzo, the thin, clear air of which was
then thought to be favorable to the birth of children of great parts. He
came of a race of grave and dignified men, who, claiming kinship with
the family of Canossa, and some color of imperial blood in their veins,
had, generation after generation, received honorable employment
under the government of Florence. His mother, a girl of nineteen
years, put him out to nurse at a country house among the hills of
Settignano, where every other inhabitant is a worker in the marble
quarries, and the child early became familiar with that strange first

stage in the sculptor's art. To this succeeded the influence of the sweetest and most placid master Florence had yet seen, Domenico Ghirlandaio. At fifteen he was at work among the curiosities of the garden of the Medici, copying and retouching antiques, winning the condescending notice of the great Lorenzo. He knew too how to excite strong hatreds; and it was at this time that in a quarrel with a fellow student he received a blow on the face which deprived him for ever of the comeliness of outward form.

It was through an accident that he came to study those works of the early Italian sculptors which suggested much of his own grandest work, and impressed it with so deep a sweetness. He believed in dreams and omens. One of his friends dreamed twice that Lorenzo, then lately dead, appeared to him in gray and dusty apparel. To Michelangeo his dream seemed to portend the troubles which afterwards really came, and with the suddenness which was characteristic of all his movements, he left Florence. Having occasion to pass through Bologna, he neglected to procure the little seal of red wax which the stranger entering Bologna must carry on the thumb of his right hand. He had no money to pay the fine, and would have been thrown into prison had not one of the magistrates interposed. He remained in this man's house a whole year, rewarding his hospitality by readings from the Italian poets whom he loved. Bologna, with its endless colonnades and fantastic leaning towers, can never have been one of the lovelier cities of Italy. But about the portals of its vast unfinished churches and its dark shrines, half hidden by votive flowers and candles, lie some of the sweetest works of the early Tuscan sculptors, Giovanni da Pisa and Jacopo della Quercia, things as winsome as flowers; and the year which Michelangelo spent in copying these works was not a lost year.* It was now, on returning to Florence, that he put forth that unique presentment of Bacchus, which expresses, not the mirthfulness of the god of wine, but his sleepy seriousness, his enthusiasm, his capacity for profound dreaming. No one ever expressed more truly than Michelangelo the notion of inspired sleep, of faces charged with dreams. A vast fragment of marble had long lain below the Loggia of Orcagna, and many a sculptor had had his thoughts of a design which should just fill this famous block of stone, cutting the diamond, as it were, without loss. Under Michel-

---

*Michelangelo added to these works three small figures, an angel, a St. Proculus and a St. Petronius on the shrine of St. Domenic, Bologna.

angelo's hand it became the *David*. . . . Michelangelo was now thirty years old, and his reputation was established. Three great works fill the remainder of his life—three works often interrupted, carried on through a thousand hesitations, a thousand disappointments, quarrels with his patrons, quarrels with his family, quarrels perhaps most of all with himself—the Sistine Chapel, the Mausoleum of Julius the Second, and the Sacristy of San Lorenzo.

In the story of Michelangelo's life the strength, often turning to bitterness, is not far to seek. A discordant note sounds throughout it which almost spoils the music. He "treats the Pope as the King of France himself would not dare to treat him": he goes along the streets of Rome "like an executioner," Raphael says of him. Once he seems to have shut himself up with the intention of starving himself to death. As we come, in reading his life, on its harsh, untempered incidents, the thought again and again arises that he is one of those who incur the judgment of Dante, as having "willfully lived in sadness." Even his tenderness and pity are embittered by their strength. What passionate weeping in that mysterious figure which, in the *Creation of Adam*, crouches below the image of the Almighty, as he comes with the forms of things to be, woman and her progeny, in the fold of his garment! What a sense of wrong in those two captive youths, who feel the chains like scalding water on their proud and delicate flesh! The idealist who became a reformer with Savonarola, and a republican superintending the fortification of Florence—the nest where he was born, as he calls it once in a sudden throb of affection—in its last struggle for liberty, yet believed always that he had imperial blood in his veins and was of the kindred of the great Matilda, had within the depths of his nature some secret spring of indignation or sorrow. We know little of his youth, but all tends to make one believe in the vehemence of its passions. Beneath the Platonic calm of the sonnets there is latent a deep delight in carnal form and color. There, and still more in the madrigals, he often falls into the language of less tranquil affections; while some of them have the color of penitence, as from a wanderer returning home. He who spoke so decisively of the supremacy in the imaginative world of the unveiled human form had not been always, we may think, a mere Platonic lover. Vague and wayward his loves may have been; but they partook of the strength of his nature. . . .

But his genius is in harmony with itself; and just as in the products of his art we find resources of sweetness within their exceeding strength, so in his own story also, bitter as the ordinary sense of it may be, there are select pages shut in among the rest—pages one might easily turn over too lightly, but which yet sweeten the whole volume. The interest of Michelangelo's poems is that they make us spectators of this struggle; the struggle of a strong nature to adorn and attune itself; the struggle of a desolating passion, which yearns to be resigned and sweet and pensive, as Dante's was. It is a consequence of the occasional and informal character of his poetry that it brings us nearer to himself, his own mind and temper, than any work done only to support a literary reputation could possibly do. His letters tell us little that is worth knowing about him—a few poor quarrels about money and commissions. But it is quite otherwise with these songs and sonnets, written down at odd moments, sometimes on the margin of his sketches, themselves often unfinished sketches, arresting some salient feeling or unpremeditated idea as it passed. And it happens that a true study of these has become within the last few years for the first time possible. A few of the sonnets circulated widely in manuscript, and became almost within Michelangelo's own lifetime a subject of academical discourses. But they were first collected in a volume in 1623 by the great nephew of Michelangelo, Michelangelo Buonarroti the younger. He omitted much, rewrote the sonnets in part, and sometimes compressed two or more compositions into one, always losing something of the force and incisiveness of the original. So the book remained, neglected even by Italians themselves in the last century, through the influence of that French taste which despised all compositions of the kind, as it despised and neglected Dante. "His reputation will ever be on the increase, because he is so little read," says Voltaire of Dante. But in 1858 the last of the Buonarroti bequeathed to the municipality of Florence the curiosities of his family. Among them was a precious volume containing the autograph of the sonnets. A learned Italian, Signor Cesare Guasti, undertook to collate this autograph with other manuscripts at the Vatican and elsewhere, and in 1863 published a true version of Michelangelo's poems, with dissertations and a paraphrase.

People have often spoken of these poems as if they were a mere cry of distress, a lover's complaint over the obduracy of Vittoria Colonna. But those who speak thus forget that though it is quite possible that Michelangelo had seen Vittoria, that somewhat shadowy figure, as early as 1537, yet their closer intimacy did not begin till about the year 1542, when Michelangelo was nearly seventy years old. Vittoria herself, an ardent neo-catholic, vowed to perpetual widowhood since

the news had reached her, seventeen years before, that her husband
. . . lay dead of the wounds he had received in the battle of Pavia, was
then no longer an object of great passion. In a dialogue written by the
painter, Francesco d'Ollanda, we catch a glimpse of them together in
an empty church at Rome, one Sunday afternoon, discussing indeed
the characteristics of various schools of art, but still more the writings
of Saint Paul, already following the ways and tasting the sunless
pleasures of weary people, whose care for external things is slacken-
ing. In a letter still extant he regrets that when he visited her after
death he had kissed her hands only. . . . It was just because Vittoria
raised no great passion that the space in his life where she reigns has
such peculiar suavity; and the spirit of the sonnets is lost if we once
take them out of that dreamy atmosphere in which men have things as
they will, because the hold of all outward things upon them is faint and
uncertain. Their prevailing tone is a calm and meditative sweetness.
The cry of distress is indeed there, but as a mere residue, a trace of
bracing chalybeate salt, just discernible in the song which rises like a
clear, sweet spring from a charmed space in his life.

This charmed and temperate space in Michelangelo's life, without
which its excessive strength would have been so imperfect, which
saves him from the judgment of Dante on those who ''willfully lived
in sadness,'' is then a well-defined period there, reaching from the
year 1542 to the year 1547, the year of Vittoria's death. In it the
lifelong effort to tranquilize his vehement emotions by withdrawing
them into the region of ideal sentiment, becomes successful; and the
significance of Vittoria is, that she realizes for him a type of affection
which even in disappointment may charm and sweeten his spirit. . . .

Above all, he resembles Dante in the warmth and intensity of his
political utterances, for the lady of one of his noblest sonnets was from
the first understood to be the city of Florence; and he avers that all
must be asleep in heaven, if she, who was created ''of angelic form,''
for a thousand lovers, is appropriated by one alone, some Piero, or
Alessandro de' Medici. Once and again he introduces Love and
Death, who dispute concerning him. For, like Dante and all the nobler
souls of Italy, he is much occupied with thoughts of the grave, and his
true mistress is death—death at first as the worst of all sorrows and
disgraces, with a clod of the field for its brain; afterwards, death in its
high distinction, its detachment from vulgar needs, the angry stains of
life and action escaping fast.

. . . [If] one is to distinguish the peculiar savor of his work, [Michelangelo] must be approached, not through his followers, but through his predecessors; not through the marbles of Saint Peter's, but through the work of the sculptors of the fifteenth century over the tombs and altars of Tuscany. He is the last of the Florentines, of those on whom the peculiar sentiment of the Florence of Dante and Giotto descended: he is the consummate representative of the form that sentiment took in the fifteenth century. . . . Up to him the tradition of sentiment is unbroken, the progress toward surer and more mature methods of expressing that sentiment continuous. But his professed disciples did not share this temper; they are in love with his strength only, and seem not to feel his grave and temperate sweetness. Theatricality is their chief characteristic.

This discipleship of Michelangelo, this dependence of his on the tradition of the Florentine schools, is nowhere seen more clearly than in his treatment of the Creation. The Creation of Man had haunted the mind of the Middle Ages like a dream; and weaving it into a hundred carved ornaments of capital or doorway, the Italian sculptors had early impressed upon it that pregnancy of expression which seems to give it many veiled meanings. As with other artistic conceptions of the Middle Ages, its treatment became almost conventional, handed on from artist to artist, with slight changes, till it came to have almost an independent and abstract existence of its own. It was characteristic of the medieval mind thus to give an independent traditional existence to a special pictorial conception, or to a legend, like that of *Tristram* or *Tannhäuser*, or even to the very thoughts and substance of a book, like the *Imitation*, so that no single workman could claim it as his own, and the book, the image, the legend, had itself a legend, and its fortunes, and a personal history; and it is a sign of the medievalism of Michelangelo, that he thus receives from tradition his central conception, and does but add the last touches, in transferring it to the frescoes of the Sistine Chapel.

But there was another tradition of those earlier, more serious Florentines, of which Michelangelo is the inheritor, to which he gives the final expression, and which centers in the sacristy of San Lorenzo, as the tradition of the Creation centers in the Sistine Chapel. It has been said that all the great Florentines were preoccupied with death.
. . . Even the gay and licentious Boccaccio gives a keener edge to his stories by putting them in the mouths of a party of people who had

taken refuge in a country house from the danger of death by plague. It was to this inherited sentiment, this practical decision that to be preoccupied with the thought of death was in itself dignifying, and a note of high quality, that the seriousness of the great Florentines of the fifteenth century was partly due; and it was reinforced in them by the actual sorrows of their times. How often, and in what various ways, had they seen life stricken down, in their streets and houses. *La bella Simonetta* dies in early youth, and is borne to the grave with uncovered face. . . . Antonio Rossellino carves his tomb in the church of San Miniato, with care for the shapely hands and feet, and sacred attire; Luca della Robbia puts his skyiest works there; and the tomb of the youthful and princely prelate became the strangest and most beautiful thing in that strange and beautiful place. After the execution of the Pazzi conspirators, Botticelli is employed to paint their portraits. This preoccupation with serious thoughts and sad images might easily have resulted, as it did, for instance, in the gloomy villages of the Rhine, or in the overcrowded parts of medieval Paris, as it still does in many a village of the Alps, in something merely morbid or grotesque, in the *Danse Macabre* of many French and German painters, or the grim inventions of Dürer. From such a result the Florentine masters of the fifteenth century were saved by the nobility of their Italian culture, and still more by their tender pity for the thing itself. . . .

Of all this sentiment Michelangelo is the achievement; and, first of all, of pity. *Pietà*, pity, the pity of the Virgin Mother over the dead body of Christ, expanded into the pity of all mothers over all dead sons, the entombment, with its cruel "hard stones": this is the subject of his predilection. He has left it in many forms, sketches, half-finished designs, finished and unfinished groups of sculpture; but always as a hopeless, rayless, almost heathen sorrow—no divine sorrow, but mere pity and awe at the stiff limbs and colorless lips. . . . The tombs in the sacristy of San Lorenzo are memorials, not of any of the other nobler and greater Medici, but of Giuliano, and Lorenzo the younger, noticeable chiefly for their somewhat early death. It is mere human nature therefore which has prompted the sentiment here. The titles assigned traditionally to the four symbolical figures, Night and Day, The Twilight and The Dawn, are far too definite for them; for these figures come much nearer to the mind and spirit of their author, and are a more direct expression of his thoughts, than any merely symbolical conceptions could possibly have been. They concentrate and express, less by way of definite conceptions than by the touches, the promptings of a piece of music, all those vague fancies, misgivings, presentiments, which shift and mix and are defined and fade again, whenever the thoughts try to fix themselves with sincerity on the conditions and surroundings of the disembodied spirit. I suppose no one would come to the sacristy of San Lorenzo for consolation; for seriousness, for solemnity, for dignity of impression, perhaps, but not for consolation. It is a place neither of consoling nor of terrible thoughts, but of vague and wistful speculation. . . .

The qualities of the great masters in art or literature, the combination of those qualities, the laws by which they moderate, support, relieve each other, are not peculiar to them; but most often typical standards, or revealing instances of the laws by which certain aesthetic effects are produced. The old masters indeed are simpler; their characteristics are written larger, and are easier to read, than the analogues of them in all the mixed, confused productions of the modern mind. But when once we have succeeded in defining for ourselves those characteristics, and the law of their combination, we have acquired a standard or measure which helps us to put in its right place many a vagrant genius, many an unclassified talent, many precious though imperfect products of art. It is so with the components of the true character of Michelangelo. That strange interfusion of sweetness and strength is not to be found in those who claimed to be his followers; but it is found in many of those who worked before him, and in many others down to our own time, in William Blake, for instance, and Victor Hugo, who, though not of his school, and unaware, are his true sons, and help us to understand him, as he in turn interprets and justifies them. Perhaps this is the chief use in studying old masters.

Seven Sonnets*

Michelangelo

THE ARTIST AND HIS WORK

How can that be, lady, which all men learn
   By long experience? Shapes that seem alive,
   Wrought in hard mountain marble, will survive
   Their maker, whom the years to dust return!
Thus to effect cause yields. Art hath her turn,
   And triumphs over Nature. I, who strive
   With Sculpture, know this well; her wonders live
   In spite of time and death, those tyrants stern.
So I can give long life to both of us
   In either way, by color or by stone,
   Making the semblance of thy face and mine.
Centuries hence when both are buried, thus
   Thy beauty and my sadness shall be shown,
   And men shall say, "For her 'twas wise to pine."

---

*The seventy-seven sonnets of Michelangelo were rendered into rhymed English for the first time by John Addington Symonds. In his introduction to his work, Symonds wrote: "[B]y far the greater number of them were composed after his sixtieth year. To whom they were addressed, we only know in a few instances. Vittoria Colonna and Tommaso de' Cavalieri, the two most intimate friends of his old age in Rome, received from him some of the most pathetically beautiful of his love poems. But to suppose that either the one or the other was the object of more than a few well-authenticated sonnets would be hazardous. . . . that the loves of his youth were not so tranquil as those of his old age, appears not only from the regrets expressed in his religious verses, but also from one or two of the rare sonnets referable to his manhood. . . . The love of beauty, the love of Florence, and the love of Christ, are the three main motives of his poetry."

ON THE PAINTING OF THE SISTINE CHAPEL
To Giovanni da Pistoia

I've grown a goitre by dwelling in this den—
  As cats from stagnant streams in Lombardy,
  Or in what other land they hap to be—
  Which drives the belly close beneath the chin:
My beard turns up to heaven; my nape falls in,
  Fixed on my spine: my breast-bone visibly
  Grows like a harp: a rich embroidery
  Bedews my face from brush-drops thick and thin.
My loins into my paunch like levers grind:
  My buttock like a crupper bears my weight;
  My feet unguided wander to and fro;
In front my skin grows loose and long; behind,
  By bending it becomes more taut and strait;
  Crosswise I strain me like a Syrian bow:
    Whence false and quaint, I know,
  Must be the fruit of squinting brain and eye;
  For ill can aim the gun that bends awry.
    Come then, Giovanni, try
  To succor my dead pictures and my fame,
  Since foul I fare and painting is my shame.

ON DANTE ALIGHIERI

From heaven his spirit came, and robed in clay,
  The realms of justice and of mercy trod:
  Then rose a living man to gaze on God,
  That he might make the truth as clear as day.
For that pure star, that brightened with his ray
  The undeserving nest where I was born,
  The whole wide world would be a prize to scorn;
  None but his Maker can due guerdon pay.
I speak of Dante, whose high work remains
  Unknown, unhonored by that thankless brood,
  Who only to just men deny their wage.
Were I but he! Born for like lingering pains,
  Against his exile coupled with his good
  I'd gladly change the world's best heritage!

ON THE LIVES OF THE PAINTERS
To Giorgio Vasari

With pencil and with palette hitherto
    You made your art high Nature's paragon;
    Nay more, from Nature her own prize you won,
    Making what she made fair more fair to view.
Now that your learned hand with labor new
    Of pen and ink a worthier work hath done,
    What erst you lacked, what still remained her own,
    The power of giving life, is gained for you.
If men in any age with Nature vied
    In beauteous workmanship, they had to yield
    When to the fated end years brought their name.
You, re-illuming memories that died,
    In spite of Time and Nature have revealed
    For them and for yourself eternal fame.

A MATCHLESS COURTESY
To Vittoria Colonna

Blest spirit, who with loving tenderness
    Quickenest my heart, so old and near to die,
    Who 'mid thy joys on me dost bend an eye,
    Though many nobler men around thee press!
As thou wert erewhile wont my sight to bless,
    So to console my mind thou now dost fly;
    Hope therefore stills the pangs of memory,
    Which, coupled with desire, my soul distress.
So finding in thee grace to plead for me—
    Thy thoughts for me sunk in so sad a case—
    He who now writes returns thee thanks for these.
Lo! it were foul and monstrous usury
    To send thee ugliest paintings in the place
    Of thy fair spirit's living phantasies.

THE MODEL AND THE STATUE
To Vittoria Colonna

When divine Art conceives a form and face,
   She bids the craftsman for his first essay
   To shape a simple model in mere clay:
   This is the earliest birth of Art's embrace.
From the live marble in the second place
   His mallet brings into the light of day
   A thing so beautiful that who can say
   When time shall conquer that immortal grace?
Thus my own model I was born to be—
   The model of that nobler self, whereto
   Schooled by your pity, lady, I shall grow.
Each overplus and each deficiency
   You will make good. What penance then is due
   For my fierce heat, chastened and taught by you?

IRREPARABLE LOSS
After the Death of Vittoria Colonna

When my rude hammer to the stubborn stone
   Gives human shape, now that, now this, at will,
   Following his hand who wields and guides it still,
   It moves upon another's feet alone:
But that which dwells in heaven, the world doth fill
   With beauty by pure motions of its own;
   And since tools fashion tools which else were none,
   Its life makes all that lives with living skill.
Now, for that every stroke excels the more
   The higher at the forge it doth ascend,
   Her soul that fashioned mine hath sought the skies:
Wherefore unfinished I must meet my end,
   If God, the great artificer, denies
   That aid which was unique on earth before.

Casting Perseus and Medusa

Benvenuto Cellini

I am called Benvenuto Cellini, [1500-1571], son of Maestro Giovanni, son of Andrea, son of Cristofano Cellini; my mother was Madonna Elisabetta, daughter to Stefano Granacci; both parents citizens of Florence. It is found written in chronicles made by our ancestors of Florence, men of old time and credibility, even as Giovanni Villani writes, that the city of Florence was evidently built in imitation of the fair city of Rome; and certain remnants of the Colosseum and the Baths can yet be traced. These things are near Santa Croce. The Capitol was where is now the Old Market. The Rotonda is entire, which was made for the temple of Mars, and is now dedicated to our S. Giovanni. That thus it was, can very well be seen, and cannot be denied; but the said buildings are much smaller than those of Rome. He who caused them to be built, they say, was Julius Caesar, in concert with some noble Romans, who, when Fiesole had been stormed and taken, raised a city in this place, and each of them took in hand to erect one of these notable edifices.

Julius Caesar had among his captains a man of highest rank and valor, who was called Fiorino of Cellino, which is a village about two miles distant from Monte Fiascone. Now this Fiorino took up his quarters under the hill of Fiesole, on the ground where Florence now stands, in order to be near the river Arno, and for the convenience of

BENVENUTO CELLINI (1500–1571), goldsmith, jeweler, sculptor, and author. His autobiography is regarded as a model of vernacular Tuscan prose and an indispensable tool in understanding the Italian renaissance. Michelangelo called him "the best goldsmith we know of," and his work delighted popes, dukes, and kings. Cellini perfected new methods of engraving, casting metal, and setting gems.

the troops. All those soldiers and others who had to do with the said captain, used then to say: "Let us go to Fiorenze"; as well because the said captain was called Fiorino, as also because the place he had chosen for his quarters was by nature very rich in flowers. Upon the foundation of the city, therefore, since this name struck Julius Caesar as being fair and apt, and given by circumstance, and seeing furthermore that flowers themselves bring good augury, he appointed the name of Florence for the town. He wished besides to pay his valiant captain this compliment; and he loved him all the more for having drawn him from a very humble place, and for the reason that so excellent a man was a creature of his own. . . .

Thus then we find; and thus we believe that we are descended from a man of worth.* . . .

Having succeeded so well with the cast of the Medusa, I had great hope of bringing my Perseus through; for I had laid the wax on, and felt confident that it would come out in bronze as perfectly as the Medusa. The waxen model produced so fine an effect, that when the Duke saw it and was struck with its beauty—whether somebody had persuaded him it could not be carried out with the same finish in metal, or whether he thought so for himself—he came to visit me more frequently than usual, and on one occasion said: "Benvenuto, this figure cannot succeed in bronze; the laws of art do not admit of it." These words of his Excellency stung me so sharply that I answered: "My lord, I know how very little confidence you have in me; and I believe the reason of this is that your most illustrious Excellency lends too ready an ear to my calumniators, or else indeed that you do not understand my art." He hardly let me close the sentence when he broke in: "I profess myself a connoisseur, and understand it very well indeed." I replied: "Yes, like a prince, not like an artist; for if your Excellency understood my trade as well as you imagine, you would trust me on the proofs I have already given. These are, first, the colossal bronze bust of your Excellency . . . ; secondly, the restoration of the Ganymede in marble, which offered so many difficulties and cost me so much trouble, that I would rather have made the whole statue new from the beginning; thirdly, the Medusa, cast by me in bronze, here now before your Excellency's eyes, the execution of which was a greater triumph of strength and skill than any of my predecessors in this fiendish art have yet achieved. Look you, my lord! I constructed that furnace anew on principles quite different

---

*Cellini's derivation from the name of his supposed ancestor is apocryphal.

from those of other founders; in addition to many technical improvements and ingenious devices, I supplied it with two issues for the metal, because this difficult and twisted figure could not otherwise have come out perfect. It is only owing to my intelligent insight into means and appliances that the statue turned out as it did; a triumph judged impossible by all the practitioners of this art. I should like you furthermore to be aware, my lord, for certain, that the sole reason why I succeeded with all those great and arduous works in France under his most admirable Majesty King Francis, was the high courage which that good monarch put into my heart by the liberal allowances he made me, and the multitude of workpeople he left at my disposal. I could have as many as I asked for, and employed at times above forty, all chosen by myself. These were the causes of my having there produced so many masterpieces in so short a space of time. Now then, my lord, put trust in me; supply me with the aid I need. I am confident of being able to complete a work which will delight your soul. But if your Excellency goes on disheartening me, and does not advance me the assistance which is absolutely required, neither I nor any man alive upon this earth can hope to achieve the slightest thing of value."

It was as much as the Duke could do to stand by and listen to my pleadings. He kept turning first this way and then that; while I, in despair, poor wretched I, was calling up remembrance of the noble state I held in France, to the great sorrow of my soul. All at once he cried: "Come, tell me, Benvenuto, how is it possible that yonder splendid head of Medusa, so high up there in the grasp of Perseus, should ever come out perfect?" I replied upon the instant: "Look you now, my lord! If your Excellency possessed that knowledge of the craft which you affirm you have, you would not fear one moment for the splendid head you speak of. There is good reason, on the other hand, to feel uneasy about this right foot, so far below and at a distance from the rest." When he heard these words, the Duke turned, half in anger, to some gentlemen in waiting, and exclaimed: "I verily believe that this Benvenuto prides himself on contradicting everything one says." Then he faced round to me with a touch of mockery, upon which his attendants did the like, and began to speak as follows: "I will listen patiently to any argument you can possibly produce in explanation of your statement, which may convince me of its probability." I said in answer: "I will adduce so sound an argument that your Excellency shall perceive the full force of it." So I began: "You must know, my lord, that the nature of fire is to ascend, and therefore I promise you that Medusa's head will come out famously; but since it is not in the nature of fire to descend, and I must force it downward six cubits by artificial means, I assure your Excellency upon this most convincing ground of proof that the foot cannot possibly come out. It will, however, be quite easy for me to restore it." "Why, then," said the Duke, "did you not devise it so that the foot should come out as well as you affirm the head will?" I answered: "I must have made a much larger furnace, with a conduit as thick as my leg; and so I might have forced the molten metal by its own weight to descend so far. Now, my pipe, which runs six cubits to the statue's foot, as I have said, is not thicker than two fingers. However, it was not worth the trouble and expense to make a larger; for I shall easily be able to mend what is lacking. But when my mold is more than half full, as I expect, from this middle point upwards, the fire ascending by its natural property, then the heads of Perseus and Medusa will come out admirably; you may be quite sure of it." After I had thus expounded these convincing arguments, together with many more of the same kind, which it would be tedious to set down here, the Duke shook his head and departed without further ceremony.

Abandoned thus to my own resources, I took new courage, and banished the sad thoughts which kept recurring to my mind, making me often weep bitter tears of repentance for having left France; for though I did so only to revisit Florence, my sweet birthplace, in order that I might charitably succor my six nieces, this good action, as I well perceived, had been the beginning my great misfortune. Nevertheless, I felt convinced that when my Perseus was accomplished, all these trials would be turned to high felicity and glorious well-being.

Accordingly I strengthened my heart, and with all the forces of my body and my purse, employing what little money still remained to me, I set to work. First I provided myself with several loads of pinewood from the forests of Serristori, in the neighborhood of Montelupo. While these were on their way, I clothed my Perseus with the clay which I had prepared many months beforehand, in order that it might be duly seasoned. After making its clay tunic (for that is the term used in this art) and properly arming it and fencing it with iron girders, I began to draw the wax out by means of a slow fire. This melted and issued through numerous air-vents I had made; for the more there are of these, the better will the mold fill. When I had finished drawing off the wax, I constructed a funnel-shaped furnace all round the model of my Perseus. It was built of bricks so interlaced, the one above the other, that numerous apertures were left for the fire to exhale. Then I began to lay on wood by degrees, and kept it burning two whole days and nights. At length, when all the wax was gone, and the mold was well baked, I set to work at digging the pit in which to sink it. This I performed with scrupulous regard to all the rules of art. When I had finished that part of my work, I raised the mold by windlasses and stout ropes to a perpendicular position, and suspending it with the greatest care one cubit above the level of the furnace, so that it hung exactly above the middle of the pit, I next lowered it gently down into the very bottom of the furnace, and had it firmly placed with every possible precaution for its safety. When this delicate operation was accomplished, I began to bank it up with the earth I had excavated; and, ever as the earth grew higher, I introduced its proper air-vents, which were little tubes of earthenware, such as folk use for drains and such-like purposes. At length, I felt sure that it was admirably fixed, and that the filling-in of the pit and the placing of the air-vents had been properly performed. I also could see that my work-people understood my method, which differed very considerably from that of all the other masters in the trade. Feeling confident, then, that I could rely upon them, I next turned to my furnace, which I had filled with numerous pigs of copper and other bronze stuff. The pieces were piled according to the laws of art, that is to say, so resting one upon the other that the flames could play freely through them, in order that the metal might heat and liquefy the sooner. At last I called out heartily to set the furnace going. The logs of pine were heaped in, and, what with the unctuous resin of the wood and the good draught I had given, my furnace worked so well that I was obliged to rush from side to side to keep it going. The labor was more than I could stand; yet I forced myself to strain every nerve and muscle. To increase my anxieties, the workshop took fire, and we were afraid lest the roof should fall upon our heads; while, from the garden, such a storm of wind and rain kept blowing in, that it perceptibly cooled the furnace.

Battling thus with all these untoward circumstances for several hours, and exerting myself beyond even the measure of my powerful constitution, I could at last bear up no longer, and a sudden fever, of the utmost possible intensity, attacked me. I felt absolutely obliged to go and fling myself upon my bed. Sorely against my will having to drag myself away from the spot, I turned to my assistants, about ten or more in all, what with master-founders, hand-workers, country-fellows, and my own special journeymen, among whom was Bernardino

Mannellini of Mugello, my apprentice through several years. To him in particular I spoke: "Look, my dear Bernardino, that you observe the rules which I have taught you; do your best with all despatch, for the metal will soon be fused. You cannot go wrong; these honest men will get the channels ready; you will easily be able to drive back the two plugs with this pair of iron crooks; and I am sure that my mold will fill miraculously. I feel more ill than I ever did in all my life, and verily believe that it will kill me before a few hours are over." Thus, with despair at heart, I left them, and betook myself to bed.

No sooner had I got to bed than I ordered my serving-maids to carry food and wine for all the men into the workshop; at the same time I cried: "I shall not be alive tomorrow." They tried to encourage me, arguing that my illness would pass over, since it came from excessive fatigue. In this way I spent two hours battling with the fever, which steadily increased, and calling out continually: "I feel that I am dying." . . . While I was thus terribly afflicted, I beheld the figure of a man enter my chamber, twisted in his body into the form of a capital S. He raised a lamentable doleful voice, like one who announces their last hour to men condemned to die upon the scaffold, and spoke these words: "O Benvenuto! your statue is spoiled, and there is no hope whatever of saving it." No sooner had I heard the shriek of that wretch than I gave a howl which might have been heard from the sphere of flame. Jumping from my bed, I seized my clothes and began to dress. The maids, and my lad, and every one who came around to help me, got kicks or blows of the fist, while I kept crying out in lamentation: "Ah! traitors! enviers! This is an act of treason, done by malice! But I swear by God that I will sift it to the bottom, and before I die will leave such witness to the world of what I can do as shall make a score of mortals marvel."

When I had got my clothes on, I strode with soul bent on mischief toward the workshop; there I beheld the men, whom I had left erewhile in such high spirits, standing stupefied and downcast. I began at once and spoke: "Up with you! Attend to me! Since you have not been able or willing to obey the directions I gave you, obey me now that I am with you to conduct my work in person. Let no one contradict me, for in cases like this we need the aid of hand and hearing, not advice." When I had uttered these words, a certain Maestro Alessandro Lastricati broke silence and said: "Look you, Benvenuto, you are going to attempt an enterprise which the laws of art do not sanction, and which cannot succeed." I turned upon him with such fury and so full of mischief, that he and all the rest of them exclaimed with one voice: "On then! Give orders! We will obey your least commands, so long as life is left in us." I believe they spoke thus feelingly because they thought I must fall shortly dead upon the ground. I went immediately to inspect the furnace, and found that the metal was all curdled; an accident which we express by "being caked." I told two of the hands to cross the road, and fetch from the house of the butcher Capretta, a load of young oak-wood, which had lain dry for above a year; this wood had been previously offered me by Madame Ginevra, wife of the said Capretta. So soon as the first armfuls arrived, I began to fill the grate beneath the furnace. Now oak-wood of that kind heats more powerfully than any other sort of tree; and for this reason, where a slow fire is wanted, as in the case of gun-foundry, alder or pine is preferred. Accordingly, when the logs took fire, oh! how the cake began to stir beneath that awful heat, to glow and sparkle in a blaze! At the same time I kept stirring up the channels, and sent men upon the roof to stop the conflagration, which had gathered force from the increased combustion in the furnace; also I caused boards, carpets, and other hangings to be set up against the garden, in order to protect us from the violence of the rain.

When I had thus provided against these several disasters, I roared out first to one man and then to another: "Bring this thing here! Take that thing there!" At this crisis, when the whole gang saw the cake was on the point of melting, they did my bidding, each fellow working with the strength of three. I then ordered half a pig of pewter to be brought, which weighed about sixty pounds, and flung it into the middle of the cake inside the furnace. By this means, and by piling on wood and stirring now with pokers and now with iron rods, the curdled mass rapidly began to liquefy. Then, knowing I had brought the dead to life again, against the firm opinion of those ignoramuses, I felt such vigor fill my veins, that all those pains of fever, all those fears of death, were quite forgotten.

All of a sudden an explosion took place, attended by a tremendous flash of flame, as though a thunderbolt had formed and been discharged amongst us. Unwonted and appalling terror astonished every one, and me more even than the rest. When the din was over and the dazzling light extinguished, we began to look each other in the face. Then I discovered that the cap of the furnace had blown up, and the bronze was bubbling over from its source beneath. So I had the mouths of my mold immediately opened, and at the same time drove in the two plugs which kept back the molten metal. But I noticed that it did not flow as rapidly as usual, the reason being probably that the fierce heat of the fire we kindled had consumed its base alloy. Accordingly I sent for all my pewter platters, porringers, and dishes, to the number of some two hundred pieces, and had a portion of them cast, one by one, into the channels, the rest into the furnace. This expedient succeeded, and every one could now perceive that my bronze was in most perfect liquefaction, and my mold was filling; whereupon they all with heartiness and happy cheer assisted and obeyed my bidding, while I, now here, now there, gave orders, helped with my own hands, and cried aloud: 'O God! Thou that by Thy immeasurable power didst rise from the dead, and in Thy glory didst ascend to heaven!'' . . . even thus in a moment my mold was filled; and seeing my work finished, I fell upon my knees, and with all my heart gave thanks to God. . . .

That evil fellow, my mortal foe, . . . majordomo of the Duke, took great pains to find out how the affair had gone. In answer to his questions, the two men whom I suspected of having caked my metal for me, said I was no man, but of a certainty some powerful devil, since I had accomplished what no craft of the art could do; indeed they did not believe a mere ordinary fiend could work such miracles as I in other ways had shown. They exaggerated the whole affair so much, possibly in order to excuse their own part in it, that the majordomo wrote an account to the Duke, who was then in Pisa, far more marvelous and full of thrilling incidents than what they had narrated.

After I had let my statue cool for two whole days, I began to uncover it by slow degrees. The first thing I found was that the head of Medusa had come out most admirably, thanks to the air-vents; for, as I had told the Duke, it is the nature of fire to ascend. Upon advancing farther, I discovered that the other head, that, namely, of Perseus, had succeeded no less admirably; and this astonished me far more, because it is at a considerably lower level than than that of the Medusa. Now the mouths of the mold were placed above the head of Perseus and behind his shoulders; and I found that all the bronze my furnace contained had been exhausted in the head of this figure. It was a miracle to observe that not one fragment remained in the orifice of the channel, and that nothing was wanting to the statue. In my great astonishment I seemed to see in this the hand of God arranging and controlling all.

I went on uncovering the statue with success, and ascertained that everything had come out in perfect order, until I reached the foot of the right leg on which the statue rests. There the heel itself was formed, and going farther, I found the foot apparently complete. This gave me great joy on the one side, but was half unwelcome to me on the other, merely because I had told the Duke that it could not come out. However, when I reached the end, it appeared that the toes and a little piece above them were unfinished, so that about half the foot was wanting. Although I knew that this would add a trifle to my labor, I was very well pleased, because I could now prove to the Duke how well I understood my business. It is true that far more of the foot than I expected had been perfectly formed; the reason of this was that, from causes I have recently described, the bronze was hotter than our rules of art prescribe; also that I had been obliged to supplement the alloy with my pewter cups and platters, which no one else, I think, had ever done before.

Having now ascertained how successfully my work had been accomplished, I lost no time in hurrying to Pisa, where I found the Duke. He gave me a most gracious reception, as did also the Duchess; and although the majordomo had informed them of the whole proceedings, their Excellencies deemed my performance far more stupendous and astonishing when they heard the tale from my own mouth. When I arrived at the foot of Perseus, and said it had not come out perfect, just as I previously warned his Excellency, I saw an expression of wonder pass over his face, while he related to the Duchess how I had predicted this beforehand. Observing the princes to be so well disposed towards me, I begged leave from the Duke to go to Rome. He granted it in most obliging terms, and bade me return as soon as possible to complete his Perseus; giving me letters of recommendation meanwhile to his ambassador. We were then in the first years of Pope Julius III, elected February, 1550.

The Astronomical Messenger

Galilio Galilei*
(1564–1642)

*Containing and setting forth Observations lately made with
aid of a newly invented* Telescope *respecting the Moon's
Surface, the Milky Way, Nebulous Stars, an
innumerable multitude of Fixed Stars, and
also respecting Four Planets never before
seen, which have been named*

The Cosmian Stars.[1]

In the present small treatise I set forth some matters of great interest
for all observers of natural phenomena to look at and consider. They
are of great interest, I think, first, from their intrinsic excellence;
secondly, from their absolute novelty; and lastly, also on account of
the instrument by the aid of which they have been presented to my
apprehension.

The number of the Fixed Stars which observers have been able to
see without artificial powers of sight up to this day can be counted. It
is therefore decidedly a great feat to add to their number, and to set
distinctly before the eyes other stars in myriads, which have never
been seen before, and which surpass the old, previously known, stars
in number more than ten times.

Again, it is a most beautiful and delightful sight to behold the body
of the Moon, which is distant from us nearly sixty *semi*-diameters of

---

*"In 1609, Galileo, then Professor of Mathematics at Padua, in the service of the
Venetian Republic, heard from a correspondent at Paris of the invention of a telescope,
and set to work to consider how such an instrument could be made. The result was his
invention of the telescope by his name, and identical in principle with the modern opera
glass. . . . In his pamphlet, *The Sidereal Messenger*, Galileo relates how he came to learn
the value of the telescope for astronomical research; and how his observations were
rewarded by numerous discoveries in rapid succession, and at length by that of Jupiter's
satellites. Galileo at once saw the value of his discovery as bearing upon the establishment
of the Copernican system of astronomy, which had met with slight acceptance. . . ."
Edward Stafford Carlos in the prefatory note to *The Sidereal Messenger*.

[1]The satellites of Jupiter are here called "the Cosmian Stars" in honor of Cosmo de'
Medici, but elsewhere Galileo calls them "the Medicean Stars."

the Earth, as near as if it was at a distance of only two of the same measures; so that the diameter of this same Moon appears about thirty times larger, its surface about nine hundred times, and its solid mass nearly 27,000 times larger than when it is viewed only with the naked eye; and consequently any one may know with the certainty that is due to the use of our senses, that the Moon certainly does not possess a smooth and polished surface, but one rough and uneven, and, just like the face of the Earth itself, is everywhere full of vast protuberances, deep chasms, and sinuosities.

Then to have got rid of disputes about the Galaxy or Milky Way, and to have made its nature clear to the very senses, not to say to the understanding, seems by no means a matter which ought to be considered of slight importance. In addition to this, to point out, as with one's finger, the nature of those stars which every one of the astronomers up to this time has called *nebulous*, and to demonstrate that it is very different from what has hitherto been believed, will be pleasant, and very fine. But that which will excite the greatest astonishment by far, and which indeed especially moved me to call the attention of all astronomers and philosophers, is this, namely, that I have discovered four planets, neither known nor observed by any one of the astronomers before my time, which have their orbits round a certain bright star, one of those previously known, like Venus and Mercury round the Sun, and are sometimes in front of it, sometimes behind it, though they never depart from it beyond certain limits. All which facts were discovered and observed a few days ago by the help of a telescope devised by me, through God's grace first enlightening my mind.

Perchance other discoveries still more excellent will be made from time to time by me or by other observers, with the assistance of a similar instrument, so I will first briefly record its shape and preparation, as well as the occasion of it being devised, and then I will give an account of the observations made by me.

About ten months ago a report reached my ears that a Dutchman had constructed a telescope, by the aid of which visible objects, although at a great distance from the eye of the observer, were seen distinctly as if near; and some proofs of its most wonderful performances were reported, which some gave credence to, but others contradicted. A few days after, I received confirmation of the report in a letter written from Paris by a noble Frenchman, Jaques Badovere, which finally determined me to give myself up first to inquire into the principle of the telescope, and then to consider the means by which I might compass the invention of a similar instrument, which a little while after I succeeded in doing, through deep study of the theory of Refraction; and I prepared a tube, at first of lead, in the ends of which I fitted two glass lenses, both plane on one side, but on the other side one spherically convex, and the other concave. Then bringing my eye to the concave lens I saw objects satisfactorily large and near, for they appeared one-third of the distance off and nine times larger than when they are seen with the natural eye alone. I shortly afterwards constructed another telescope with more nicety, which magnified objects more than sixty times. At length, by sparing neither labor nor expense, I succeeded in constructing for myself an instrument so superior that objects seen through it appear magnified nearly a thousand times, and more than thirty times nearer than if viewed by the natural powers of sight alone.

It would be altogether a waste of time to enumerate the number and importance of the benefits which this instrument may be expected to confer, when used by land or sea. But without paying attention to its use for terrestrial objects, I betook myself to observations of the heavenly bodies; and first of all, I viewed the Moon as near as if it was scarcely two *semi*-diameters of the Earth distant. After the Moon, I frequently observed other heavenly bodies, both fixed stars and planets, with incredible delight; and, when I saw their very great number, I began to consider about a method by which I might be able to measure their distances apart, and at length I found one. And here it is fitting that all who intend to turn their attention to observations of this kind should receive certain cautions. For, in the first place, it is absolutely necessary for them to prepare a most perfect telescope, one which will show very bright objects distinct and free from any mistiness, and will magnify them at least 400 times, for then it will show them as if only one-twentieth of their distance off. For unless the instrument be of such power, it will be in vain to attempt to view all the things which have been seen by me in the heavens, or which will be enumerated hereafter.

But in order that any one may be a little more certain about the magnifying power of his instrument, he shall fashion two circles, or two square pieces of paper, one of which is 400 times greater than the other, but that will be when the diameter of the greater is twenty times the length of the diameter of the other. Then he shall view from a distance simultaneously both surfaces, fixed on the same wall, the smaller with one eye applied to the telescope, and the larger with the other eye unassisted; for that may be done without inconvenience at one and the same instant with both eyes open. Then both figures will appear of the same size, if the instrument magnifies objects in the desired proportion. . . . But let it suffice for the present to have thus slightly touched, and as it were just put our lips to these matters, for on some other opportunity I will publish the theory of this instrument in completeness.

Sentence of Galileo by the Supreme Inquisition of the Holy Roman Catholic Church, June 22, 1633*

On Wednesday, 22nd June, 1633, in the forenoon, Galileo was conducted to the large hall . . . in the Dominican Convent of St. Maria [Rome] where, in the presence of his judges and a large assemblage of cardinals and prelates of the Holy Congregation, the following sentence was read to him:

We, . . . by the grace of God, cardinals of the Holy Roman Church, Inquisitors General, by the Holy Apostolic see specially deputed, against heretical depravity throughout the whole Christian Republic.

Whereas you, Galileo, son of the late Vincenzo Galilei, Florentine, aged seventy years, were in the year 1615 denounced to this Holy Office for holding as true the false doctrine taught by many, that the sun is the center of the world and immovable, and that the earth moves, and also with a diurnal motion; for having disciples to whom you taught the same doctrine; for holding correspondence with certain mathematicians of Germany concerning the same; for having printed certain letters, entitled "On the Solar Spots," wherein you developed the same doctrine as true; and for replying to the objections from the Holy Scriptures, which from time to time were urged against it, by glossing the said Scriptures according to your own meaning: and whereas there was thereupon produced the copy of a document in the form of a letter, purporting to be written by you to one formerly your

---

*Presiding in 1979 at the Vatican ceremony commemorating the centenary of the birth of Albert Einstein, Pope John Paul II declared Galileo "had suffered greatly, and we cannot hide it, from [the persecution of] his fellow men and organs of the church." The Pope invited the attending theologists, scientists, and historians to re-examine the events surrounding the life of Galileo.

disciple, and in this divers propositions are set forth, following the hypothesis of Copernicus, which are contrary to the true sense and authority of Holy Scripture:

This Holy Tribunal being therefore desirous of proceeding against the disorder and mischief thence resulting, which went on increasing to the prejudice of the Holy Faith, by command of his Holiness and of the most eminent Lords Cardinals of this supreme and universal Inquisition, the two propositions of the stability of the sun and the motion of the earth were by the theological "Qualifiers" qualified as follows:

The proposition that the sun is the center of the world and does not move from its place is absurd and false philosophically and formally heretical, because it is expressly contrary to the Holy Scripture.

The proposition that the earth is not the center of the world and immovable, but that it moves, and also with a diurnal motion, is equally absurd and false philosophically, and theologically considered, at least erroneous in faith.

But whereas it was desired at that time to deal leniently with you, it was decreed at the Holy Congregation held before his Holiness on the 25th February, 1616, that his Eminence the Lord Cardinal Bellarmine should order you to abandon altogether the said false doctrine, and, in the event of your refusal, that an injunction should be imposed upon you by the Commissary of the Holy Office, to give up the said doctrine, and not to teach it to others, nor to defend it, nor even discuss it; and failing your acquiescence in this injunction, that you should be imprisoned. And in execution of this decree, on the following day, at the Palace, and in the presence of his Eminence, the said Lord Cardinal Bellarmine, after being gently admonished by the said Lord Cardinal, the command was intimated to you by the Father Commissary of the Holy Office for the time before a notary and witnesses, that you were altogether to abandon the said false opinion, and not in future to defend or teach it in any way whatsoever, neither verbally nor in writing; and upon your promising to obey you were dismissed.

And in order that a doctrine so pernicious might be wholly rooted out and not insinuate itself further to the grave prejudice of Catholic truth, a decree was issued by the Holy Congregation of the Index, prohibiting the books which treat of this doctrine, and declaring the doctrine itself to be false and wholly contrary to sacred and divine Scripture.

And whereas a book appeared here recently, printed last year at Florence, the title of which shows that you were the author, this title being: *Dialogue of Galileo Galilei on the Two Principal Systems of the World, the Ptolemaic and the Copernican*; and whereas the Holy Congregation was afterwards informed that through the publication of the said book, the false opinion of the motion of the earth and the stability of the sun was daily gaining ground; the said book was taken into careful consideration, and in it there was discovered a patent violation of the aforesaid injunction that had been imposed upon you, for in this book you have defended the said opinion previously condemned and to your face declared to be so, although in the said book you strive by various devices to produce the impression that you leave it undecided, and in express terms as probable: which however is a most grievous error, as an opinion can in no wise be probable which has been declared and defined to be contrary to Divine Scripture:

Therefore by our order you were cited before this Holy Office, where, being examined upon your oath, you acknowledged the book to be written and published by you. You confessed that you began to write the said book about ten or twelve years ago, after the command had been imposed upon you as above; that you requested license to print it, without however intimating to those who granted you this license that you had been commanded not to hold, defend, or teach in any way whatever the doctrine in question.

You likewise confessed that the writing of the said book is in various places drawn up in such a form that the reader might fancy that the arguments brought forward on the false side are rather calculated by their cogency to compel conviction than to be easy of refutation; excusing yourself for having fallen into an error, as you alleged, so foreign to your intention, by the fact that you had written in dialogue, and by the natural complacency that every man feels in regard to his own subtleties, and in showing himself more clever than the generality of men, in devising, even on behalf of false propositions, ingenious and plausible arguments.

And a suitable term having been assigned to you to prepare your defense, you produced a certificate in the handwriting of his Eminence the Lord Cardinal Bellarmine, procured by you, as you asserted, in order to defend yourself against the calumnies of your enemies, who gave out that you had abjured and had been punished by the Holy Office; in which certificate it is declared that you had not abjured and had not been punished, but merely that the declaration made by his Holiness and published by the Holy Congregation of the Index, had been announced to you, wherein it is declared that the doctrine of the motion of the earth and the stability of the sun is contrary to the Holy Scriptures, and therefore cannot be defended or held. And as in this certificate there is no mention of the two articles of the injunction, namely, the order not "to teach" and "in any way," you represented that we ought to believe that in the course of fourteen or sixteen years you had lost all memory of them; and that this was why you said nothing of the injunction when you requested permission to print your book. And all this you urged not by way of excuse for your error, but that it might be set down to a vainglorious ambition rather than to malice. But this certificate produced by you in your defense has only aggravated your delinquency, since although it is there stated that the said opinion is contrary to Holy Scripture, you have nevertheless dared to discuss and defend it and to argue its probability; nor does the license artfully and cunningly extorted by you avail you anything, since you did not notify the command imposed upon you.

And whereas it appeared to us that you had not stated the full truth with regard to your intention, we thought it necessary to subject you to a rigorous examination, at which (without prejudice, however, to the matters confessed by you, and set forth as above, with regard to your said intention) you answered like a good Catholic. Therefore, having seen and maturely considered the merits of this your cause, together with your confessions and excuses above mentioned, and all that ought justly to be seen and considered, we have arrived at the underwritten final sentence against you:

Invoking, therefore, the most holy name of our Lord Jesus Christ and of His most glorious Mother, and ever Virgin Mary, by this our final sentence, which sitting in judgment, with the counsel and advice of the Reverend Masters of sacred theology and Doctors of both Laws, our assessors, we deliver in these writings, in the cause and causes presently before us between the magnificent Carlo Sinceri, Doctor of both Laws, Proctor Fiscal of this Holy Office, of the one part, and you Galileo Galilei, the defendant, here present, tried and confessed as above, of the other part—we say, pronounce, sentence, declare, that you, the said Galileo, by reason of the matters adduced in process, and by you confessed as above, have rendered yourself in the judgment of this Holy Office vehemently suspected of heresy, namely, of having believed and held the doctrine—which is false and contrary to the sacred and divine Scriptures—that the sun is the center of the world and does not move from east to west, and that the earth moves and is not the center of the world; and that an opinion may be held and defended as probable after it has been declared and defined to be contrary to Holy Scripture; and that consequently you have incurred all the censures and penalties imposed and promulgated in the sacred canons and other constitutions, general and particular, against such delinquents. From which we are content that you be absolved, provided that first, with a sincere heart, and unfeigned faith, you abjure, curse, and detest the aforesaid errors and heresies, and every other error and heresy contrary to the Catholic and Apostolic Roman Church in the form to be prescribed by us.

And in order that this your grave and pernicious error and transgression may not remain altogether unpunished, and that you may be more cautious for the future, and an example to others, that they may abstain from similar delinquencies—we ordain that the book of the *Dialogues of Galileo Galilei* be prohibited by public edict.

We condemn you to the formal prison of this Holy Office during our pleasure, and by way of salutary penance, we enjoin that for three years to come you repeat once a week the seven penitential Psalms.

Reserving to ourselves full liberty to moderate, commute, or take off, in whole or in part, the aforesaid penalties and penance.

And so we say, pronounce, sentence, declare, ordain, condemn and reserve, in this and any other better way and form which we can and may lawfully employ.

So we the undersigned Cardinals pronounce.

F. Cardinalis de Asculo.
G. Cardinalis Bentiuolus.
Fr. Cardinalis de Cremona.
Fr. Antonius Cardinalis S. Honuphrii.
B. Cardinalis Gypsius.
Fr. Cardinalis Verospius.
M. Cardinalis Ginettus.

Recantation of Galileo

"I, Galileo Galilei, son of the late Vincenzo Galilei, Florentine, aged seventy years, arraigned personally before this tribunal, and kneeling before you, most Eminent and Reverend Lord Cardinals, Inquisitors general against heretical depravity throughout the whole Christian Republic, having before my eyes and touching with my hands, the holy Gospels—swear that I have always believed, do now believe, and by God's help will for the future believe, all that is held, preached, and taught by the Holy Catholic and Apostolic Roman Church. But whereas—after an injunction had been judicially intimated to me by this Holy Office, to the effect that I must altogether abandon the false opinion that the sun is the center of the world and immovable, and that the earth is not the center of the world, and moves, and that I must not hold, defend, or teach in any way whatsoever, verbally or in writing, the said doctrine, and after it had been notified to me that the said doctrine was contrary to Holy Scripture—I wrote and printed a book in which I discuss this doctrine already condemned, and adduce arguments of great cogency in its favor, without presenting any solution of these; and for this cause I have been pronounced by the Holy Office to be vehemently suspected of heresy, that is to say, of having held and believed that the sun is the center of the world and immovable, and that the earth is not the center and moves:

"Therefore, desiring to remove from the minds of your Eminences, and of all faithful Christians, this strong suspicion, reasonably conceived against me, with sincere heart and unfeigned faith I abjure, curse, and detest the aforesaid errors and heresies, and generally every other error and sect whatsoever contrary to the said Holy Church; and I swear that in future I will never again say or assert, verbally or in writing, anything that might furnish occasion for a similar suspicion regarding me; but that should I know any heretic, or person suspected of heresy, I will denounce him to this Holy Office, or to the Inquisitor and ordinary of the place where I may be. Further, I swear and promise to fulfil and observe in their integrity all penances that have been, or that shall be, imposed upon me by this Holy Office. And, in the event of my contravening, (which God forbid!) any of these my promises, protestations, and oaths, I submit myself to all the pains and penalties imposed and promulgated in the sacred canons and other constitutions, general and particular, against such delinquents. So help me God, and these His holy Gospels, which I touch with my hands.

"I, the said Galileo Galilei, have abjured, sworn, promised, and bound myself as above; and in witness of the truth thereof I have with my own hand subscribed the present document of my abjuration, and recited it word for word at Rome, in the Convent of Minerva, this twenty-second day of June, 1633.

"I, Galileo Galilei, have abjured as above with my own hand."

PART 3

THE NINETEENTH-CENTURY PILGRIMAGE

THE OLD BRIDGE AT FLORENCE

Taddeo Gaddi built me. I am old,
    Five centuries old. I plant my foot of stone
    Upon the Arno, as St. Michael's own
Was planted on the dragon. Fold by fold

Beneath me as it struggles, I behold
    Its glistening scales. Twice hath it overthrown
    My kindred and companions. Me alone
It moveth not, but is by me controlled.

I can remember when the Medici
    Were driven from Florence; longer still ago
    The final wars of Ghibelline and Guelf.
Florence adorns me with her jewelry;
    And when I think that Michel Angelo
    Hath leaned on me, I glory in myself.

Henry Wadsworth Longfellow

Stendhal, 1817

(Marie-Henri Beyle)

Florence, *22nd January* [1817]. The day before yesterday, as I descended upon Florence from the high ridges of the Apennine, my heart was leaping wildly within me. What utterly childish excitement! At long last, at a sudden bend in the road, my gaze plunged downward into the heart of the plain, and there, in the far distance, like some darkling mass, I could distinguish the somber pile of Santa Maria del Fiore with its famous Dome, the masterpiece of Brunelleschi.

"Behold the home of Dante, of Michelangelo, of Leonardo da Vinci" I mused within my heart. "Behold then this noble city, the Queen of medieval Europe! Here, within these walls, the civilization of mankind was born anew!...As the minutes passed, so these memories came crowding and jostling one against the other within my soul, and soon I found myself grown incapable of rational thought, but rather surrendered to the sweet turbulence of fancy, as in the presence of some beloved object. Upon approaching the San Gallo gate, with its unbeautiful Triumphal Arch, I could gladly have embraced the first inhabitants of Florence whom I encountered.

...So often have I studied views of Florence, that I was familiar with the city before I ever set foot within its walls; I found that I could thread my way through the streets without a guide. Turning to the left, I passed before a bookseller's shop, where I bought a couple of descriptive surveys of the town. Twice only was I forced to enquire my way of passers-by, who answered me with a politeness which was wholly French and with a most singular accent; and at last I found myself before the facade of Santa Croce. Within, upon the right of the doorway, rises the tomb of Michelangelo; beyond, lo! there stands Canova's effigy of Alfieri; I needed no *cicerone* to recognize the features of the great Italian writer. Further still, I discovered the tomb of Machiavelli; while facing Michelangelo lies Galileo. What a race of men! And to these already named, Tuscany might further add Dante, Boccaccio and Petrarch. What a fantastic gathering! The tide of emotion which overwhelmed me flowed so deep that it scarce was to be distinguished from religious awe. The mystic dimness which filled the church, its plain, timbered roof, its unfinished facade—all these things spoke volumes to my soul. . . . A Friar moved silently towards me; and I, in the place of that sense of revulsion all but bordering on physical horror which usually possesses me in such circumstances, discovered in my heart a feeling which was almost friendship. Was not he likewise a Friar, Fra Bartolomeo di San Marco, that great painter who invented the art of chiaroscuro, and showed it to Raphael, and was the forefather of Coreggio? I spoke to my tonsured acquaintance, and found in him an exquisite degree of politeness. Indeed, he was delighted to meet a Frenchman. I begged him to unlock for me the chapel in the northeast corner of the church, where are preserved the frescoes of Volterrano. He introduced me to the place, then left me to my own devices. There, . . . with my head thrown back to rest upon the desk, so that I might let my gaze dwell on the ceiling, I underwent, through the medium of Volterrano's Sybils, the profoundest experience of ecstasy that, as far as I am aware, I ever encountered through the painter's art. My soul, affected by the very notion of being in Florence, and by the proximity of those great men whose tombs I had just beheld, was already in a state of trance. Absorbed in the contemplation of sublime beauty, I could perceive its very essence close at hand; I could, as it were, feel the stuff of it beneath my fingertips. I had attained to that supreme degree of sensibility where the divine intimations of art merge with the impassioned sensuality of emotion. As I emerged from the porch of Santa Croce, I was seized with a fierce palpitation of the heart; . . . the wellspring of life was dried up within me, and I walked in constant fear of falling to the ground. . . . *23rd January*. Yesterday, all the livelong day, I roamed about in a sort of melancholy, historical abstraction. My first excursion led me to the church of Santa Maria del Carmine, which contains the Masaccio frescoes; after which, feeling myself ill-disposed properly to appreciate the oil paintings of the Palazzo Pitti or of the Uffizi, I decided rather to visit the tombs of the Medici at San Lorenzo, together with the Michelangelo Chapel, so called on account of the sculptures executed by this great man. Emerging from San Lorenzo, I began to wander aimlessly about the streets, contemplating, from the wordless depths of my own emotion (with my eyes wide-staring, and the power of speech utterly gone from me), those massive *palazzi*—those veritable fortresses and castle-keeps—built toward the year 1300 by the merchants of Florence. On the perimeter of that vast piazza, whose center is occupied by the Cathedral of Santa Maria del Fiore (built in 1293), my glance lighted upon those long arcades, whose arches, with their distant hint of gothic inspiration, rise to an elegant apex formed by the junction of two curves (similar to the upper section of the fleur-de-lis design which you may find engraved upon a five-franc piece). This style of design is found repeated above the door of every house in Florence; but a modern generation has built a wall to block the ancient arcades which used to encircle the immensity of that open space, in the midst of which, in splendid isolation, rises the mass of Santa Maria del Fiore.

I experienced a great joy for knowing no one, for having no fear of being forced to make conversation. The power of this . . . architecture took undisputed possession of all my faculties; I could believe that Dante was the companion of my steps. Today, since waking, I doubt whether so many as a dozen thoughts have crossed my mind for which I might not find a ready formulation in the lines of this great poet. I feel ashamed of these observations, which will surely earn me the reputation of an egoist. . . .

Florence, whose thoroughfares are paved with massive blocks of white granite, irregular in shape, is of a cleanliness rarely encountered elsewhere; her streets are perfumed with a curious and characteristic odor. With the unique exception of one or two townships in the Low Countries, Florence bids fair to be acclaimed the cleanest city in the universe; and undoubtedly she is to be numbered among the most elegant. Her greco-gothic architecture has all the clean finish and the consummate artistry of a perfect miniature. Happily for the tangible beauty of Florence, her citizens, at the same instant when they forfeited their liberty, did not likewise forfeit the energy which inspires the building of such massive structures . . . nor does anything disturb the exquisite harmony of these streets, instinct with Ideal Beauty. . . . There are a score of odd corners in Florence—for instance, as you come down from the Ponte della Trinità to pass before the Palazzo Strozzi—where the traveler may well believe himself to be living in the year 1500.

Yet despite the rare beauty of these countless streets, so richly steeped in grandeur and in melancholy, there is nothing which bears comparison to the Palazzo Vecchio. This fortress, built in 1298 by the freely offered contributions of the merchant guilds, surges upward, with its brickwork battlements and its fantastically towering walls, not in some solitary and deserted spot, but in the very center of the finest piazza in Florence. Southward, it looks down upon Vasari's noble Gallery; northward, it is set off by an equestrian statue of one of the Medici; while in a cluster about its foot stand Michelangelo's David and Benvenuto Cellini's Perseus, together with the charming Loggia dei Lanzi—in a word, all the artistic masterpieces of Florence and all the activity of her civilization. By a fortunate circumstance, this piazza has grown to be the constant thoroughfare for all and sundry. What monument of Grecian architecture could tell so many tales of men and deeds as this grim medieval fortress, rough-hewn, implacable and energetic as the century which gave it birth? "Up there," observed my *cicerone*, "from that high window on the northern face, they hanged Archbishop Pazzi in all his solemn pontifical attire." . . .

In Florence, the Palazzo Vecchio—this stark, contrasting incarnation of the stern realities of medieval times set square amid the artistic glories of the past . . . —creates an impression of unparalleled grandeur and truth. Here, for the instruction of the philosophic mind, stand the masterpieces of those arts, whose genius was fired by violence of passion and bore fruit, only to wither in a later century and fade, becoming petty, insignificant and misshapen when the tempest of desire ceased to swell the sails by which alone that frail craft, the human soul, so impotent when passion falters and evaporates, leaving it bereft alike of vice and virtue, is driven across the stormy seas of life.

This evening, seated on a cane chair in front of the coffee-house in the center of the great piazza facing the Palazzo Vecchio, neither the crowd nor the cold—the one as inconsiderable as the other—could prevent my eye from beholding the whole tapestry of incident which had been unfolded upon this same piazza. Here, on these very stones, Florence had risen a score of times in the name of liberty, while blood had flowed in the cause of an unworkable constitution. And now the rising moon, by imperceptible degrees, began to print the massive shadow of the Palazzo Vecchio upon the scoured flagstones of the piazza, and to lend her magic touch of mystery to the colonnades of the Uffizi, beneath whose arches gleamed the lights of houses, distant beyond the Arno. . . .

Seated at the Leghorn Gate, where I . . . idle away many a long
hour, it has been my pastime to observe the peasant women, and to
note the rare degree of beauty in their eyes; yet there is no trace in their
expression of that dreamy sensuality, no sign of that susceptibility to
passion which characterizes the women of Lombardy. Here, in
Tuscany, the one quality which you may never discover is that strange
capacity for exaltation; instead, by way of compensation, you may
discern no lack of mental alertness, of pride, of rational intelligence,
together with an elusive hint of provocative malice. I know of nothing
so captivating as the glance of these handsome peasant women,
beneath their delicious headdress with its black plume nodding and
curtseying above their mannish hats. Yet I sense in such sharp and
glittering eyes a deeper power of criticism than of adoration. I can
never mistake that rational, speculative glint, nor discern in their look
the potential irrationality of love. These madonna-eyes flash with the
mocking light of battle rather than with the softer fires of passion.

The countryfolk of Tuscany, as I most readily believe, form the
oddest and the wittiest peasantry in Italy. They may well be ac-
counted, within the bounds of their condition, the most civilized race
in all the world. They look upon religion much rather as a social
convention, whose ill-observance would constitute a breach of good
manners, than as a faith; and Hell holds few terrors for such as they. . . .

In painting, the great masters of the Florentine school have gradually led me, by a different path, to an identical verdict concerning the
national character. Those old citizens of Florence, as they are portrayed by Masaccio and Ghirlandaio, would seem like figures out of
Bedlam were they to tread the earth today and invade the fashionable
coffeehouse which flourishes in the shadow of Santa Maria del Fiore;
yet, compared with the figures depicted by Paolo Veronese or by
Tintoretto (I have deliberately chosen two painters who never idealize
their subjects), the frost seems already to have bitten deep into their
souls; their features reflect a hint of desiccation, of narrowness, of
pedestrian rationality, of squeamish decorousness; in a word, not one
but seems to lack that finer capacity for EXALTATION. They stand
much closer in spirit to the true meaning of civilization, yet infinitely
further removed from those qualities which alone awaken my interest
in any individual member of the human race. . . .

Milan is a riverless city, circular in shape, set in the center of a
plain, whose level expanse, devoid of undulation, is threaded by a
hundred streamlets of fresh-running water. Florence, by contrast, lies

in the hollow of a narrowish valley cut deep in the contours of high and barren ranges, and set hard against the rampart of hills which flank it on the south. This latter city, which, by the pattern of her streets, is in some ways reminiscent of Paris, is set astride the Arno much as Paris is built astride the Seine. Likewise the Arno—a mere mountain torrent, artifically swollen, by means of a transverse causeway constructed to work a mill wheel, to the dimensions of a self-respecting river beneath the bridges of Florence—flows from east to west. If you mount the southern hillside, climbing through the gardens of the Palazzo Pitti and from thence embarking upon a circuit of the walls as far as the highroad to Arezzo, you may gain some notion of the countless multitude of little hills which compose the domain of Tuscany; carpeted with olive groves, with vineyards and with narrow strips of cereal, the undulating surface of the land is cultivated like a garden. And indeed, agriculture is a pursuit most admirably suited to the placid, pacific, husbanding genius of the Tuscan race.

The landscape—just as we may observe it in paintings by Leonardo or by Raphael in his early manner—often terminates in a perspective of dark foliage against the clear blue of a cloudless sky.

The famous Cascine—the common rendezvous whither all resort, to see or to be seen—are situated much as the Champs Elysees in relation to Paris. The displeasing aspect of these gardens, as far as I am concerned, is that I find them constantly encumbered with some six hundred or so foreign visitors, English and Russian predominating. Florence is nothing better than a vast museum full of foreign tourists; and each nationality brings with it its own manners and customs. The English, with their rigid caste system, their meticulous observance of it and their firm resolve never to depart from it, even by a hair's-breadth, provide the material for countless satirical anecdotes. . . .

29th January. The city of Florence possesses four fine bridges, which span the Arno at more or less regular intervals; and these, in juxtaposition to the quays of the embankment and the hill-slopes to the south, with their frieze of cypresses cut out sharply against the sky, form a most pleasing prospect. The scene admits of less grandeur than the setting of the famous bridge at Dresden; but the effect is infinitely more charming. The second of these Florentine bridges (following the current of the Arno) is overbuilt with goldsmiths' shops. Here it was, this morning, that I renewed my acquaintance with a dealer in precious stones, Nathan, a Jew in whose company, once, in days gone by, I ran most imminent danger of drowning. . . .

Tonight, Nathan introduced me into the society of a group of wealthy merchants and their wives—the pretext being that he desired me to witness a play performed by marionettes in their own charming little theatre. This delightful miniature stage measures no more than five feet across the proscenium arch, and yet affords an exact copy of the Teatro alla Scala. Before the curtain rose, all lights were extinguished in the drawing room where the performance was to take place; and indeed, the décor was most impressive, for the reason that, in spite of its lilliputian scale, it was not treated *as a* miniature. ...There were tiny lamps proportionate to all the rest, and each change of set was carried out rapidly, neatly and by means exactly copied from La Scala. I can conceive of nothing more enchanting. A company of four-and-twenty marionettes, each eight inches tall, equipped with leaden legs and costing a sequin apiece, performed a delicious, if somewhat indelicate comedy which proved to be an abridged version of Machiavelli's *Mandragola*. Subsequently, these same marionettes proceeded to dance a miniature ballet, with considerable style and elegance.

But the experience which afforded me still greater delight than the puppet show was the genial manner and polished intelligence of the conversation which reigned amid this Florentine assembly, the tone of unforced politeness which characterized the welcome which they designed to accord to myself....In Florence the aura of curiosity which surrounds a newcomer carries the battle by storm against the opposing preoccupations of love. Besides, is there not all the time in the world to talk to one's lover?

James Fenimore Cooper, 1828-30

Florence is full of noble hotels, which are termed palaces in the language of the country, and few families still retaining a sufficient portion of the ancient wealth to occupy the whole of such huge edifices, apartments are let in them, furnished, or not, as it may happen, on the French plan. Hunting for lodgings gives one a good idea of the domestic economy of a place, for we entered some twenty or thirty of these palaces with this object. Rooms are unusually cheap, notwithstanding the number of strangers who resort to the place, for the town has shrunk to less than half its ancient population, and probably to a tithe of its ancient magnificence.

We became fully impressed with the changes that time produces, not only in things, but in the moral aspect of the world, by seeing a town like Florence. In our age, the man who should dream of making an inland place, in the heart of the Apennines, the focus of trade, would be set down as a simpleton; nor could any powers of combination or of wealth now overcome the efforts of those who would naturally resort to more favorable positions.

These old merchants, however, men who truly ennobled commerce, and not commerce them, have left behind them more durable remains of their ascendency than can be seen in almost any other place. As they were not particularly pacific, however, the constant struggles of factions in the streets induced a style of architecture that is almost peculiar to Florence, for every palace is a sort of fortress. We took an apartment in one that belongs to an ancient family who still inhabit a portion of the building, and as our rooms are on the street, we may be said to occupy the fortress. The great gate is of iron, and the great stairs, of course, massive and solid. The lower floor is occupied only for the offices and stables. Then comes what is called a *mezzinino*, or a low story, with small windows, but which has some very good rooms. Above this is our apartment, with ceilings nearly twenty feet high, large rooms all *en suite*, and windows, to look out of which we ascend two steps. The walls would bear considerable battering, though the position of the house protected it from any danger of such a nature. Forty or fifty stouthearted retainers, and the number would not be great for the old Florentines, must have been able to stand a respectable siege in such an abode.

You will ask me what are my impressions, on finding myself entrenched behind such works, with a thousand recollections of the Medici and the Strozzi, and the Capponi, to awaken the love of the romantic and interesting? Alas! I am filled with the consciousness of the impotency of man, who, after rearing these piles, and guarding against the violence and ungovernable passions of his fellows, is obliged to allow that all his resources cannot keep out the mosquitoes.

We have two noble bedrooms, besides several smaller; a large drawing room, and a larger dining room; a good cabinet for myself; an antechamber, and baths, offices, &c. &c. all furnished, for the moderate sum of sixty dollars a month. We have ten good rooms in all, besides the offices.

Our hotel has a small court, and, I believe, a garden; though I have not had access to the latter. By the side of the great gate is a small hole in the wall, closed in general by a shutter. At eleven o'clock every day, people come to the shutter and rap, and it is opened by a steward of the family. The applicant puts in an empty flask and a paul (ten cents), receiving in return a flask filled with wine. In this manner, I understand, most of the grand families of Florence now dispose of the products of their vines! It would be curious to learn if the Medici carried on this trade. The wine of our palace is among the best of Tuscany, and I drink it with great satisfaction; the more so because its cost is about four cents the bottle. It is positively much better wine than half the claret that is drunk in Paris. Twice a week, a donkey appears in the court, dragging a little cart filled with flasks from the estate, and carrying away the "dead soldiers." We are, however, a little above the market, as our wine commands fully a cent a flask, or about four nills a bottle, more than most of the Tuscan liquor.

We burn in our lamps oil that you would be happy to get on your lobsters and salads. In other respects the market is good, and cloths are both fine and cheap, finer and cheaper than I remember to have seen them anywhere else, and yet they are imported! The shopkeepers are moderate in their wishes, preferring the *dolce far niente* to the more terrible energies of trade.

There is a sleepy indolence in these Italians that singularly suits my humor. They seem too gentlemanlike to work, or to be fussy, but appear disposed to make a siesta of life, and to enjoy the passing moment. The Tuscans seem full of sentiment, and though the poor, as is the case all over the continent of Europe, are very poor, the class immediately above them have as much satisfaction, I fancy, as they who dream dollars and talk dollars from "the rising of the sun unto the going down of the same." If you ask me if I would exchange populations and habits, I shall answer, we cannot afford it. It would check our career short of perfect civilization. We have arts to acquire, and tastes to form, before we could enter at all into the enjoyments of these people; one half of their pleasures depending on recollections that possibly may have had their origin in the energies of the first of the Medici; and there are things that must be created, but which give more satisfaction in after ages than during the period of their formation. For myself, I begin to feel I could be well content to vegetate here for half my life, to say nothing of the remainder. All who travel know that the greatest pleasure is in their recollections; and I fancy that nations in their decline enjoy more true happiness than nations in their advance.

Of course, I have visited the Venus, and the Pitti, and all the other marvels of art that Florence contains. These things have been so often described that my remarks shall be limited to such gleanings as others appear to have left, or as are suggested by my own passing feelings. The tribune of the gallery contains the most precious collection of ancient art, perhaps, in the world. Everything in it is a *chef-d' oeuvre* in its way; though I am far from seeing the necessity of believing that every old statue that is exhumed is an original. When I was introduced into this place, I felt as if approaching a presence of illustrious personages, and stood, hat in hand, involuntarily bowing to the circle of marble figures that surrounded me, as if they were endowed with sensibilities to appreciate my homage. You are not, however, to suppose that a love of art was so much at the bottom of this reverence, as association. There was a set of engravings in my father's house that represented most of the antique statues, and for these I had imbibed the respect of a child. The forms had become familiar by years of observation, and the Venus, the wrestlers, the dancing faun, and the knife-grinder, four of my oldest acquaintances on paper, now stood before my eyes, looking like living beings. . . .

Economy, the galleries, the facility with which one obtains lodgings, caprice, and the court, unite to make Florence a favorite residence with foreigners. The court has a little more of air and pretension than it might otherwise possess, from the circumstance of the sovereign being an archduke. Tuscany, however, is a respectable state, having nearly a million and a half subjects. . . .

Among the foreigners the English and Russians predominate; especially the former, who are found in swarms, on the Continent, in all the most agreeable places of residence. The policy of the Tuscan government encourages diplomatic appointments, and I believe all the great courts of Europe have ministers here. The French, Russians, English, Austrians, and Prussians have ministers plenipotentiaries, and many others chargés d'affaires. All these things contribute to render the place gay; nor is it without brilliancy at times, the little court appearing at the festivals and other ceremonies with sufficient pomp. I shall not philosophize on these things, but I fancy they do more good and less harm than is commonly thought by us democrats. I have often compared the *agréments* of this little town with those of one of our own larger cities. New York, which is four times as large as Florence, and ten times as rich, does not possess a tithe—nay, not a hundredth part of its attractions. To say nothing of taste, or of the stores of ancient art, or of the noble palaces and churches, and the other historical monuments, the circle of living creatures here affords greater sources of amusement and instruction than are to be found in all of the five great American towns put together. Every one appears to be at leisure, and the demon money seems to be forgotten, unless, indeed, he occasionally shows his talons at the gaming table. . . .

We left our palazzo within the walls, and went to a villa, called St. Illario, just without them. All the eminences around Florence are dotted with these retreats, many of which are large and princely. That we occupy is on a smaller scale; but it has numerous rooms. is near the town, and has many conveniences. Among other recommendations, it has two covered belvederes, where one can sit in the breeze and overlook the groves of olive trees, with all the crowded objects of an Italian landscape.

But, to give you some idea of the region in which we dwell: The valley of the Arno, though sufficiently wide, and cultivated chiefly with the spade, is broken by many abrupt and irregular heights, the advanced spurs of the ranges of the Appennines that bound it. On nearly all of these eminences, stands a stone edifice topped by a belvedere; sometimes with and sometimes without terraces; here and there a tree, and with olive groves beneath. The whole country is intersected by narrow roads leading up the heights; and these lanes usually run between high walls. They are commonly paved to prevent the wash of the rains, and nothing can be less attractive than the objects they present; though we find the shade of the walls beginning to be necessary as the season advances. To obtain a view, one is obliged to ascend to some one of the lookouts on the hills, of which there are a good many; though the rides and walks on the level land that lies above and behind us occasionally furnish us glorious glimpses. We are much in the habit of going to one of these places, which is rightly enough called Bellosguardo, for a better bird's-eye view of a town is not often had than this affords of Florence. In addition, we get the panorama of the valley and mountains, and the delicate lights and shades of the misty Apennines. Some of the latter I rank among the best things in their way that I have seen. These mountains are generally to be distinguished from the lower ranges of the Alps, or those whose elevation comes nearest to their own, by a softer and more sunny hue, which is often rendered dreamy and indolent by the sleepy haziness of the atmosphere. Indeed, everything in these regions appears to invite to contemplation and repose at this particular season. There is an admixture of the savage and the refined in the ragged ravines of the hills, the villas, the polished town, the cultivated plain, the distant and chestnut-covered peaks, the costumes, the songs of the peasants, the Oriental olive, the monasteries and churches, that keeps the mind constantly attuned to poetry. . . .

This is not the only music I get gratis. One of the narrow lanes separates my end of the house from the church of St. Illario and the dwelling of the priest. From the belvedere, which communicates with my own room, we have frequent passages of civility across the lane with the good old *curato*, who discusses the weather and the state of the crops with unction. The old man has some excellent figs, and our cook having discovered it, lays his trees under contribution. And here I will record what I conceive to be the very perfection of epicurism, or rather of taste, in the matter of eating. A single fresh fig, as a corrective after the soup, I hold to be one of those sublime touches of art that are oftener discovered by accident than by the investigations of knowledge. I do not mean that I have even the equivocal merit of this accidental discovery, for I was told the secret, and I believe French ingenuity had got pretty near it already, in the way of the melons. But no melon is like a fig; nor will a French fig, certainly not a Paris fig, answer the purpose at all. It must be such a fig as one gets in Italy. At Paris you are always offered a glass of Madeira after the soup, the only one taken at table; but it is a pitiful substitute for the fig. After communicating this improvement on human happiness, let me add that it is almost destructive of the pleasure derived from the first, to take a second. *One* small, green-coated, fresh fig is the precise point of gastronomic felicity in this respect.

But the good *curato*, besides his figs, has a pair of uneasy bells in his church tower, which are exactly forty-three feet from my ears, and which invariably ring in pairs six or eight times daily. There are matins, noontide, angelus, vespers, and heaven knows what, regularly; to say nothing of extramasses, christenings, funerals, and weddings. The effect of the bells is often delightful when heard in the distance, for they are ringing all over the valley and on the heights, morning, noon, and night; but these are too near. Still, I get, now and then, rare touches of the picturesque from this proximity to the church. The *contadini* assemble in their costumes beneath my belvedere, and I have an excellent opportunity of overlooking, and overhearing them too. . . .

In one of the dreamy walks that I take in company with a Florentine, I strolled near a league along the road to Rome. The country is broken; the road winding among naked and abrupt hills that constantly remind me of the scenery that one usually finds attached to subjects painted from Holy Writ. On a small bit of tableland, that rises in one of the valleys, is a Carthusian convent; and finding ourselves beneath its walls, my companion proposed entering.

The ascent was easy, and the outer gate open. We saw no one, but, following a carriage way that resembled the approach to an ancient castle, we soon reached the door that communicates with the cloisters. Here we accidently met with a lay brother, who amused himself with cooking for the worthy fathers, and our application for admission was favorably, but silently received. The place was the image of solitude and silence; not a soul besides the lay brother was visible, and even he soon disappeared.

You may imagine the effect of strolling through vast, tenantless, echoing, monastic cloisters, corridors and halls, on a sleepy Italian day, grateful for the shade and coolness, but wondering for whom these vast edifices were constructed. We positively entered, remained an hour, and left this structure without seeing a soul but the lay brother. The gates were open, apparently, for all who chose to enter; the chapel, sacristy, and cloisters were all accessible, not a door or a gate requiring the hand, and yet no one was visible. We departed as we had come; and the only evidence we had that there was a fraternity within, was to be found in a list of the fathers who were to perform certain masses. . . .

Herman Melville, 1857*

March 23rd . . . At 5½ P.M took cars for Florence. Level plain richly cultivated. Mountains. At 8 P.M arrived at Florence. Hotel du Nord. Caffe Doney near it. To bed early, no sleep for 2 nights past.

Tuesday March 24th. Cold & raining all day. To Pitti Palace[1]—"It's as bad as too much pain: it gets to be pain at last" Heard this broken latter part of sentence from wearied lady coming from Uffizi Palace. —She was talking no doubt about excess of pleasure in these galleries.—Florence is a lovely city even on a cold rainy day. Ufezzi Palace. The Perrseus of Cellini. Wandered about after leaving gallery Pitti. To the Duomo & Campanile. Came upon them unexpectedly. Amazed at their magnificance. Could not enter. Bought fine mosaics for one Napoleon.—Breakfasted to day at Caffe Doney.

*The publication of Melville's *Journal* preserves the vagaries of spelling and the syntax of his cryptic entries.

[1] Both the Pitti and Uffizi world-famous art galleries were open daily, except Sundays and holidays, the former from 10 to 3, the latter from 9 to 3, and no fees, tips, or other gratuities were expected. The Pitti was still the Grand Ducal residence, and its rooms were magnificantly furnished and well-heated, but the Uffizi, across the Arno, and reached by a connecting arcade built atop the Ponte Vecchio, vied with it in comfort and provisions for displaying the paintings to best advantage. The Pitti had the better collection of paintings, and of course, the Louvre and Vatican were larger, but all things considered, the Uffizi possessed the richest and most varied collection of art in the world. The "Perseus of Cellini" mentioned by Melville a few lines later was in the cabinet of modern bronzes. There were actually two, a wax and a bronze copy of the original.

Wednesday March 25th. Festa, galleries closed. To Pitti gardens, rather Boboli. Noble views of Florence & country. Strolled about generally to churches, piazzas &c. At Santa Croce saw tombs of Dante, M. Angelo, Alfieri, and Machiavelli. Preacher near M.'s tomb. M. said naught. Crucifix held out towards him. Campo Santa here.—At Annunziata saw fine frescoes of A. del Sarto. Gamblers struck by lightning.—Animated appearance of streets. Walked over to Romana Gate, outside to Bellesgardo. Striking view from this hill of city & Vale d'Arno. Roundabout walk to get to it. Abruptly came upon it, by a narrow lane between high walls of gardens. The tower on the Vecchio palace[2] the grand feature.—Came on violent rain; & walked home in it.

Thursday March 26th. Sunned myself after breakfast in Grand Ducal square. To the Uffizi gallery. Idle to enumerate. Grand view of tower of Vechio palace from head of gallery. View of covered way that crosses the Vechio bridge.—Not pleased with the Venus de Medici, but very much astonished at the Wrestlers & charmed with Titian's Venus. The Portraits of painters interesting.—To the Accademia de B. Arti.[3]—Giotto's paintings. Rich effect of gilding & raised parts. Here are predicessors of the Peruginos & Raphaels. Saw a large painting, not referred to in my hand book, which contained many faces, attitudes, expressions & groupings I had noted at Rome in Raphael. Undoubtedly Raphael took from this, or some yet older painting. But still more, the *whole spirit* was the same.—Could not get access to all parts of the Accademia.—But saw the statues,—such as they are. Returning, passed Ricardi palace—Immense arched & lowering pile, with massive and impending cornice.—Raining pretty much all day, at times violently.—At dinner table accosted by singu-

---

[2]The great tower was built, not over the line of the walls of this vast building in the heart of the city, but out upon the machicolations, proverbially built in the air. At the time of Melville's visit, the famous *David* of Michelangelo still stood outside the door, but he seems not to have noticed it.

[3]The Accademia delle Belle Arti, founded in 1350, was most famous for its unique series of early Tuscan paintings, ranging chronologically from Cimabue and Giotto to Fra Bartolomeo. Among the Giottos were a series from the life of St. Francis, a Madonna, and a series from the life of Christ, to which Hawthorne's reactions, as in so many cases, were the reverse of Melville's. The large painting which reminded Melville of Raphael cannot be positively identified, but it is more than likely one of Fra Angelico's, a collection of whose work was displayed separately.

lar young man who speaks 6 or 8 languages. He presented me with a flower, and talked like one to whom the world was delightful. May it prove so.

Friday March 27th. At Caffe after breakfast sat musing upon caffes in general, & the young men frequenting them. Something good might be written on the "Caffe Doney", including that "Henry" & the flower-girls.—To the Museum of Natural History.[4] Immense collection. Lapis lazuli—chrystal vessels, (dragons?) [flagons?], (perfumers) &c &cc. Wax plants, seeds & germinations. Anatomacl [Anatomical] preparations. Terrible cases & wilderness of rooms of them.—The Sicilian's work. No 1. Interior of case, broken arches, skeleton thrown under arch—head of statue—dead expression—crown & scepter among bones—medallion—Death & scythe—pointing—tossed skeletons—tools. horrible humiliation. Cleft shows (more) temples & pyramid. *No. 2* Vault—heaps—all colors from deep green to buff—all ruins—detached bones—mothers children old men, intricacy of heaps. Man with cloth over face bringing down another body whose buff contrasts with the putrid green.
No. 3. In a cavernous ruin. Superb mausoleum like Pope's, lid removed shows skeleton & putridity. Roman sarcophagus—joyous triumphal procession—putrid corpse thrown over it.—grating—rats, vampires—insects. slime & ooze of corruption.—Moralist, this Sicilian.—The final collection.—Revisited Pitti Gallery. The 3 Fates of M. Angelo. Admirable expression. The way the one Fate looks at other—Shall I?—The expectancy of the 3. (Transition from splendid humanity of gallery to the Sicilian) The inlaid tables & pictures. S.

---

[4]The museum adjoining the Pitti Palace housed the collections of the Medicis; both the mineralogical and the botanical series were especially rich, the latter including meticulous wax reproductions by Amici. The collection of wax works illustrating human anatomy, principally in various stages of decay, was prepared by a Sicilian named Zummo for Cosimo III. "But to the casual visitor, at least, the most striking part of the collection are the models in wax, which are distributed through fifteen apartments. They comprise preparations of every possible variety, colored with the utmost fidelity, and elaborated with the most patient minuteness of detail . . . Zummo's genius, like that of Rabelais and Swift, had a diseased fondness for revelling in those disgusting images, from the contemplation of which most men instinctively recoil. The representations which he has left of the plagues of Florence are doubtless hideously and repulsively real; certainly, it is difficult to look at them a second time . . . Indeed, were they of the size of life, they could not be looked at all."(Hillard, *Six Months in Italy*)

Rosa's portraits (one autograph) Battle Peice.—To Powers'[5] studio.
His America. Il Penseroso, Fisher Boy.—Saw him. Open, plain man.
Fine specimen of an American.—To the Cascine.[6]—Dined at the
Luna with the young Polyglot. Walk along river & home.

Saturday 28th March. Before breakfast ascended Duomo.[7] Entered
Ball. Fine morning & noble view. Parapet round the building. Fresco
of dome. Immense foot five feet long by measurement.—Magnitude
of dome.—After breakfast at caffe Doney, did some business & then
to Ufizzi gallery for last look. Afterwards to Fiesole.[8] Boccaccio's
villa—Medicis villa. Franciscan convent. View from windows. Old
maps,—behind the age.—Etruscan wall.—To the Cascine & home.
After dinner packed carpet bag & wrote this.

[5]Hiram Powers (1805-1873), born in Vermont, spent his youth in Ohio where poverty
forced him into all kinds of jobs; six years in a Cincinnati clock and organ factory
developed much of his mechanical ingenuity, five more years with a wax museum
developed his skill at sculpture. After some initial adversity in Italy where he had
arrived in 1837, he spent the remainder of his life there among influential and
interesting friends, with increasing prosperity. In Florence he became the center of a
famous circle of friends because of his frank, open, and genial nature, though on the
subject of sculpture he was dogmatic and opinionated. All Americans who saw him
were deeply impressed and his *Greek Slave* (1843) was the most celebrated single
statue of the day. The *Il Penseroso* (1856) was modeled according to Milton's
description, while his *Fisher Boy* (1846) was a slender little boy, standing holding a
shell to his ear.

[6]The large, parklike region north of the city along the river, part of the Grand Ducal
dairies, was the "Hyde Park" of Florence. There was a racecourse, many avenues,
groves, etc., where the fashionable society of Florence promenaded or rode.

[7]The grand feature of the Cathedral was Brunelleschi's great dome, the precursor of
St. Peter's. Excepting the smaller building which it surmounted, it was the highest in
the world, higher than St. Peter's. 463 easy steps led up between the usual double shell
to the upper gallery, from which one might climb a ladder of 57 more steps to the cross
on the summit. The frescoes on the interior of the dome were designed by Vasari,
representing Paradise, Prophets, Angels, Saints, etc., in bold and gigantic figures.

[8]Fiesole, atop a high hill three miles from Florence, still preserved in the northern
walls huge blocks of Etruscan quarrying. In the center, where the citadel once stood, a
Franciscan convent looked out over the length of the Arno valley a thousand feet
below. At the foot of the hill were the Villa dei tri Visi, where Boccaccio located his
group of storytellers in the *Decameron*, and the Villa Mozzi, favorite retreat of
Lorenzo Medici. Anciently, it was the site of the villa to which Cataline fled from
Rome, and there still remained the terrace and groves where Lorenzo engaged in his
philosophical debates.

Nathaniel Hawthorne, 1858

Florence at first struck me as having the aspect of a very new city in comparison with Rome; but, on closer acquaintance, I find that many of the buildings are antique and massive, though the still clear atmosphere, the bright sunshine, the light, cheerful hues of the stucco, and—as much as anything else, perhaps—the vivacious character of the human life in the streets, take away the sense of its being an ancient city. The streets are delightful to walk in after so many penitential pilgrimages as I have made over those little square, uneven blocks of the Roman pavement, which wear out the boots and torment the soul. I absolutely walk on the smooth flags of Florence for the mere pleasure of walking, and live in its atmosphere for the mere pleasure of living; and, warm as the weather is getting to be, I never feel that inclination to sink down in a heap and never stir again, which was my dull torment and misery as long as I stayed in Rome. I hardly think there can be a place in the world where life is more delicious for its own simple sake than here.

I went today into the Baptistery, which stands near the Duomo, and, like that, is covered externally with slabs of black and white marble, now grown brown and yellow with age. The edifice is octagonal, and on entering, one immediately thinks of the Pantheon—the whole space within being free from side to side, with a dome above; but it differs from the severe simplicity of the former edifice, being elaborately ornamented with marble and frescoes, and lacking that great eye in the roof that looks so nobly and reverently heavenward from the Pantheon. I did little more than pass through the Baptistery, glancing at the famous bronze doors, some perfect and admirable casts of which I had already seen at the Crystal Palace.

The entrance of the Duomo being just across the piazza, I went in there after leaving the Baptistery, and was struck anew—for this is the third or fourth visit—with the dim grandeur of the interior, lighted as it is almost exclusively by painted windows, which seem to me worth all the variegated marbles and rich cabinetwork of St. Peter's. The Florentine cathedral has a spacious and lofty nave, and side aisles divided from it by pillars; but there are no chapels along the aisles, so that there is far more breadth and freedom of interior, in proportion to the actual space, than is usual in churches. It is woeful to think how the vast capaciousness within St. Peter's is thrown away, and made to seem smaller than it is by every possible device, as if on purpose. The pillars and walls of this Duomo are of a uniform brownish, neutral tint; the pavement, a mosaic work of marble; the ceiling of the dome itself is covered with frescoes, which, being very imperfectly lighted, it is impossible to trace out. Indeed, it is but a twilight region that is enclosed within the firmament of this great dome, which is actually larger than that of St. Peter's, though not lifted so high from the pavement. But looking at the painted windows, I little cared what dimness there might be elsewhere; for certainly the art of man has never contrived any other beauty and glory at all to be compared to this.

This dome sits, as it were, upon three smaller domes—smaller, but still great—beneath which are three vast niches, forming the transepts of the cathedral and the tribune behind the high alter. All round these hollow, dome-covered arches or niches are high and narrow windows crowded with saints, angels, and all manner of blessed shapes, that turn the common daylight into a miracle of richness and splendor as it passes through their heavenly substance. And just beneath the swell of the great central dome is a wreath of circular windows quite round it, as brilliant as the tall and narrow ones below. It is a pity anybody should die without seeing an antique painted window, with the bright Italian sunshine glowing through it. This is "the dim, religious light" that Milton speaks of; but I doubt whether he saw these windows when he was in Italy, or any but those faded or dusty and dingy ones of the English cathedrals, else he would have illuminated that word "dim" with some epithet that should not chase away the dimness, yet should make it shine like a million of rubies, sapphires, emeralds, and topazes—bright in themselves, but dim with tenderness and reverence. . . .

June 7th. Saturday evening we walked . . . into the city, and looked at the exterior of the Duomo with new admiration. Since my former view of it, I have noticed—which, strangely enough, did not strike me before—that the facade is but a great, bare, ugly space, roughly plastered over, with the brickwork peeping through it in spots, and a faint, almost invisible fresco of colors upon it. This front was once nearly finished with an incrustation of black and white marble, like the rest of the edifice; but one of the city magistrates . . . demolished it three hundred years ago, with the idea of building it again in better style. He failed to do so, and ever since the magnificence of the great church has been marred by this unsightly roughness of what should have been its richest part; nor is there, I suppose, any hope that it will ever be finished now.

The campanile, or bell tower, stands within a few paces of the cathedral, but entirely disconnected from it, rising to a height of nearly three hundred feet, a square tower of light marbles, now discolored by time. It is impossible to give an idea of the richness of effect produced by its elaborate finish; the whole surface of the four sides, from top to bottom, being decorated with all manner of statuesque and architectural sculpture. It is like a toy of ivory, which some ingenious and pious monk might have spent his lifetime in adorning with scriptural designs and figures of saints; and when it was finished, seeing it so beautiful, he prayed that it might be miraculously magnified from the size of one foot to that of three hundred. This idea somewhat satisfied me, as conveying an impression how gigantesque the campanile is in its mass and height, and how minute and varied in its detail. Surely these medieval works have an advantage over the classic. They combine the telescope and the microscope. . . .

June 8th. I went this morning to the Uffizi gallery. The entrance is from the great court of the palace, which communicates with Lungarno at one end, and with the Grand Ducal Piazza at the other. The gallery is in the upper story of the palace, and in the vestibule are some busts of the princes and cardinals of the Medici family—none of them beautiful, one or two so ugly as to be ludicrous, especially one who is all but buried in his own wig. I at first traveled slowly through the whole extent of this long, long gallery, which occupies the entire length of the palace on both sides of the court, and is full of sculpture and pictures. The latter, being opposite to the light, are not seen to the best advantage; but it is the most perfect collection, in a chronological series, that I have seen, comprehending specimens of all the masters since painting began to be an art. Here are Giotto, and Cimabue, and Botticelli, and Fra Angelico, and Filippo Lippi, and a hundred others, who have haunted me in churches and galleries ever since I have been in Italy, and who ought to interest me a great deal more than they do. . . .

There were so many beautiful specimens of antique, ideal sculpture all along the gallery—Apollos, Bacchuses, Venuses, Mercurys, Fauns—with the general character of all of which I was familiar enough to recognize them at a glance. The mystery and wonder of the gallery, however, the Venus di Medici, I could nowhere see, and indeed was almost afraid to see it; for I somewhat apprehended the extinction of another of those lights that shine along a man's pathway, and go out in a snuff the instant he comes within eyeshot of the fulfilment of his hopes. My European experience has extinguished many such. I was pretty well contented, therefore, not to find the famous statue in the whole of my long journey from end to end of the gallery, which terminates on the opposite side of the court from that where it commences. The ceiling, by the by, through the entire length, is covered with frescos, and the floor paved with a composition of stone smooth and polished like marble. The final piece of sculpture, at the end of the gallery, is a copy of the Laocoön, considered very fine. I know not why, but it did not impress me with the sense of mighty and terrible repose—a repose growing out of the infinitude of trouble— that I had felt in the original.

Parallel with the gallery, on both sides of the palace-court, there runs a series of rooms devoted chiefly to pictures, although statues and bas-reliefs are likewise contained in some of them. I remember an unfinished bas-relief by Michelangelo of a Holy Family, which I touched with my finger, because it seemed as if he might have been at work upon it only an hour ago. . . .

I could not quite believe that I was not to find the Venus di Medici; and still, as I passed from one room to another, my breath rose and fell a little, with the half-hope, half-fear, that she might stand before me. Really, I did not know that I cared so much about Venus, or any possible woman of marble. At last, when I had come from among the Dutchmen, I believe, and was looking at some works of Italian artists, chiefly Florentines, I caught a glimpse of her through the door of the next room. It is the best room of the series, octagonal in shape, and hung with red damask, and the light comes down from a row of windows, passing quite round, beneath an octagonal dome. The Venus stands somewhat aside from the center of the room, and is surrounded by an iron railing, a pace or two from her pedestal in front, and less behind. I think she might safely be left to the reverence her womanhood would win, without any other protection. She is very beautiful, very satisfactory; and has a fresh and new charm about her unreached by any cast or copy. The hue of the marble is just so much mellowed by time, . . . warming her almost imperceptibly, making her an inmate of the heart, as well as a spiritual existence. I felt a kind of tenderness for her; an affection, not as if she were one woman, but all womanhood in one. Her modest attitude, which, before I saw her, I had not liked, deeming that it might be an artificial shame, is partly what unmakes her as the heathen goddess, and softens her into woman. There is a slight degree of alarm, too, in her face; not that she really thinks anybody is looking at her, yet the idea has flitted through her mind, and startled her a little. Her face is so beautiful and intellectual, that it is not dazzled out of sight by her form. Methinks this was a triumph for the sculptor to achieve. I may as well stop here. It is of no use to throw heaps of words upon her; for they all fall away, and leave her standing in chaste and naked grace, as untouched as when I began.

She has suffered terribly by the mishaps of her long existence in the marble. Each of her legs has been broken into two or three fragments, her arms have been severed, her body has been broken quite across at the waist, her head has been snapped off at the neck. Furthermore, there have been grievous wounds and losses of substance in various tender parts of her person. But on account of the skill with which the statue has been restored, and also because the idea is perfect and indestructable, all these injuries do not in the least impair the effect, even when you see where the dissevered fragments have been reunited. She is just as whole as when she left the hands of the sculptor. I am glad to have seen this Venus, and to have found her so tender and so chaste. On the wall of the room, and to be taken in at the same glance, is a painted Venus by Titian, reclining on a couch, naked and lustful.

The room of the Venus seems to be the treasure place of the whole Uffizi Palace, containing more pictures by famous masters than are to be found in all the rest of the gallery. There were several by Raphael, and the room was crowded with the easels of artists. I did not look half enough at anything, but merely took a preliminary taste, as a prophecy of enjoyment to come.

The most beautiful picture in the world, I am convinced, is Raphael's *Madonna della Seggiola*. I was familiar with it in a hundred engravings and copies, and therefore it shone upon me as with a familiar beauty, though infinitely more divine than I had ever seen it before. An artist was copying it, and producing certainly something very like a facsimile, yet leaving out, as a matter of course, that mysterious something that renders the picture a miracle. It is my present opinion that the pictorial art is capable of something more like magic, more wonderful and inscrutable in its methods than poetry, or any other mode of developing the beautiful. But how does this accord with what I have been saying only a minute ago? How then can the decayed picture of a great master ever be restored by the touches of an inferior hand? Doubtless it never can be restored; but let some devoted worshipper do his utmost, and the whole inherent spirit of the divine picture may pervade his restorations likewise. . . .

Sophia Amelia Hawthorne, 1858

This day [June 8] has been memorable by my seeing Mr. and Mrs. Browning for the first time. At noon Mr. Browning called upon us. . . . His grasp of the hand gives a new value to life, revealing so much fervor and sincerity of nature. He invited us most cordially to go at eight and spend the evening . . . and so at eight we went to the illustrious Casa Guidi. We found a little boy in an upper hall, with a servant. . . . In the dim light he looked like a waif of poetry, drifted up into the dark corner, with long, curling, brown hair, and buff silk tunic, embroidered with white. He took us through an anteroom, into the drawing room, and out upon the balcony. In a brighter light he was lovelier still, with brown eyes, fair skin, and a slender, graceful figure. In a moment Mr. Browning appeared, and welcomed us cordially. In a church near by, opposite the house, a melodious choir was chanting. The balcony was full of flowers in vases, growing and blooming. In the dark blue fields of space overhead, the stars, flowers of light, were also blossoming, one by one, as evening deepened. The music, the stars, the flowers, Mr. Browning and his child, all combined to entrance my wits. Then Mrs. Browning came out to us—very small, delicate, dark, and expressive. She looked like a spirit. A cloud of hair falls on each side of her face in curls, so as partly to veil her features. But out of the veil look sweet, sad eyes, musing and far-seeing and weird. Her fairy fingers seem too airy to hold, and yet their pressure was very firm and strong. The smallest possible amount of

SOPHIA AMELIA HAWTHORNE (1809–71) was painter, sculptor, illustrator, before becoming an author. She was also editor of the notebooks of her husband, Nathaniel Hawthorne.

substance encloses her soul, and every particle of it is infused with heart and intellect. I was never conscious of so little unredeemed, perishable dust in any human being. I gave her a branch of small pink roses, twelve on the stem, in various stages of bloom, which I had picked from our terrace vine, and she fastened it in her black-velvet dress with most lovely effect to her whole aspect. Such roses were fit emblems of her. We soon returned to the drawing room—a lofty, spacious apartment, hung with gobelin tapestry and pictures, and filled with carved furniture and object of vertu. Everything harmonized—poet, poetess, child, house, the rich air and the starry night. . . . Tea was brought and served on a long, narrow table, placed before a sofa, and Mrs. Browning presided. . . . Mr. Browning introduced the subject of spiritism, and there was an animated talk. Mr. Browning cannot believe, and Mrs. Browning cannot help believing. They kindly expressed regret that they were going to the seaside in a few weeks, since we were to stay in Florence, and hoped to find us here on their return. . . .

Let me not forget to record a wonder I met with today—Fra Angelico's Madonna and Child, of life-size, surrounded with angels in choir. It is in three parts—a tryptich—and on the folding doors are saints. The backgrounds are gold. The wreath of angels, each one with a different instrument of music, and one, over Mary's head, with hands folded in prayer, are worthy of the holy friar. I do not know in what he dips his pencil, unless in the rainbow; but the robes of this celestial band are glorious in color: gold circles are round their heads, fretted with points that catch the light—a brighter gold than gold. Their hair is still another shade, and their instruments also are gold, and their wings purple and crimson and azure, mingled with plumes of shining gold. The hues of their faces have his peculiar transparency and softness of tint; and it must be the complexion of celestial beings, for there is no earth in it. The grace, splendor, and state of this garland of divine choristers give an idea of the heavenly world, which Fra Angelico alone reveals. The Virgin Mary sits in the center, with the babe standing upon her knees, with both little arms extended in blessing. From his fair face and blue eyes suns seem to radiate and actually dazzle. . . . How paltry are words in the presence of such an apocalypse of boundless grace to all! Two artists were each copying an angel, and their backgrounds being fresh gold just laid on, showed how gorgeous the original picture must have been when first executed. When Fra Angelico first unfolded the doors of the tryptich, the beholder must have thought the heavens opened upon him. . . .

We went to the Pitti this morning early, . . . but we gained admittance into the palace: first, into the Entrance Hall of Stuccoes, long, wide, and lofty—the walls and arched ceilings covered with stucco figures and ornaments of every device. In the center, a door upon the right admitted us into another anteroom equally lofty, and not so large, entirely painted in fresco by Porchetti (or Porcetti); but the custodian did not tell us what subjects were illustrated. Now the guard took out his keys, and unlocked a door and ushered us into a bedchamber, high, but small—the walls hung with satin damask of deep dahlia-red, illumined with lines of bright gold. The bed, doors, and windows were hung with the same material. It is a fine custom of these southern kingdoms to drape the doors with sweeping folds. It probably obtains all over Europe.

The next room was hung with gobelin tapestry—one whole side a charming scene of gardening and husbandry, carried on by a troupe of little genii of loveliest baby-forms and sweet faces, all full of earnestness, and as busy as so many bees. They made labor soar and sing. The brilliant, fresh coloring, the careful drawing, and living expression of these tapestries amazed me; for the softest, round cheek is rendered as by enamel-painting. Several apartments followed one another, filled with similar beautiful hangings—sometimes landscapes; and one was particularly delicate in its aerial perspective. In England, and even in Rome, the arras we saw was always somewhat faded; but these were as radiant as if this moment woven. Every room contained tables of Florentine mosaic, in *pietra dura*, as well as of the most precious marbles; and superb cabinets of ebony, with small columns of oriental alabaster and of lapis lazuli, and of the rare Blue John (which however is purple)—inlaid with flowers, birds, and shells, composed of pearls and gems, in infinitely varied devices, and with no end of beauty. Each cabinet differed from every other in form, and they were of all varieties of substance. The flowers can never fade that are composed of jewels and marbles—lilies, passionflowers, roses, jessamines, morning-glories, trailing in long vines with lapis-lazuli petals, forget-me-nots of turquoise, and other blossoms of earth, together with birds of the air, involved in graceful arabesques, winding and wreathing about. After the tapestries ceased, velvet and satin-damask took their place, so thick and solid that my hand could scarcely clutch it. It had the thickness and richness of Genoa velvet, with the sheen of the satin added—woven into flowers and leaves, like embossed work. Just fancy the walls made up of this gorgeousness, and full, trailing curtains at all the doors and windows.

At last we came to the chamber of the grand duchess. The bed was hung with white satin, heavily embroidered with gold—the satin seeming to be an eighth of an inch in thickness. The walls, windows, and doors were draped with light-blue satin and gold—as well as the chairs and couches. On the toilet were candlesticks entirely of flowers in wreaths, in enamel. A chandelier of the same design hung from the center of the frescoed ceiling. A priedieu, near the bed, was inlaid with *pietra dura* and gems, and cushioned with white satin rayed with gold. But the dressing room! On a marble table, of Greek form, stood a small gothic-shaped glass, framed in enameled flowers. Taborets of white satin, embroidered with flowers, stood against the walls, which were encased in azure damask. And so we went on, in splendid mazes lost, till we opened upon an anteroom or hall of audience, and then I supposed we were at the end. But behold! the custodian unlocked another door, and we began upon a suite of winter apartments, which were carpeted. Our feet seemed sinking in deep moss, and we crushed down fresh blooming flowers at every step. Hitherto we had walked over marble and inlaid floors. Now, each room showed a new variety of carpet—a new color for groundwork, and new designs elaborated upon it. In each was also a clock of some rare device. One was made entirely on gold and Blue John. Some were of gold and oriental alabaster, and all were clicking. One struck while we were near by, and it was like fairy music. The cabinets seemed to become more and more superb, and the tables richer, as we went on. In the grand duke's bedroom hung the only oil painting we saw, a Madonna by Carlo Dolci, a replica of the original one, in the Borghese Palace in Rome, entirely different from any other Madonna, very beautiful and highly finished. Wonderful eyes has the Virgin, with tender, deep shadows, as from long lashes. I liked it extremely at Rome, but this is more lovely still. The priedieu here was particularly exquisite, in Florentine mosaic, and one table in the room had marvelous groups of faces and figures, inlaid. Inlaying certainly can go no further than in this Florentine work. The walls of all the winter suite were covered with satin and velvet damask—one was again entirely azure. . . . now we had really finished the circuit. . . .

Soon after five [we went] to the Boboli gardens. They are open to the public two days in the week. We soon found a lake with swans . . . and so I sat down on a marble seat, . . . The grounds extend for an immense distance, and include hill, plain and valley, groves, avenues, lawns, fountains, lakes, islands, statues, flowers, conservatories—impenetrable shades and sunny open spaces—extensive views from the heights—temples, bowers, grottoes—in short, "enormous bliss" of every green, flowery, and bosky kind. They are the gardens of the palace, and have an entrance from the piazza in front, as well as this other entrance, nearer to our Casa del Bello. In the swans' lake was a rough rock, upon which sat a marble Ariadne, stretching out her fair arms wildly for help against a horrible green dragon, who was creeping out of the water on one side, while an enormous frog—probably antediluvian—was opening his jaws upon her from the other.

From [the Medici] chapel we went to the Laurentian Library, which is over the cloisters. We were guided to a vestibule, planned by Michelangelo, in which a staircase leads up into the library. It was much smaller than I expected, but yet big enough to hold the nine or ten thousand precious manuscripts deposited there. It is a long apartment, with a great many windows on each side, painted in bright arabesques. The ceiling is carved in oak, I think—as it is brown—though I should suppose it would be stone for safety, and the pavement is a mosaic of red, brown, and yellow terracotta. A broad aisle in the center runs the whole length, between long, pewlike seats, with desks, upon which the manscripts are chained. In the aisle are tables at intervals, at many of which men were copying manuscripts. . . . We saw the famous earliest manuscript of Virgil; and the *Decameron*, much interlined, with many notes on the margin; Cicero's epistles, copied by Petrarch; Aristotle, in a dozen folios; Horatius Flaccus, with an autograph of Petrarch, showing it to have been his property, . . . and beautiful colored contemporaneous portraits of Petrarch and Laura, as illuminations in the *Canzoniere*. Laura is beautiful, with a very stately head, and proud, refined expression, entirely satisfactory. Opening from the library is a rotonda, surrounded by glass cases, in which are placed all the first books printed after the invention of printing—Plato, Aristotle, Cicero, Horace, and all the other classics in all languages. Many of the manuscripts are richly illuminated; and we saw the first map by Ptolemy, with ultramarine seas, of the eastern hemisphere, then the whole of the known world. This collection is the most valuable there is, except that of the Vatican. . . .

Henry James, 1877

I had never known Florence more herself, or in other words more attaching, than I found her for a week in that brilliant October. She sat in the sunshine beside her yellow river like the little treasure-city she has always seemed, without commerce, without other industry than the manufacture of mosaic paperweights and alabaster Cupids, without actuality or energy or earnestness or any of those rugged virtues which in most cases are deemed indispensable for civic cohesion; with nothing but the little unaugmented stock of her medieval memories, her tender-colored mountains, her churches and palaces, pictures and statues. There were very few strangers; one's detested fellow-pilgrim was infrequent, the native population itself seemed scanty; the sound of wheels in the streets was but occasional; by eight o'clock at night, apparently, everyone had gone to bed, and the musing wanderer, still wandering and still musing, had the place to himself—had the thick shadow-masses of the great palaces, and the shafts of moonlight striking the polygonal paving stones, and the empty bridges, and the silvered yellow of the Arno, and the stillness broken only by a homeward step, a step accompanied by a snatch of song from a warm Italian voice. My room at the inn looked out on the river and was flooded all day with sunshine. There was an absurd orange-colored paper on the walls; the Arno, of a hue not altogether different, flowed beneath; and on the other side of it rose a line of sallow houses, of extreme antiquity, crumbling and moldering, bulging and protruding over the stream. (I seem to speak of their fronts; but what I saw was their shabby backs, which were exposed to the cheerful flicker of the river, while the fronts stood for ever in the deep damp shadow of a narrow medieval street.) All this brightness and yellowness was a perpetual delight; it was a part of that indefinably charming color which Florence always seems to wear as you look up and down at it from the river, and from the bridges and quays. This is a kind of grave radiance—a harmony of high tints—which I scarce know how to describe. There are yellow walls and green blinds and red roofs, there are intervals of brilliant brown and natural-looking blue; but the picture is not spotty nor gaudy, thanks to the distribution of the colors in large and comfortable masses, and to the washing-over of the scene by some happy softness of sunshine. The riverfront of Florence is in short a delightful composition. Part of its charm comes of course from the generous aspect of those high-based Tuscan palaces which a renewal of acquaintance with them has again commended to me as the most dignified dwellings in the world. Nothing can be finer than that look of giving up the whole immense ground floor to simple purposes of vestibule and staircase, of court and high-arched entrance; as if this were all but a massive pedestal for the real habitation and people weren't properly housed unless, to begin with, they should be lifted fifty feet above the pavement. The great blocks of the basement; the great intervals, horizontally and vertically, from window to window (telling of the height and breadth of the rooms within); the armorial shield hung forward at one of the angles; the wide-brimmed roof, overshadowing the narrow street; the rich old browns and yellows of the walls: these definite elements put themselves together with admirable art.

Take a Tuscan pile of this type out of its oblique situation in the town; call it no longer a palace, but a villa; set it down by a terrace on one of the hills that encircle Florence, place a row of high-waisted cypresses beside it, give it a grassy courtyard and a view of the Florentine towers and the valley of the Arno, and you will think it perhaps even more worthy of your esteem. It was a Sunday noon, and brilliantly warm, when I again arrived; and after I had looked from my windows a while at that quietly basking riverfront I have spoken of I took my way across one of the bridges and then out of one of the gates—that immensely tall Roman Gate in which the space from the top of the arch to the cornice (except that there is scarcely a cornice, it is all a plain massive piece of wall) is as great, or seems to be, as that from the ground to the former point. Then I climbed a steep and winding way—much of it a little dull if one likes, being bounded by mottled, mossy garden walls—to a villa on a hilltop, where I found various things that touched me with almost too fine a point. Seeing them again, often, for a week, both by sunlight and moonshine, I never quite learned not to covet them; not to feel that not being a part of them was somehow to miss an exquisite chance. What a tranquil, contented life it seemed, with romantic beauty as a part of its daily texture!—the sunny terrace, with its tangled *podere* beneath it; the bright gray olives against the bright blue sky; the long, serene, horizontal lines of other villas, flanked by their upward cypresses, disposed upon the neighboring hills; the richest little city in the world in a softly scooped hollow at one's feet, and beyond it the most appealing of views, the most majestic, yet the most familiar. Within the villa was a great love of art and a painting room full of felicitous work, so that if human life there confessed to quietness, the quietness was mostly but that of the intent act. A beautiful occupation in that beautiful position, what could possibly be better? That is what I spoke just now of envying—a way of life that doesn't wince at such refinements of peace and ease. When labor self-charmed presents itself in a dull or an ugly place we esteem it, we admire it, but we scarce feel it to be the ideal of good fortune. When, however, its votaries move as figures in an ancient, noble landscape, and their walks and contemplations are like a turning of the leaves of history, we seem to have before us an admirable case of virtue made easy; meaning here by virtue contentment and concentration, a real appreciation of the rare, the exquisite though composite, medium of life. You needn't want a rush or a crush when the scene itself, the mere scene, shares with you such a wealth of consciousness.

It is true indeed that I might after a certain time grow weary of a regular afternoon stroll among the Florentine lanes; of sitting on low parapets, in intervals of flower-topped wall, and looking across at Fiesole or down the rich-hued valley of the Arno; of pausing at the open gates of villas and wondering at the height of cypresses and the depth of loggias; of walking home in the fading light and noting on a dozen westward-looking surfaces the glow of the opposite sunset. But for a week or so all this was delightful. The villas are innumerable, and if you're an aching alien half the talk is about villas. This one has a story; that one has another; they all look as if they had stories—none in truth predominantly gay. Most of them are offered to rent (many of them for sale) at prices unnaturally low; you may have a tower and a garden, a chapel and an expanse of thirty windows, for five hundred dollars a year. In imagination you hire three or four; you take possession and settle and stay. Your sense of the fineness of the finest is of something very grave and stately; your sense of the bravery of two or three of the best something quite tragic and sinister. From what does this latter impression come? You gather it as you stand there in the early dusk, with your eyes on the long, pale-brown facade, the enormous windows, the iron cages fastened to the lower ones. Part of the brooding expression of these great houses comes, even when they have not fallen into decay, for their look of having outlived their original use. Their extraordinary largeness and massiveness are a satire on their present fate. They weren't built with such a thickness of wall and depth of embrasure, such a solidity of staircase and superfluity of stone, simply to afford an economical winter residence to English and American families. I don't know whether it was the appearance of these stony old villas, which seemed so dumbly conscious of a change of manners, that threw a tinge of melancholy over the general prospect; . . . "Lovely, lovely, but it makes me 'blue,' " the sensitive stranger couldn't but murmur to himself as, in the late afternoon, he looked at the landscape from over one of the low parapets, and then, with his hands in his pockets, turned away indoors to candles and dinner.

Below, in the city, through all frequentation of streets and churches and museums, it was impossible not to have a good deal of the same feeling; but here the impression was more easy to analyze. It came from a sense of the perfect separateness of all the great productions of the Renaissance from the present and the future of the place, from the actual life and manners, the native ideal. I have already spoken of the way in which the vast aggregation of beautiful works of art in the Italian cities strikes the visitor nowadays—so far as present Italy is concerned—as the mere stock-in-trade of an impecunious but thrifty people. It is this spiritual solitude, this conscious disconnection of the great works of architecture and sculpture that deposits a certain weight upon the heart; when we see a great tradition broken we feel something of the pain with which we hear a stifled cry. But regret is one thing and resentment is another. Seeing one morning, in a shopwindow, the series of *Mornings in Florence* published a few years since by Mr. Ruskin, I made haste to enter and purchase these amusing little books, some passages of which I remembered formerly to have read. I couldn't turn over many pages without observing that the "separateness" of the new and old which I just mentioned had produced in their author the liveliest irritation. With the more acute phases of this condition it was difficult to sympathize, for the simple reason, it seems to me, that it savors of arrogance to demand of any people, as a right of one's own, that they shall be artistic. "Be artistic yourselves!" is the very natural reply that young Italy has at hand for English critics and censors. When a people produces beautiful statues and pictures, it gives us something more than is set down in the bond, and we must thank it for its generosity; and when it stops producing them or caring for them we may cease thanking, but we hardly have a right to begin and rail. The wreck of Florence, says Mr. Ruskin, "is now too ghastly and heartbreaking to any human soul that remembers the days of old"; and these desperate words are an allusion to the fact that the little square in front of the cathedral, at the foot of Giotto's Tower, with the grand Baptistery on the other side, is now the resort of a number of hackney coaches and omnibuses. This fact is doubtless lamentable, and it would be a hundred times more agreeable to see among people who have been made the heirs of so priceless a work of art as the sublime campanile some such feeling about it as would keep it free even from the danger of defilement. A cab-stand is a very ugly and dirty thing, and Giotto's Tower should have nothing in common with such conveniences. But there is more than one way of taking such things, and the sensitive stranger who has been walking about for a week with his mind full of the sweetness and suggestiveness of a hundred Florentine places may feel at last in looking into Mr. Ruskin's little tracts that, discord for discord, there isn't much to choose between the importunity of the author's personal ill-humor and the incongruity of horse pails and bundles of hay. And one may say this without being at all a partisan of the doctrine of the inevitableness of new desecrations. For my own part, I believe there are few things in this line that the new Italian spirit isn't capable of, and not many indeed that we aren't destined to see. Pictures and buildings won't be completely destroyed, because in that case the *forestieri*, scatterers of cash, would cease to arrive and the turnstiles at the doors of the old palaces and convents, with the little patented slit for absorbing your half-franc, would grow quite rusty, would stiffen with disuse. But it's safe to say that the new Italy growing into an old Italy again will continue to take her elbowroom wherever she may find it.

I am almost ashamed to say what I did with Mr. Ruskin's little books. I put them into my pocket and betook myself to Santa Maria Novella. There I sat down and, after I had looked about for a while at the beautiful church, drew them forth one by one and read the greater part of them. Occupying one's self with light literature in a great religious edifice is perhaps as bad a piece of profanation as any of those rude dealings which Mr. Ruskin justly deplores; but a traveler has to make the most of odd moments, and I was waiting for a friend in whose company I was to go and look at Giotto's beautiful frescoes in the cloister of the church. My friend was a long time coming, so that I had an hour with Mr. Ruskin, whom I called just now a light *littérateur* because in these little *Mornings in Florence* he is for ever making his readers laugh. I remembered of course where I was, and in spite of my latent hilarity felt I had rarely got such a snubbing. I had really been enjoying the good old city of Florence, but I now learned from Mr. Ruskin that this was a scandalous waste of charity. I should have gone about with an imprecation on my lips, I should have worn a face three yards long. I had taken great pleasure in certain frescoes by Ghirlandaio in the choir of that very church; but it appeared from one of the little books that these frescoes were as naught. I had much admired Santa Croce and had thought the Duomo a very noble affair; but I had now the most positive assurance I knew nothing about them. After a while, if it was only ill-humor that was needed for doing honor to the city of the Medici, I felt that I had risen to a proper level; only now it was Mr. Ruskin himself I had lost patience with, not the stupid Brunelleschi, not the vulgar Ghirlandaio. Indeed I lost patience altogether, and asked myself by what right this informal votary of form pretended to run riot through a poor charmed *flâneur*'s quiet contemplations, his attachment to the noblest of pleasures, his enjoyment of the loveliest of cities. The little books seemed invidious and insane, and it was only when I remembered that I had been under no obligation to buy them that I checked myself in repenting of having done so.

Then at last my friend arrived and we passed together out of the church, and, through the first cloister beside it, into a smaller enclosure where we stood a while to look at the tomb of the Marchesa Strozzi-Ridolfi, upon which the great Giotto has painted four superb little pictures. It was easy to see the pictures were superb; but I drew forth one of my little books again, for I had observed that Mr. Ruskin spoke of them. Hereupon I recovered my tolerance; for what could be better in this case, I asked myself, than Mr. Ruskin's remarks? They are in fact excellent and charming—full of appreciation of the deep and simple beauty of the great painter's work. I read them aloud to my companion; but my companion was rather, as the phrase is, "put off" by them. One of the frescoes—it is a picture of the birth of the Virgin—contains a figure coming through a door. "Of ornament," I quote, "there is only the entirely simple outline of the vase which the servant carries; of color two or three masses of sober red and pure white, with brown and gray. That is all," Mr. Ruskin continues. "And if you are pleased with this you can see Florence. But if not, by all means amuse yourself there, if you find it amusing, as long as you like; you can never see it." *You can never see it.* This seemed to my friend insufferable, and I had to shuffle away the book again, so that we might look at the fresco with the unruffled geniality it deserves. We agreed afterwards, when in a more convenient place I read aloud a good many more passages from the precious tracts, that there are a great many ways of seeing Florence, as there are of seeing most beautiful and interesting things, and that it is very dry and pedantic to say that the happy vision depends upon our squaring our toes with a certain particular chalkmark. We see Florence wherever and whenever we enjoy it, and for enjoying it we find a great many more pretexts than Mr. Ruskin seems inclined to allow. My friend and I convinced ourselves also, however, that the little books were an excellent purchase, on account of the great charm and felicity of much of their incidental criticism; to say nothing, as I hinted just now, of their being extremely amusing. Nothing in fact is more comical than the familiar asperity of the author's style and the pedagogic fashion in which he pushes and pulls his unhappy pupils about, jerking their heads toward this, rapping their knuckles for that, sending them to stand in corners and giving them Scripture texts to copy. But it is neither the felicities nor the aberrations of detail, in Mr. Ruskin's writings, that are the main affair for most readers; it is the general tone that, as I have said, puts them off or draws them on. For many persons he will never bear the test of being read in this rich old Italy, where art, so long as it really lived at all, was spontaneous, joyous, irresponsible. If the reader is in daily contact with those beautiful Florentine works which do still, in a way, force themselves into notice through the vulgarity and cruelty of modern profanation, it will seem to him that this commentator's comment is pitched in the strangest falsetto key. "One may read a hundred pages of this sort of thing," said my friend, "without ever dreaming that he is talking about *art.* You can say nothing worse about him than that." Which is perfectly true. Art is the one corner of human life in which we may take our ease. To justify our presence there the only thing demanded of us is that we shall have felt the representational impulse. In other connections our impulses are conditioned and embarrassed; we are allowed to have only so many as are consistent with those of our neighbors; with their convenience and well-being, with their convictions and prejudices, their rules and regulations. Art means an escape from all this. Wherever her shining standard floats the need for apology and compromise is over; there it is enough simply that we please or are pleased. There the tree is judged only by its fruits. If these are sweet the tree is justified—and not less so the consumer.

PART 4

FLORENCE IN ENGLISH LITERATURE

BY THE ARNO

The oleander on the wall
   Grows crimson in the dawning night,
   Though the gray shadows of the light
Lie yet on Florence like a pall.

The dew is bright upon the hill,
   And bright the blossoms overhead;
   But ah! the grasshoppers have fled,
The little Attic song is still.

Only the leaves are gently stirred
   By the soft breathing of the gale,
   And in the almost-scented vale
The lonely nightingale is heard.

The day will make thee silent soon;
   O nightingale sing on for love!
   While yet upon the shadowy grove
Splinter the arrows of the moon,

Before across the silent lawn
   In sea-green mist the morning steals,
   And to love's frightened eyes reveals
The long white fingers of the dawn

Fast climbing up the eastern sky
   To grasp and slay the shuddering night,
   All careless of my heart's delight,
Or if the nightingale should die.

Oscar Wilde

Childe Harold's Pilgrimage
Canto IV (Abridged)

Lord Byron

But Arno wins us to the fair white walls,
    Where the Etrurian Athens claims and keeps
    A softer feeling for her fairy halls:
    Girt by her theatre of hills, she reaps
    Her corn, and wine, and oil—and Plenty leaps
    To laughing life, with her redundant Horn.
    Along the banks where smiling Arno sweeps
    Was modern Luxury of Commerce born,
And buried Learning rose, redeemed to a new Morn.*

There, too, the Goddess loves in stone, and fills**
    The air around with Beauty—we inhale
    The ambrosial aspect, which, beheld, instils
    Part of its immortality—the veil
    Of heaven is half undrawn—within the pale
    We stand, and in that form and face behold
    What mind can make, when Nature's self would fail;

*The wealth which permitted the Florentine nobility to indulge their taste for luxury was derived from success in trade. Giovanni de' Medici (1360–1428), the father of Cosmo and great-grandfather of Lorenzo de' Medici, was a banker and Levantine merchant. As for the Renaissance, to say nothing of Petrarch of Florentine parentage, two of the greatest Italian scholars and humanists—Ficino, born 1430, and Politian, born 1454—were Florentines; and Poggio, born 1380, at Terra Nuova on Florentine soil.

**The Venus de' Medici statue, which stands in the tribune of the Uffizi Gallery, had been deported to Paris by Napoleon, but when Lord Byron spent a day in Florence in April, 1817, and returned "drunk with Beauty," the Venus was once more in the Tribune.

And to the fond Idolaters of old
Envy the innate flash which such a Soul could mould:

We gaze and turn away, and know not where,
　　Dazzled and drunk with Beauty, till the heart
　　Reels with its fulness; there—for ever there—
　　Chained to the chariot of triumphal Art,
　　We stand as captives, and would not depart.
　　Away!—there need no words, nor terms precise,
　　The paltry jargon of the marble mart,
　　Where Pedantry gulls Folly—we have eyes:
Blood—pulse—and breast confirm the Dardan Shepherd's prize.

In Santa Croce's holy precincts lie
　　Ashes which make it holier, dust which is
　　Even in itself an immortality,
　　Though there were nothing save the past, and this,
　　The particle of those sublimities
　　Which have relapsed to chaos:—here repose
　　Angelo's—Alfieri's bones*—and his
　　The starry Galileo, with his woes;
Here Machiavelli's earth returned to whence it rose.

These are four minds, which, like the the elements,
　　Might furnish forth creation:—Italy!
　　Time, which hath wronged thee with ten thousand rents
　　Of thine imperial garment, shall deny
　　And hath denied, to every other sky,
　　Spirits which soar from ruin:—thy Decay
　　Is still impregnate with divinity,
　　Which gilds it with revivifying ray;
Such as the great of yore, Canova is today.

But where repose the all Etruscan three—
　　Dante, and Petrarch, and, scarce less than they,

---

*Vittorio Alfieri (1749–1803) is one of numerous real and ideal personages with whom, as Byron tells us, he was compared. The resemblance, as Byron admits, ''related to our apparent personal dispositions.'' Both were noble, both were poets, both were ''patrician republicans,'' and both were lovers of pleasure as well as lovers and students of literature.

The Bard of Prose, creative Spirit! he
Of the Hundred Tales of Love—where did they lay
Their bones, distinguished from our common clay
In death as life? Are they resolved to dust,
And have their Country's Marbles nought to say?
Could not her quarries furnish forth one bust?
Did they not to her breast their filial earth entrust?

Ungrateful Florence! Dante sleeps afar,*
Like Scipio, buried by the upbraiding shore:
Thy factions, in their worse than civil war,
Proscribed the Bard whose name for evermore
Their children's children would in vain adore
With the remorse of ages; and the crown
Which Petrarch's laureate brow supremely wore,
Upon a far and foreign soil had grown,
His Life, his Fame, his Grave, though rifled—not thine own.

Boccaccio** to his parent earth bequeathed
His dust,—and lies it not her Great among,
With many a sweet and solemn requiem breathed
O'er him who formed the Tuscan's siren tongue?
That music in itself, whose sounds are song,

---

*Dante died at Ravenna, September 14, 1321, and was buried in the Church of S. Francesco. His remains were afterwards transferred to a mausoleum in the friars' cemetery, which was raised to his memory by his friend and patron, Guido da Polenta. On the occasion of Dante's sexcentenary, in 1865, it was discovered that the skeleton had been placed for safety in a wooden box, and enclosed in a wall of the Braccioforte Chapel. The house which Byron occupied during his first visit to Ravenna, June 8–August 9, 1819, is close to the chapel. In January 1820, he wrote in the Fourth Canto of Don Juan: "I pass each day where Dante's bones are laid."

**Giovanni Boccaccio died and was buried in Certaldo, where his family is supposed to have originated, in 1375. His sepulchre, which stood in the center of the Church of S. Michele and S. Giovanni, was removed in 1783 on the plea that a recent edict forbidding burial in churches applied to ancient interments. The stone was broken and thrown aside as useless. But it is improbable that the "hyena bigots," that is, the ecclesiastical authorities, were ignorant that Boccaccio was a bitter satirist of Churchmen, or that "he transferred the functions and histories of Hebrew prophets and Christian saints...the highest mysteries and most awful objects of Christian faith, to the names and drapery of Greek and Roman mythology." (Note of S. T. Coleridge in his copy of Boccaccio's *Opere*.)

The poetry of speech? No;—even his tomb
Uptorn, must bear the hyena bigot's wrong,
No more amidst the meaner dead find room,
Nor claim a passing sigh, because it told for *whom*!

And Santa Croce wants their mighty dust;
   Yet for this want more noted, as of yore
   The Caesar's pageant shorn of Brutus' bust
   Did but of Rome's best Son remind her more:
   Happier Ravenna! on thy hoary shore,
    Fortress of falling Empire! honoured sleeps
   The immortal Exile;—Arqua, too, her store
   Of tuneful relics proudly claims and keeps
While Florence begs her banished dead and weeps.

What is her Pyramid of precious stones?
   Of porphyry, jasper, agate, and all hues
   Of gem and marble, to encrust the bones
   Of merchant-dukes? the momentary dews*
   Which, sparkling to the twilight stars, infuse
   Freshness in the green turf that wraps the dead,
   Whose names are Mausoleums of the Muse,
   Are gently prest with far more reverent tread
Than ever paced the slab which paves the princely head.

There be more things to greet the heart and eyes
   In Arno's dome of Art's most princely shrine,
   Where Sculpture with her rainbow Sister vies;
   There be more marvels yet—but not for mine;
   For I have been accustomed to entwine
   My thoughts with Nature rather in the fields,
   Than Art in galleries: though a work divine
   Calls for my Spirit's homage, yet it yields
Less than it feels, because the weapon which it wields

Is of another temper. . . .

---

*"I also went to the Medici Chapel—fine frippery in great slabs of various expensive stones, to commemorate fifty rotten and forgotten carcasses. It is unfinished, and will remain so." (Bryon's letter to Murray, April 26, 1917.)

Ode to the West Wind*

Percy Bysshe Shelley

O Wild West Wind, thou breath of Autumn's being;
Thou, from whose unseen presence the leaves dead
Are driven, like ghosts from an enchanter fleeing,

Yellow, and black, and pale, and hectic red,
Pestilence-stricken multitudes: O thou,
Who chariotest to their dark wintry bed

The wingèd seeds, where they lie cold and low,
Each like a corpse within its grave, until
Thine azure sister of the Spring shall blow

Her clarion o'er the dreaming earth, and fill
(Driving sweet buds like flocks to feed in air)
With living hues and odors plain and hill:

Wild Spirit, which art moving everywhere;
Destroyer and preserver; hear, Oh hear!

*This poem was conceived and chiefly written in a wood that skirts the Arno, near
Florence, and on a day when that tempestuous wind, whose temperature is at once mild
and animating, was collecting the vapors which pour down the autumnal rains. They
began, as I foresaw, at sunset with a violent tempest of hail, and rain, attended by that
magnificent thunder and lightning peculiar to the Cisalpine regions.

The phenomenon alluded to at the conclusion of the third stanza is well known to
naturalists. The vegetation at the bottom of the sea, of rivers, and of lakes, sym-
pathizes with that of the land in the change of seasons, and is consequently influenced
by the winds which announce it.—Shelley's Note.

II

Thou on whose stream, 'mid the steep sky's commotion,
Loose clouds like earth's decaying leaves are shed,
Shook from the tangled boughs of Heaven and Ocean,

Angels of rain and lightning: there are spread
On the blue surface of thine airy surge,
Like the bright hair uplifted from the head

Of some fierce Maenad, even from the dim verge
Of the horizon to the zenith's height
The locks of the approaching storm. Thou dirge

Of the dying year, to which this closing night
Will be the dome of a vast sepulchre,
Vaulted with all thy congregated might

Of vapors, from whose solid atmosphere
Black rain, and fire, and hail will burst: Oh hear!

III

Thou who didst waken from his Summer dreams
The blue Mediterranean, where he lay,
Lulled by the coil of his crystalline streams,

Beside a pumice isle in Baiae's bay,
And saw in sleep old palaces and towers
Quivering within the wave's intenser day,

All overgrown with azure moss and flowers
So sweet, the sense faints picturing them! Thou
For whose path the Atlantic's level powers

Cleave themselves into chasms, while far below
The sea-blooms and the oozy woods which wear
The sapless foliage of the ocean, know

Thy voice, and suddenly grow gray with fear,
And tremble and despoil themselves: Oh hear!

IV

If I were a dead leaf thou mightest bear;
If I were a swift cloud to fly with thee;
A wave to pant beneath thy power, and share

The impulse of thy strength, only less free
Than thou, O uncontrollable! If even
I were as in my boyhood, and could be

The comrade of thy wanderings over heaven,
As then, when to outstrip the skiey speed
Scarce seemed a vision; I would ne'er have striven

As thus with thee in prayer in my sore need.
Oh, lift me as a wave, a leaf, a cloud!
I fall upon the thorns of life! I bleed!

A heavy weight of hours has chained and bowed
One too like thee: tameless, and swift, and proud.

V

Make me thy lyre, even as the forest is:
What if my leaves are falling like its own?
The tumult of thy mighty harmonies

Will take from both a deep, autumnal tone,
Sweet though in sadness. Be thou, Spirit fierce,
My spirit! Be thou me, impetuous one!

Drive my dead thoughts over the universe
Like withered leaves to quicken a new birth!
And, by the incantation of this verse,

Scatter, as from an unextinguished hearth
Ashes and sparks, my words among mankind!
Be through my lips to awakened earth

The trumpet of a prophecy! O Wind,
If Winter comes, can Spring be far behind?

Casa Guidi Windows
(Abridged)

Elizabeth Barrett Browning

For me who stand in Italy today
Where worthier poets stood and sang before,
  I kiss their footsteps yet their words gainsay.
I can but muse in hope upon this shore
  Of golden Arno as it shoots away
Through Florence' heart beneath her bridges four:
  Bent bridges, seeming to strain off like bows,
And tremble while the arrowy undertide
  Shoots on and cleaves the marble as it goes
And strikes up palace walls on either side,
  And froths the cornice out in glittering rows,
With doors and windows quaintly multiplied,
  And terrace-sweeps, and gazers upon all,
By whom if flower or kerchief were thrown out
  From any lattice there, the same would fall
Into the river underneath, no doubt,
  It runs so close and fast 'twixt wall and wall.
How beautiful! the mountains from without
  In silence listen for the word said next.
What word will men say,—here where Giotto planted
  His campanile like an unperplexed
Fine question Heavenward, touching the things granted
  A noble people who, being greatly vexed
In act, in aspiration keep undaunted?
  What word will God say? Michael's Night and Day
And Dawn and Twilight wait in marble scorn

Like dogs upon a dunghill, couched on clay
From whence the Medicean stamp's outworn,
　　The final putting off of such sway
By all such hands, and freeing of the unborn
　　In Florence and the great world outside Florence.
Three hundred years his patient statues wait
　　In that small chapel of the dim Saint Lawrence:
Day's eyes are breaking bold and passionate
　　Over his shoulder, and will flash abhorrence
On darkness and with level looks meet fate,
　　When once loose from that marble film of theirs;
The Night has wild dreams in her sleep, the Dawn
　　Is haggard as the sleepless, Twilight wears
A sort of horror; as the veil withdrawn
　　'Twixt the artist's soul and works had left them heirs
Of speechless thoughts which would not quail nor fawn,
　　Of angers and contempts, of hope and love:
For not without a meaning did he place
　　The princely Urbino on the seat above
With everlasting shadow on his face,
　　While the slow dawns and twilights disapprove
The ashes of his long-extinguished race
　　Which never more shall clog the feet of men.
I do believe, divinest Angelo,
　　That winter-hour in Via Larga, when
They bade thee build a statue up in snow
　　And straight that marvel of thine art again
Dissolved beneath the sun's Italian glow,
　　Thine eyes, dilated with the plastic passion,
Thawing too in drops of wounded manhood, since,
　　To mock alike thine art and indignation,
Laughed at the palace-window the new prince,—
　　("Aha! this genius needs for exaltation,
When all's said and howe'er the proud may wince,
　　A little marble from our princely mines!")
I do believe that hour thou laughedst too
　　For the whole sad world and for thy Florentines,
After those few tears, which were only few!
　　That as, beneath the sun, the grand white lines
Of thy snow-statue trembled and withdrew,—

The head, erect as Jove's, being palsied first,
The eyelids flattened, the full brow turned blank,
    The right-hand, raised but now as if it cursed,
Dropt, a mere snowball, (till the people sank
    Their voices, though a louder laughter burst
From the royal window)—though couldst proudly thank
    God and the prince for promise and presage,
And laugh the laugh back, I think verily,
    Thine eyes being purged by tears of righteous rage
To read a wrong into prophecy,
    And measure a true great man's heritage
Against a mere great-duke's posterity.
    I think thy soul said then, "I do not need
A princedom and its quarries, after all;
    For if I write, paint, carve a word, indeed,
On book or board or dust, on floor or wall,
    The same is kept of God who taketh heed
That not a letter of the meaning fall
    Or ere it touch and teach His world's deep heart,
Outlasting, therefore, all your lordships, sir!
    So keep your stone, beseech you, for your part,
O cover up your grave-place and refer
    The proper titles; *I* live by my art.
The thought I threw into this snow shall stir
    This gazing people when their gaze is done;
And the tradition of your act and mine,
    When all the snow is melted in the sun,
Shall gather up, for unborn men, a sign
    Of what is the true princedom,—ay, and none
Shall laugh that day, except the drunk with wine."

*****

    Meanwhile, from Casa Guidi windows, we
Beheld the armament of Austria flow
    Into the drowning heart of Tuscany:
And yet none wept, none cursed, or, if 't was so,
    They wept and cursed in silence. Silently
Our noisy Tuscans watched the invading foe;
    They had learnt silence. Pressed against the wall,

And grouped upon the church steps opposite,
   A few pale men and women stared at all.
God knows what they were feeling, with their white
   Constrainéd faces, they, so prodigal
Of cry and gesture when the world goes right,
   Or wrong indeed. But here was depth of wrong,
And here, still water; they were silent here;
   And through that sentient silence, struck along
That measured tramp from which it stood out clear,
   Distinct the sound and silence, like a gong
At midnight, each by the other awfuller,—
   While every soldier in his cap displayed
A leaf of olive. Dusty, bitter thing!
   Was such plucked at Novara, is it said?

*****

O Magi of the east and of the west,
Your incense, gold and myrrh are excellent!—
   What gifts for Christ, then, bring ye with the rest?
Your hands have worked well: is your courage spent
   In handwork only? Have you nothing best,
Which generous souls may perfect and present,
   And He shall thank the givers for? no light
Of teaching, liberal nations, for the poor
   Who sit in darkness when it is not night?
No cure for wicked children? Christ,—no cure!
   No help for women sobbing out of sight
Because men made the laws? no brothel-lure
   Burnt out by popular lightnings? Hast thou found
No remedy, my England, for such woes?
   No outlet, Austria, for the scourged and bound,
No entrance for the exiled? no repose,
   Russia, for knouted Poles worked underground,
And gentle ladies bleached among the snows?
   No mercy for the slave, America?
No hope for Rome, free France, chivalric France?
   Alas, great nations have great shames, I say.
No pity, O world, no tender utterance
   Of benediction, and prayers stretched this way

For poor Italia, baffled by mischance?
    O gracious nations, give some ear to me!
You all go to your Fair, and I am one
    Who at the roadside of humanity
Beseech your alms,—God's justice to be done.
    So, prosper!

*****

    The sun strikes, through the windows, up the floor;
Stand out in it, my own young Florentine,
    Not two years old, and let me see thee more!
It grows along thy amber curls, to shine
    Brighter than elsewhere. Now, look straight before,
And fix thy brave blue English eyes on mine,
    And from my soul, which fronts the future so,
With unabashed and unabated gaze,
    Teach me hope for, what the angels know
When they smile clear as thou dost. Down God's ways
    With just alighted feet, between the snow
And snowdrops, where a little lamb may graze,
    Thou hast no fear, my lamb, about the road,
Albeit in our vain-glory we assume
    That, less than we have, thou hast learnt of God.
Stand out, my blue-eyed prophet!—thou, to whom
    The earliest world-day light that ever flowed,
Through Casa Guidi Windows chanced to come!
    Now shake the glittering nimbus of thy hair,
And be God's witness that the elemental
    New springs of life are gushing everywhere
To cleanse the watercourses, and prevent all
    Concrete obstructions which infest the air!
That earth's alive, and gentle or ungentle
    Motions within her, signify but growth!—
The ground swells greenest o'er the laboring moles.

    Howe'er the uneasy world is very vexed and wroth,
Young children, lifted high on parent souls,
    Look round them with a smile upon the mouth,
And take for music every bell that tolls;

(WHO said we should be better if like these?)
But *we* sit murmuring for the future though
    Posterity is smiling on our knees,
Convicting us of folly. Let us go—
    We will trust God. The blank interstices
Men take for ruins, He will build into
    With pillared marbles rare, or knit across
With generous arches, till the fane's complete.
    This world has no perdition, if some loss.

Such cheer I gather from thy smiling, Sweet!
    The self-same cherub-faces which emboss
The Vail, lean inward to the Mercy-seat.

Old Pictures in Florence

Robert Browning

The morn when first it thunders in March,
   The eel in the pond gives a leap, they say:
As I leaned and looked over the aloed arch
   Of the villa-gate this warm March day,
No flash snapped, no dumb thunder rolled
   In the valley beneath where, white and wide
And washed by the morning water-gold,
   Florence lay out on the mountain-side.

River and bridge and street and square
   Lay mine, as much as my beck and call,
Through the live translucent bath of air,
   As the sights in the magic crystal ball.
And of all I saw and of all I praised,
   The most to praise and the best to see
Was the startling bell-tower Giotto raised:
   But why did it more than startle me?

Giotto, how, with that soul of yours,
   Could you play me false who loved you so?
Some slights if a certain heart endures
   Yet it feels, I would have your fellows know!
I' faith, I perceive not why I should care
   To break a silence that suits them best,
But the thing grows somewhat hard to bear
   When I find a Giotto join the rest.

On the arch where olives overhead
   Print the blue sky with twig and leaf,
(That sharp-curled leaf which they never shed)
   'Twixt the aloes, I used to leaf in chief,
And mark through the winter afternoons,
   By a gift God grants me now and then,
In the mild decline of those suns like moons,
   Who walked in Florence, besides her men.

Romola

George Eliot

It was the seventeenth of November, 1494: more than eighteen months since Tito and Romola had been finally united in the joyous Easter time, and had had a rainbow-tinted shower of comfits thrown over them, after the ancient Greek fashion, in token that the heavens would shower sweets on them through all their double life.

Since that Easter time a great change had come over the prospects of Florence; and as in the tree that bears a myriad of blossoms, each single bud with its fruit is dependent on the primary circulation of the sap, so the fortunes of Tito and Romola were dependent on certain grand political and social conditions which made an epoch in the history of Italy.

In this very November, little more than a week ago, the spirit of the old centuries seemed to have re-entered the breasts of Florentines. The great bell in the Palace tower had rung out the hammer-sound of alarm, and the people had mustered with their rusty arms, their tools and impromptu cudgels, to drive out the Medici. The gate of San Gallo had been fairly shut on the arrogant, exasperating Piero, galloping away toward Bologna with his hired horsemen frightened behind him, and his keener young brother, the cardinal, escaping in the disguise of a Franciscan monk; and a price had been set on their heads. After that, there had been some sacking of houses, according to old precedent; the ignominious images, painted on the public buildings, of the men who had conspired against the Medici in days gone by, were effaced; the exiled enemies of the Medici were invited home. The half-fledged tyrants were fairly out of their splendid nest in the Via Larga, and the Republic had recovered the use of its will again.

But now, a week later, the great palace in the Via Larga had been prepared for the reception of another tenant; and if drapery roofing the streets with unwonted color, if banners and hangings pouring out from the windows, if carpets and tapestry stretched over all steps and pavement on which exceptional feet might tread, were an unquestionable proof of joy, Florence was very joyful in the expectation of its new guest. . . .

An unexampled visitor! . . . For he had come across the Alps with the most glorious projects: he was to march through Italy amidst the jubilees of a grateful and admiring people; he was to satisfy all conflicting complaints at Rome; he was to take possession, by virtue of hereditary right and a little fighting, of the kingdom of Naples; and from that convenient starting-point he was to set out on the conquest of the Turks, who were partly to be cut to pieces and partly converted to the faith of Christ. It was a scheme that seemed to befit the Most Christian King, head of a nation which, thanks to the devices of a subtle Louis the Eleventh, who had died in much fright as to his personal prospects ten years before, had become the strongest of Christian monarchies; and this antitype of Cyrus and Charlemagne was no other than the son of that subtle Louis—the young Charles the Eighth of France.

Surely, on a general statement, hardly anything could seem more grandiose, or fitter to revive in the breasts of men the memory of great dispensations by which new strata had been laid in the history of mankind. And there was a very widely spread conviction that the advent of the French King and his army into Italy was one of those events at which marble statues might well be believed to perspire, phantasmal fiery warriors to fight in the air, and quadrupeds to bring forth monstrous births—that it did not belong to the usual order of Providence, but was in a peculiar sense the work of God. It was a conviction that rested less on the necessarily momentous character of a powerful foreign invasion than on certain moral emotions to which the aspect of the times gave the form of presentiments: emotions which had found a very remarkable utterance in the voice of a single man.

That man was Fra Girolamo Savonarola, Prior of the Dominican convent of San Marco in Florence. On a September morning, when men's ears were ringing with the news that the French army had entered Italy, he had preached in the Cathedral of Florence from the text, "Behold I, even I, do bring a flood of waters upon the earth." He believed it was by supreme guidance that he had reached just so far in his exposition of Genesis the previous Lent; and he believed the "flood of waters"—emblem at once of avenging wrath and purifying mercy—to be the divinely indicated symbol of the French army. His audience, some of whom were held to be among the choicest spirits of the age—the most cultivated men in the most cultivated of Italian cities—believed it too, and listened with shuddering awe. For this man had a power rarely paralleled, of impressing his beliefs on others, and of swaying very various minds. And as long as four years ago he had proclaimed from the chief pulpit of Florence that a scourge was about to descend on Italy, and that by this scourge the Church was to be purified. Savonarola appeared to believe, and his hearers more or less waveringly believed, that he had a mission like that of the Hebrew prophets, and that the Florentines amongst whom his message was delivered were in some sense a second chosen people. The idea of prophetic gifts was not a remote one in that age: seers of visions, circumstantial heralds of things to be, were far from uncommon either outside or inside the cloister; but this very fact made Savonarola stand out the more conspicuously as a grand exception. While in others the gift of prophecy was very much like a farthing candle illuminating small corners of human destiny with prophetic gossip, in Savonarola it was like a mighty beacon shining far out for the warning and guidance of men. And to some of the soberest minds the supernatural character of his insight into the future gathered a strong attestation from the peculiar conditions of the age. . . .

But the real force of demonstration for Girolamo Savonarola lay in his own burning indignation at the sight of wrong; in his fervent belief in an Unseen Justice that would put an end to the wrong, and in an Unseen Purity to which lying and uncleanness were an abomination. To his ardent, power-loving soul, believing in great ends, and longing to achieve those ends by the exertion of its own strong will, the faith in a supreme and righteous Ruler became one with the faith in a speedy divine interposition that would punish and reclaim.

. . .In 1493 the rumor spread and became louder that Charles the Eighth of France was about to cross the Alps with a mighty army; and the Italian populations, accustomed, since Italy had ceased to be the heart of the Roman empire, to look for an arbitrator from afar, began vaguely to regard his coming as a means of avenging their wrongs and redressing their grievances.

And in that rumor Savonarola had heard the assurance that his prophecy was being verified. What was it that filled the ear of the prophets of old but the distant tread of foreign armies, coming to do the work of justice? He no longer looked vaguely to the horizon for the coming storm: he pointed to the rising cloud. The French army was that new deluge which was to purify the earth from iniquity; the French king, Charles VIII, was the instrument elected by God, as Cyrus had been of old, and all men who desired good rather than evil were to rejoice in his coming. For the scourge would fall destructively on the impenitent alone. Let any city of Italy, let Florence above all—Florence beloved of God, since to its ear the warning voice had been specially sent—repent and turn from its ways, like Nineveh of old, and the storm-cloud would roll over it and leave only refreshing raindrops. . . .

The preparations for the equivocal guest were not entirely those of a city resigned to submission. Behind the bright drapery and banners symbolical of joy, there were preparations of another sort made with common accord by government and people. Well hidden within walls there were hired soldiers of the Republic, hastily called in from the surrounding districts; there were old arms newly furbished, and sharp tools and heavy cudgels laid carefully at hand, to be snatched up on short notice; there were excellent boards and stakes to form barricades upon occasion, and a good supply of stones to make a surprising hail from the upper windows. Above all, there were people very strongly in the humor for fighting any personage who might be supposed to have designs of hectoring over them, having lately tasted that new pleasure with much relish. This humor was not diminished by the sight of occasional parties of Frenchmen, coming beforehand to choose their quarters, with a hawk, perhaps, on their left wrist, and, metaphorically speaking, a piece of chalk in their right hand to mark Italian doors withal; especially as credible historians imply that many sons of France were at that time characterized by something approaching to a swagger, which must have whetted the Florentine appetite for a little stone-throwing.

And this was the temper of Florence on the morning of the seventeenth of November, 1494.

When Baldassarre, with his hands bound together, and the rope round his neck and body, pushed his way behind the curtain, and saw the interior of the Duomo before him, he gave a start of astonishment, and stood still against the doorway. He had expected to see a vast nave empty of everything but lifeless emblems—side altars with candles unlit, dim pictures, pale and rigid statues—with perhaps a few worshipers in the distant choir following a monotonous chant. That was the ordinary aspect of churches to a man who never went into them with any religious purpose.

And he saw, instead, a vast multitude of warm, living faces, upturned in breathless silence toward the pulpit, at the angle between the nave and the choir. The multitude was of all ranks, from magistrates and dames of gentle nurture to coarsely clad artisans and country people. In the pulpit was a Dominican monk, with strong features and dark hair, preaching with the crucifix in his hand.

For the first few minutes Baldassarre noted nothing of his preaching. Silent as his entrance had been, some eyes near the doorway had been turned on him with surprise and suspicion. The rope indicated plainly enough that he was an escaped prisoner, but in that case the church was a sanctuary which he had a right to claim; his advanced years and look of wild misery were fitted to excite pity rather than alarm; and as he stood motionless, with eyes that soon wandered absently from the wide scene before him to the pavement at his feet, those who had observed his entrance presently ceased to regard him, and became absorbed again in the stronger interest of listening to the sermon.

Among the eyes that had been turned toward him were Romola's: she had entered late through one of the side doors, and was so placed that she had a full view of the main entrance. . . .

Baldassarre quivered and looked up. He was too distant to see more than the general aspect of the preacher standing, with his right arm outstretched, lifting up the crucifix; but he panted for the threatening voice again as if it had been a promise of bliss. There was a pause before the preacher spoke again. He gradually lowered his arm. He deposited the crucifix on the edge of the pulpit, and crossed his arms over his breast, looking round at the multitude as if he would meet the glance of every individual face.

"All ye in Florence are my witnesses, for I spoke not in a corner. Ye are my witnesses, that four years ago, when there were yet no signs of war and tribulation, I preached the coming of the scourge. I lifted up my voice as a trumpet to the prelates and princes and people of Italy and said, The cup of your iniquity is full. Behold, the thunder of the

Lord is gathering, and it shall fall and break the cup, and your iniquity, which seems to you as pleasant wine, shall be poured out upon you, and shall be as molten lead. . . .

"But hyprocites who cloak their hatred of the truth with a show of love have said to me, 'Come now, Frate, leave your prophesyings: it is enough to teach virtue.' To these I answer: Yes, you say in your hearts, God lives afar off, and his work is as a parchment written by dead men, and he deals not as in the days of old, rebuking the nations, and punishing the oppressors, and smiting the unholy priests as he smote the sons of Eli. But I cry again in your ears: God is near and not afar off; His judgments change not. He is the God of armies; the strong men who go up to battle are his ministers, even as the storm, and fire, and pestilence. He drives them by the breath of His angels, and they come upon the chosen land which has forsaken the covenant. And thou, O Italy, art the chosen land; has not God placed his sanctuary within thee, and thou has polluted it? Behold! the ministers of his wrath are upon thee—they are at thy very doors."

Savonarola's voice had been rising in impassioned force up to this point, when he became suddenly silent, let his hands fall, and clasped them quietly before him. His silence, instead of being the signal for small movements amongst his audience, seemed to be as strong a spell to them as his voice. Through the vast area of the cathedral men and women sat with faces upturned, like breathing statues, till the voice was heard again in clear low tones.

"Yet there is a pause—even as in the days when Jerusalem was destroyed there was a pause that the children of God might flee from it. There is a stillness before the storm: lo, there is blackness above, but not a leaf quakes: the winds are stayed, that the voice of God's warning may be heard. Hear it now, O Florence, chosen city in the chosen land! Repent and forsake evil: do justice: love mercy: put away all uncleanness from among you, that the spirit of truth and holiness may fill your souls and breathe through all your streets and habitations, and then the pestilence shall not enter, and the sword shall pass over you and leave you unhurt.

"For the sword is hanging from the sky; it is quivering; it is about to fall! The sword of God upon the earth, swift and sudden! Did I not tell you, years ago, that I had beheld the vision and heard the voice? And behold, it is fulfilled! Is there not a king with his army at your gates? Does not the earth shake with the tread of horses and the wheels of swift cannon? Is there not a fierce multitude that can lay bare the land as with a sharp razor? I tell you the French king with his army is the minister of God: God shall guide him as the hand guides a sharp sickle, and the joints of the wicked shall melt before him, and they shall be mown down as stubble: he that fleeth of them shall not flee away, and he that escapeth of them shall not be delivered. And the tyrants who make to themselves a throne out of the vices of the multitude, and the unbelieving priests who traffic in the souls of men and fill the very sanctuary with fornication, shall be hurled from their soft couches into burning hell; and the pagans and they who sinned under the old covenant shall stand aloof and say: 'Lo! these men have brought the stench of a new wickedness into the everlasting fire.'

"But thou, O Florence, take the offered mercy. See! the Cross is held out to you: come and be healed. Which among the nations of Italy has had a token like unto yours? The tyrant is driven out from among you: the men who held a bribe in their left hand and a rod in their right are gone forth, and no blood has been spilled. And now put away every other abomination from among you, and you shall be strong in the strength of the living God. Wash yourselves from the blackpitch of your vices, which have made you even as the heathens: put away the envy and hatred that have made your city as a nest of wolves. And there shall no harm happen to you: and the passage of armies shall be to you as the flight of birds, and rebellious Pisa shall be given to you again, and famine and pestilence shall be far from your gates, and you shall be as a beacon among the nations. But, mark! while you suffer the accursed thing to lie in the camp you shall be afflicted and tormented, even though a remnant among you may be saved."...

In the great sob of the multitude Baldassarre's had mingled. Among all the human beings present, there was perhaps not one whose frame vibrated more strongly than his to the tones and words of the preacher; but it had vibrated like a harp of which all the strings had been wrenched away except one. That threat of a fiery inexorable vengeance—of a future into which the hated sinner might be pursued and held by the avenger in an eternal grapple, had come to him like the promise of an unquenchable fountain to unquenchable thirst. The doctrines of the sages, the old contempt for priestly superstitions, had fallen away from his soul like a forgotten language: if he could have remembered them, what answer could they have given to his great need like the answer given by this voice of energetic conviction? The thunder of denunciation fell on his passion-wrought nerves with all the force of self-evidence: his thought never went beyond it into questions—he was possessed by it as the warhorse is possessed by the clash of sounds. No word that was not a threat touched his consciousness; he had no fiber to be thrilled by it. But the fierce exultant delight to which he was moved by the idea of perpetual vengeance found at once a climax and a relieving outburst in the preacher's words. . . . To Baldassarre those words only brought the vague triumphant sense that he too was devoting himself—signing with his own blood the deed by which he gave himself over to an unending fire, that would seem but coolness to his burning hatred.

Romola had seemed to hear, as if they had been a cry, the words repeated to her by many lips—the words uttered by Savonarola when he took leave of those brethren of San Marco who had come to witness his signature of the confession: "Pray for me, for God has withdrawn from me the spirit of prophecy."

Those words had shaken her with new doubts as to the mode in which he looked back at the past in moments of complete self-possession. And the doubts were strengthened by more piteous things still, which soon reached her ears.

The nineteenth of May had come, and by that day's sunshine there had entered into Florence the two Papal Commissioners, charged with the completion of Savonarola's trial. They entered amid the acclamations of the people, calling for the death of the Frate. For now the popular cry was, "It is the Frate's deception that has brought on all our misfortunes; let him be burned, and all things right will be done, and our evils will cease."

The next day it is well certified that there was fresh torture of the shattered sensitive frame; and now, at the first threat and first sight of the horrible implements, Savonarola, in convulsed agitation, fell on his knees, and in brief, passionate words, *retracted his confession*, declared that he had spoken falsely in denying his prophetic gift, and that if he suffered, he would suffer for the truth—"The things that I have spoken, I had them from God."

But not the less the torture was laid upon him, and when he was under it he was asked why he had uttered those retracting words. Men were not demons in those days, and yet nothing but confessions of guilt were held a reason for release from torture. The answer came: "I said it that I might seem good; tear me no more, I will tell you the truth."

There were Florentine assessors at this new trial, and those words of
twofold retractation had soon spread. They filled Romola with dis-
mayed uncertainty.

"But"—it flashed across her—"there will come a moment when
he may speak. When there is no dread hanging over him but the dread
of falsehood, when they have brought him into the presence of death,
when he is lifted above the people, and looks on them for the last time,
they cannot hinder him from speaking a last decisive word. I will be
there."

Three days after, on the 23rd of May, 1498, there was again a long
narrow platform stretching across the great piazza, from the Palazzo
Vecchio towards the Tetta de'Pisani. But there was no grove of fuel as
before: instead of that, there was one great heap of fuel placed on the
circular area which made the termination of the long narrow platform.
And above this heap of fuel rose a gibbet with three halters on it; a
gibbet which, having two arms, still looked so much like a cross as to
make some beholders uncomfortable, though one arm had been trun-
cated to avoid the resemblance.

On the marble terrace of the Palazzo were three tribunals; one near
the door for the Bishop, who was to perform the ceremony of degradation of Fra Girolamo and the two brethren who were to suffer as his
followers and accomplices; another for the Papal Commissioners,
who were to pronounce them heretics and schismatics, and deliver
them over to the secular arm; and a third, close to Marzocco, at the
corner of the terrace where the platform began, for the Gonfaloniere,
and the Eight who were to pronounce the sentence of death.

Again the piazza was thronged with expectant faces: again there
was to be a great fire kindled. In the majority of the crowd that pressed
around the gibbet the expectation was that of ferocious hatred, or of
mere hard curiosity to behold a barbarous sight. But there were still
many spectators on the wide pavement, on the roofs, and at the
windows, who . . . were not without a lingering hope, even at this
eleventh hour, that God would interpose, by some sign, to manifest
their beloved prophet as His servant. And there were yet more who
looked forward with trembling eagerness, as Romola did, to that final
moment when Savonarola might say, "O people, I was innocent of
deceit."

Romola was at a window on the north side of the piazza, far away
from the marble terrace where the tribunals stood; and near her, also
looking on in painful doubt concerning the man who had won his early

reverence, was a young Florentine of two-and-twenty, named Jacopo Nardi, afterwards to deserve honor as one of the very few who, feeling Fra Girolamo's eminence, have written about him with the simple desire to be veracious. He had said to Romola, with respectful gentleness, when he saw the struggle in her between her shuddering horror of the scene and her yearning to witness what might happen in the last moment.

"Madonna, there is no need for you to look at these cruel things. I will tell you when he comes out of the Palazzo. Trust to me; I know what you would see."

Romola covered her face, but the hootings that seemed to make the hideous scene still visible could not be shut out. At last her arm was touched, and she heard the words, "He comes." She looked toward the Palace, and could see Savonarola led out in his Dominican garb; could see him standing before the Bishop, and being stripped of the black mantle, the white scapulary and long white tunic, till he stood in a close woolen under-tunic, that told of no sacred office, no rank. He had been degraded, and cut off from the Church Militant.

The baser part of the multitude delight in degradations, apart from any hatred; it is the satire they best understand. There was a fresh hoot of triumph as the three degraded Brethren passed on to the tribunal of the Papal Commissaries, who were to pronounce them schismatics and heretics. Did not the prophet look like a schismatic and heretic now? It is easy to believe in the damnable state of a man who stands stripped and degraded.

Then the third tribunal was passed—that of the Florentine officials who were to pronounce sentence. . . .

Then the three figures, in their close white raiment, trod their way along the platform, amidst yells and grating tones of insult.

"Cover your eyes, madonna," said Jacopo Nardi; "Fra Girolamo will be the last."

It was not long before she had to uncover them again. Savonarola was there. He was not far off her now. He had mounted the steps; she could see him look round on the multitude.

But in the same moment expectation died, and she only saw what he was seeing—torches waving to kindle the fuel beneath his dead body, faces glaring with a yet worse light; she only heard what *he* was hearing—gross jests, taunts, and curses.

The moment was past. Her face was covered again, and she only knew that Savonarola's voice had passed into eternal silence.

The Tower of Taddeo

Ouida
(Louise de la Ramée)

It was a high square tower, brown and gray, standing in a narrow street; one of the oldest of the once numerous towers of Florence. It was of great height, and dark with age, and rose above the lofty houses which surrounded it; its machicolated roofs and its iron vane and wooden flagstaff looked black against the sky. But warlike, and stalwart, and austere as it was, it had been given both grace and poetry by its builders, who had belonged to that age in which men knew so well how to unite the useful and the beautiful, how to harmonize the lovely with the formidable, and how to use the sports of peace to hide the strength of war. For it had been built by the great builder of its neighbor, the Jeweler's Bridge, and it was called now, as it had been called in the days of its rising, the Tower of Taddeo.

Tradition indicated it also was at one time his residence, but this rested only on rumor; that he had been its architect the archives of the city proved beyond any doubt. He had built it as he built and painted so much else that was beautiful. He built the Campanile, and it is called Giotto's; he built San Michele, and it is called Orcagna's. True, those masters did design both belfry and church; but he built them, and all alone he both designed and built the Ponte Vecchio, the Goldsmith's Bridge, which has no rival anywhere except the arch named after the

OUIDA (1839–1908) was the pseudonym of Louise de la Ramée, a prolific English writer who chose in mid-career to live in Florence. She is best known for her novels, among them *Under Two Flags* (1867) and *In Maremma* (1882), and children's stories, including the popular *Dog of Flanders* (1872).

alta Riva of Venice, and which has stood the sieges and floods and storms of six hundred years, and will stand six centuries more unless the accursed greed of municipal speculation seizes on its stones. Taddeo Gaddi led one of the loveliest, happiest, manliest lives ever led on earth, such a life as it is impossible to lead now, because the atmosphere which then made it possible nowhere now exists. But of fame in the mouths of posterity he has not had his full portion. Of the many thousands who every season pass over his bridge, scarce one Florentine, or one foreigner, in a million remembers its architect. Beauty in those days was necessary as air to those men, so much greater in every art than are the men of these days; and the makers of all these mighty medieval streets of Italy loved to decorate them with marble and majolica and terra cotta, and to put niches in them for Madonna's shrines and statues of the saints, and allegorical devices, and inscriptions in the Latin tongue and iron scrollwork made by hand into the utmost delicacy of flower and foliage.

This tower was rich in all such decoration, and was sometimes called as well the House of the Loves from the winged children, by Luca della Robbia, which clustered together over its archway, and held aloft the shield of the great family for whom it had been built, a Tuscan branch of those Brancaleone who once were lords of Cesena and Imola.

Above their shield was a shrine, with the Virgin and Child seated beneath a canopy, which had, it was said, wrought a miracle in the plague, and a framework of white and green lilies was around them. Above these were other winged children, and other garlands of lilies, and above these, again, was the figure of a bishop with a lamb at his feet; and all this ornament went upward, upward, upward, until figures and flowers mounted as high as the lines of the battlements, and were full of bright color, and wholly unspoiled, although four centuries, if one, had gone by since they had been placed there to brighten the dark and gruesome walls, which were pierced with ogive windows and kneeling windows, barred with iron gratings, while below these were iron rings for torches, and iron sconces for lamps, and one massive oaken iron-studded door.

A narrow and dark staircase of stone, very steep, went from top to bottom of the tower; half its lower chambers served as a store place for oils, cheeses, and pastes to a chandler; and a seller of fuel had the other half filled with his charcoal wood and pine cones; on the narrow *mezzanina* above lived a cabinet maker, a tailor, and a shoemaker, whilst the first, second, and third floors were occupied by a bookseller and librarian, and were known in the quarter as the Libreria Ardiglione.

On these floors every yard of space was filled to overflowing with books. There was a little kitchen, a little sitting room, two little bedrooms, mere closets; and all the rest served as storage for books, books, books, nothing but books—and old books all of them, moreover—for their owner would no more have sold new books than he would have sold daily newspapers; either were abominations in his sight. A place of business might easily have been put in a more accessible locality than the Tower of Taddeo. But his father had been there before him, and his grandfather also; and if the dark steep, breakneck stairs deterred customers from mounting them, its present proprietor, Francesco Ardiglione, commonly called Ser Checchi, had more leisure time in which to pore over his treasures, and chase the mice away from them, and add to them by visits to bookstalls in the town, and to any remote ancient rural place where it was known that there were any volumes of interest or age to be purchased. Books, even choice and antique ones, fetch but little in Italy; and many scores of valuable volumes rot away in old rooms or granaries, or cellars, no one noticing them except the rats. In the country which once produced the noblest literature in the world, books are in the present era the least esteemed, are read the least, and are regarded with the most indifference and contempt.

Ardiglione was a man of some sixty-five years; he had the true scholar's stoop of the throat and shoulders, and the true scholar's eyes, luminous and benign and dreamy; his head was fine, with white hair which fell softly off a broad and noble forehead, and a complexion smooth, pale, and delicate, of the faint yellow hue of old ivory. In stature he was short, and in build frail and spare. His clothes were always very shabby, and his gait was awkward; but no one who looked on him could doubt that he had gentle blood in his veins and vast learning in his brain.

Everyone called him Ser Checchi, which is the Tuscan diminutive of Francesco, and he was the jest of the neighborhood for his absence of mind and his simplicity in money matters; but no one, not the boldest and most impudent little rascal of the streets, would have dared to joke at him to his face, and the rudest rough of the populace stood aside respectfully to let him go by on the curbstone.

It was three o'clock, and the June day was hot. Ser Checchi was tired, for he had strolled more miles than he had counted along the fragrant hillside, where nightingales sang under the bay thickets and the yellow gorse was blossoming and the wild rose.

"You are fatigued, sir; rest for an hour or two," said the black-smith, a big, good-tempered, middle-aged man, with his reaping-hook in his hand and his shirt-sleeves rolled up to his shoulder.

"Thanks to you, I will do so," said Ser Checchi; "at least, if you will promise me to go back to your field work, for your corn is overripe, and I fear that there is rain in the air for this evening, and your grain is not half cut."

"Sit and rest, then, and we will go and finish cutting the corner field," said Iorio to him; "and, by the way, Ser Checchi, there is an old chest which you may like to look over—there are papers and such-like in it. I found it under a heap of old hay in the loft. It has been there, I be bound, as many years as the house is old. We hoped there was something good in it; but there was nothing but an odd lot of books, so we threw them back again, being spited not to have laid our hand heartily on something better. You are welcome to it if there be any paper or book as may please you; they are only a pack of rubbish, I fear—copybooks and ciphering-books and the like; but if you care to look over them the house is yours, and we will get, by your leave, to our reaping."

Ser Checchi thanked him and looked longingly toward a dusty, worm-eaten old wooden chest of solid nutwood, with a coat-of-arms carved heavily on its lid, and with rusty iron handles.

Old books!—the sound of the word was as sweet to him as the promise of bridal gifts to a maiden, or winter toys to a child by the fireside. They might most probably be of no value, but old volumes were always of interest, were they only records of household expenditure or of clerkly memoranda. . . .

He took the volumes out and brushed from them tenderly the dust, the dirt, and the seeds of hay with which they were covered. They were all books of the same date, the seventeenth century, to which the ledgers and household books belonged; there were prayer books, lives of saints, copies of ecclesiastical works, in all some dozen volumes, none of any rarity or especial mark, none of any uncommon binding or unusual typography. But one volume much longer and larger than the others, with a binding of another epoch, caught his instructed eyes where it lay in a corner of the chest, more than half hidden under the loose and dusty hayseed.

His hands trembled as he drew it forth. His sight swam as he opened its pages. His hands shook, his whole person quivered, his eyes were full of longing and light; they were the eyes of a man of twenty years.

Learned in such things as he was, he knew its antiquity and its value at a glance. To find such a treasure moldering neglected in a dusty chest in a cottage had been the dream of his whole life. Indignation, amaze, awe, delight, all held him breathless and entranced before the worm-eaten bench on which it lay. Oh, how happy the scribe who had penned it, though long ago his hand had crumbled to ashes!

The sun poured in through the strings of flowering beans which were running up the window, and the gentle air blew the yellow dry leaves to and fro irreverently. He remained on his knees before the manuscript, gazing with a lover's ardor and a devotee's devotion at the marvelous fine regular lines of the penman, the serried ranks of this black letter, in which not a blot, nor a deviation, nor an erasure was visible. Oh, the marvel of it! Look what the handwriting of men had become since the days of printing! Who wrote now what would be clear and beautiful for ever as this was? What would the sprawled, careless, hurried, blotted calligraphy of the present age tell men, as this work told them, of the beauty and holiness of ardor, of persever-ance, and of labor, where the hand was but the instrument of the soul?

It was a codex of the *Divina Commedia*, dated under the colophon as finished at Ravenna in May, 1320.

There are but few such in the world, and those few are numbered and known to all bibliophiles, like the folios of Shakespeare. To have discovered one other was to a lover and student of books what the discovery of a new world was to navigators of old—an ecstasy, an honor, a miracle, an intoxication of happiness.

He examined the parchment, the capitals, the writing, the head-piece, the colophon, the binding, which was of leather much eaten and gnawed by mice, with some unpolished cornelians, cut and mounted on silver, on its clasps; he scarcely breathed as he bent over it, whilst the full sun fell warm and golden on to these pages, which had once, like enough, been touched and seen by Dante's self. There could be no question of its age and its authenticity; indeed, the finding of it in such a place was proof enough of these. How many other treasures there are, doubtless, lying unknown in attic and cellar, in granary and wood-house in remote country places, where even the tireless feet of the collector and the dealer never wander, and the wand of the modern Hermes of the book-mart is unknown! . . .

For the first time in all his pure and upright life, a great temptation to an act of dishonor, of dishonesty, assailed him as he knelt there before it. No one knew that it was there; no one around him even beholding it would see in it anything more than an old book, quite worthless, only fit, perhaps, to be torn up to kindle a fire or to stop a leak in a cask. Nothing could be simpler, nothing more easy, than to put it in his pocket or take it away under his arm. No one on that hillside would ever know or care. Unless his learning enlightened their ignorance, no one of the people around him would ever dream that this old brown volume, moth-eaten and mice-gnawed, would be worth its weight in gold to the libraries of great cities and great men. There was not a soul near, not even in sight; all the family were out in the fields; there was not even a child asleep in the cradle, nor a dog, save his own by the threshold. He had only to walk out of the open doorway along the grass paths of the hillside towards his own home, and carry the precious manuscript with him.

Never was any temptation made more easy and more alluring to an innocent soul!

He bent over the codex, his hands pressed around it lovingly as a woman's hands round the body of her child; his was no cold appetite of a dry as dust, but a passion infinitely tender, and yearning, and even romantic; beside all that old books said to him as a scholar, they awoke his affections and his imagination; to hold thus, what likely enough Dante once had held, thrilled him to his utmost soul; he could never see a volume which had weathered centuries, a manuscript which had been written in other ages, without a strong emotion as of tears.

He would have given half the few years remaining to him to have had this one in his own possession, safe locked under his own keys; and to so possess it he had nothing to do but to put it under his arm and walk quietly away down the hillside; no one would ever have known.

It was so intense a temptation that the dew stood on his temples, and the blue veins swelled in his throat, as he knelt there, his hands about the old dark rusty cover of it. There it had lain so long, and no eyes but his could have recognized it for what it was. It was his own by all right of affinity, all title of sympathy. What was it to those who owned it?

He stayed there gazing on it so long that his limbs grew cramped and stagnated, and he lost all sense of nerve and pulse whilst the sun sank down out of sight behind the mountain afar off in the west.

The sound of voices laughing and talking and singing came to his ear as the reapers approached from the fields. Then he arose slowly, for his knees were stiff and bruised by the bricks on which he had so long knelt.

He took the volume in his hand, and crossed the kitchen, and met the peasants at the threshold.

"My friend! my friend!" he said to the blacksmith. "Here is a treasure I have found for you in that which you thought was a mere heap of rubbish. This volume is worth its weight in gold, if it be truly that which I think. Tomorrow we will go together into the city and have it fully appraised."

Iorio drew near with startled round eyes, alight with joy and covetousness, and the women with him pressed close also in excitement and wonder, expecting to see some vessels of gold and silver or some jewelled pyx or cross.

"An old book! a leather book!" said the smith's wife with derision and disappointment. 'You are joking, Ser Checchi! You are so fond of books that your head gets turned about them. Any rubbish bewitches you."

"You mistake," said Ser Checchi almost harshly, for his temptation to say otherwise was almost greater than his strength. "Take my word on a matter of which you are yourself utterly ignorant. This book is so old, and of such a nature, that it is extremely valuable. Keep it carefully all the night, and tomorrow I will take you to those in the town who will confirm what I say. You will learn from them precisely its worth. Only, good man," he added, as he clasped the volume in both hands and gazed at it with swimming, reverent eyes, "if that value be what I can pay you, you will let me become the purchaser of it at its due price, will you not?"

The smith, brawny, bare-legged, bare-armed, sunburnt till he was almost black, stared sheepishly at the volume, which to him looked worth no more than, nay, not half as much as, a clod of good brown earth. The other men, with the women and children, were all gaping with wide-open mouths, and nudging one another, and whispering that it was commonly said that the good Ser Checchi was in his dotage on certain matters.

"You will find what I say is true," said the old man abruptly; "and—and—you will give me the preference over other buyers, if the price come within my means?"

"About what might be the price?" asked Iorio in a shamefaced, awed tone, the avarice of the Tuscan peasant beginning to stir in him at the idea of a possible gain.

"That I would rather not say, since I intend to be, if possible, a buyer," replied Ser Checchi a little austerely, for what he had done had cost him a sharp effort, and he suffered at the idea of this precious treasure-trove going away from his own hands, even for this one short summer night.

"Keep it as the apple of your eye," he said to the smith, and reluctantly relinquished it to the dirty rough hand outstretched to take it.

"Lord! It's been in that chest, I will be bound, for hundreds and hundreds of years," said the smith, staring confusedly down on this dingy, mouse-nibbled, leathern folio, of which such wonders were told him.

"I will meet you at the foot of the hill at daybreak," said Ser Checchi, hastily averting his eyes from the sight of the volume in those ignorant and impious hands.

Then he turned his back on them and went down the steep grass path under the olive boughs, through the sheaves of wheat.

"Lead us not into temptation," he thought. "Who has not need to say that?"

All the night he could not sleep for the memory of the manuscript confided to the stupid care of a peasant ignorant and contemptuous of its value, and it made him restless and ashamed to feel how nearly, how closely, the temptation to secrecy had assailed him.

"We are wretched creatures, and can find fair sophisms to cover all our evil-doing," he thought sadly as he lay wide awake looking at the clouds sweeping slowly past his moonlit casement, and hearing the prolonged and harmonious call of the owl through the shadows.

In the morning he kept his word, and went down with the blacksmith into the city, Iorio wholly incredulous, but carrying with him, wrapped in a bit of cotton stuff which his wife had given him, the dingy volume. . . .

After long and careful examination the book was pronounced by those most competent to judge on such matters to be undoubtedly one of the very earliest copies of the great poem extant, worth many thousand francs in private sale, likely to be sold for its weight in gold in an auction room. . . .

"Iorio," said Ser Checchi at that moment, "you see what I said is true. You have heard from sound judges the value of your volume. Now, what will you do with it? Will you offer it to the State, or will you let me have it, or will you wait your chance to meet with some great fancier and collector of these things?"

He spoke quietly, but his hands shook as they had done when he had first touched the precious manuscript, and his eyes dwelt longingly on it where it lay wrapped in the piece of flowered cotton.

"Why, Ser Checchi, sure the volume is half yours already, for you found it," began Iorio, who was a simple and amiable man, but he was checked suddenly by his wife, who said quickly:

"Of course, sir, we would sooner sell it to you than to any mortal creature, so crazy fond of these things as you are, and no offense meant; but we are very poor people, as your honor knows, and with nine children and times so bad and taxes what they are, we cannot follow just the first wish of our hearts, sir, and the book these gentlemen seem to say is worth ten times its weight in gold and more."

"Nay, nay—not so much as that," murmured Iorio.

Ser Checchi was very pale. He saw that the folio was slipping from his hands. His staunch rectitude forced him to admit the truth of what the woman had said.

"You may realize a fancy price by it, certainly," he answered; "but to make one of those sensational prices you must wait the propitious season, and find the willing purchaser. If you would like to sell it to me for the small sum which the public libraries here would give you, I will buy it at that. If you prefer to take your chance, you must wait till you find your rich amateur. But amateurs do not come up in your hills. You will have to trust to some dealer to find you one, and you may trust unwisely."

Iorio opened his mouth to speak, but his wife spoke before him.

"Quite so, sir, we can see that," she said, taking up the volume in its flowered wrapper. "But a waiting race is always a safe race to ride. We will wait about this rare book. It lay long years enough in the old walnut chest, and it can go back there, and no harm done. I will clean up the red stones on it a bit, and we will ponder well what is best to be done. I saw Vestuccio just now, and he spoke of our sending it to Paris. But there's time enough for Paris, say I."

"You have shown it to Vestuccio?" asked Ser Checchi, with anxious lines on his brow, his eyes resting longingly on the treasure where it lay in the woman's stout arms.

"He had heard of it somehow already," replied the smith with some confusion, "and asked to be allowed to look at it. 'Ser Checchi would give you a barrowload of gold plate for it,' says he; but you know, sir, he always has a merry way. One never knows if he be in joke or in earnest."

"I have no gold plate to give, nor silver," said Ser Checchi sadly. "Truly, to those who honor the things of the spirit the volume were worth more than many tons' weight of either."

He murmured the last words rather to himself than to the man and woman. His heart was heavy. He had dealt by them with all candor, loyalty, and honor. He had hoped that they would show some sensibility of what he had done. He offered the fair library price; it seemed to him hard that they would not give it him for that, when but for him they would never have known that it was theirs at all.

"Good-day," he said to them with a swelling heart, and turned away. He was proud, and he was, like all sensitive people, quickly rebuffed.

Their colloquy had taken place in the piazza of San Lorenzo, in front of the warehouse where there are sold terra-cotta images, and flowerpots, and lemon-vases. The cart waited for the smith and his wife, with the patient horse in the dusty shafts dropping his nose over his bag of chaff and shaking his worsted tassels. Ser Checchi went on toward the Canto di'Nelli with slow steps and head hung down. He longed inexpressibly for the Dante, with that love of the bibliophile which has in it all the tenderness of a lover, all the eagerness of a child, all the devotion of a slave, all the hunger of a miser. He had found it, he had aroused it from its slumber beneath the dust of centuries, and restored it to the light of earth, and yet he could have no share in it . . . But he felt, what honest men feel sadly, often, that honesty costs very dear.

"It's cruel to take it from him, when he loves the senseless old parcel so, God knows why," whispered Iorio, with an uneasy sense that there must be something uncanny in the volume of which he knew nothing . . . He was a good-hearted man, though his means were small and his cupidity was excited by the idea of these vast sums circling in the air above this strange, darksome old volume. He overtook Ser Checchi with a few quick strides. . . .

"Ser Checchi," he whispered, "if it be really that your heart is set on this book, why, it would be a shame that you should not have it, if you will pay the price the dealers here would give. You pay that, sir, and you shall have it. No, do not say any more now . . . I would give it to you, sir," he added, "give it you and right welcome, for nothing; but a man with a wife and children is always a man bound; he cannot help himself. . . ."

Then and Now

W. Somerset Maugham

The sun was shining from a blue sky, there was still snow in the fields, but the road was crisp under the horses' hooves and Machiavelli, well wrapped up, was pleasantly exhilarated by the activity of invention. He felt strangely exalted. There was in his mind as yet no more than a theme; the facts were too tame for his purpose, and he was aware that he needed to think of a comic stratagem that would give him a coherent plot on which he could string his scenes. What he was looking for was a fantastic idea that would make an audience laugh and not only lead naturally to the resolution of his intrigue, but allow him to show the simplicity of Aurelia, the foolishness of Bartolomeo, the rascality of Piero, the wantonness of Monna Caterina and the knavery of Fra Timoteo. For the monk was to be an important character. In imagination Machiavelli rubbed his hands as he thought how he would show him in his true colors, with his avarice, his lack of scruple, his cunning and his hypocrisy. He would give false names to all of them, but he would leave Fra Timoteo his own so that all should know what a false and wicked man he was.

But he remained at a loss for the idea that should set his puppets in motion. It must be unexpected, outrageous even, for it was a comedy that he proposed to write, and so funny that people would gasp with astonishment and then burst into a roar of laughter. He knew his Plautus and his Terence well and he surveyed them in his memory to see whether there was not in their plays some ingenious fancy that would serve his purpose. He could think of nothing. And what made it more difficult to apply his mind to the problem was that his thoughts willy-nilly presented odd scenes to him here and there, amusing bits of dialogue and ridiculous situations. The time passed so quickly that he was surprised when they arrived at the place where they had decided to spend the night.

"To hell with love," he muttered as he got off his horse. "What is love beside art!"

The place was called Castiglione Aretino and there was an inn which at all events looked no worse than any of those he had slept at since leaving home. What with the exercise in the open air and his fancy running wild he had developed a healthy appetite, and the first thing he did on entering was to order his supper. Then he washed his feet, which, being a cleanly man, he liked to do every four or five days, and having dried them he wrote a short letter to the Signory which he sent off at once by a courier. The inn was full, but the innkeeper told him there would be room for him in the large bed he and his wife slept in. Machiavelli gave her a glance and said that if they could put a couple of sheepskins on the kitchen floor he would rest comfortably enough. Then he sat down to a great dish of macaroni.

"What is love in comparison with art?" he repeated. "Love is transitory, but art is eternal. Love is merely Nature's device to induce us to bring into this vile world creatures who from the day of their birth to the day of their death will be exposed to hunger and thirst, sickness and sorrow, envy, hatred and malice. This macaroni is better-cooked than I could have expected and the sauce is rich and succulent. Chicken livers and giblets. The creation of man was not even a tragic mistake, it was a grotesque mischance. What is its justification? Art, I suppose. Lucretius, Horace, Catullus, Dante and Petrarch. And perhaps they would never have been driven to write their divine works if their lives had not been full of tribulation, for there is no question that if I had gone to bed with Aurelia I should never have had the idea of writing a play. So when you come to look at it, it's all turned out for the best. I lost a trinket and picked up a jewel fit for a king's crown."

The good meal and these reflections restored Machiavelli to his usual amiability. He played a game of cards with a travelling friar who was on his way from one monastery to another and lost a trifle to him with good grace. Then, settling himself down on his sheepskins, he quickly fell asleep and slept without a break till dawn.

The sun had only just risen when he set out again, and it looked as though it were going to be a fine day. He was in high spirits. It was good to think that in a few hours he would be once more in his own house; he hoped Marietta would be too glad to see him to reproach him for his neglect of her, Biagio would come round after supper, dear kind Biagio, and tomorrow he would see Piero Soderini and the gentlemen of the Signory. Then he would go and see his friends. Oh, what a joy it would be to be back in Florence, to have the Chancery to go to every day and to walk those streets he had known since childhood, knowing by name, if not to speak to, almost everyone he passed!

"Welcome back, Messere," from one and "Well, well, Niccolo, where have you sprung from?" from another. "I suppose you've come back with your pockets bulging with money," from a third, and "When is the happy event to be?" from a friend of his mother's.

Home. Florence. Home. . . .

How pretty the Tuscan landscape was! In another month the almond trees would be in flower.

He began once more to think of the play that was simmering in his head. It made him feel happy and young and as lightheaded as though he had drunk wine on an empty stomach. He repeated to himself the cynical speeches he would put in the mouth of Fra Timoteo. Suddenly he pulled his horse up. The servants came up with him to see if there was anything he wanted and to their surprise saw that he was shaking with silent laughter. He saw the look on their faces and laughed all the more, then without a word clapped his spurs to the horse's flanks and galloped hell for leather down the road till the poor brute, unaccustomed to such exuberance, slackened down to its usual steady amble. The idea had come to him, the idea he had racked his brains to invent, and it had come on a sudden, he could not tell how or why or whence, and it was the very idea he wanted, ribald, extravagant and comic. It was almost a miracle. Everyone knew that credulous women bought the mandrake root to promote conception; it was a common superstition and many were the indecent stories told about its use. Now he would persuade Bartolomeo—to whom by then he had given the name of Messer Nicia—that his wife would conceive if she drank a potion made from it, but that the first man who had connection with her after she had done so would die. How to persuade him of that? It was easy. He, Callimaco, would disguise himself as a doctor who had studied in Paris and prescribe the treatment. It was obvious that Messer Nicia would hesitate to give his life to become a father and so a stranger must be found to take his place for one night. This stranger, under another disguise, would of course be Callimaco, that is to say Machiavelli.

Now that he had a plot the scenes succeeded one another with inevitability. They fell into place like the pieces of a puzzle. It was as though the play were writing itself and he, Machiavelli, were no more than an amanuensis. If he had been excited before, when the notion of making a play out of his misadventure had first come to him, he was doubly excited now that it all lay clear before his mind's eye like a garden laid out with terraces and fountains, shady walks and pleasant arbors. When they stopped to dine, absorbed in his characters he paid no attention to what he ate; and when they started off again he was unconscious of the miles they traveled; they came nearer to Florence and the countryside was as familiar to him, and as dear, as the street he was born in, but he had no eyes for it; the sun, long past its meridian, was making its westering way to where met earth and sky, but he gave no heed to it. He was in a world of make-believe that rendered the real world illusory. He felt more than himself. He *was* Callimaco, young, handsome, rich, audacious, gay; and the passion with which he burnt for Lucrezia was of a tempestuous violence that made the desire Machiavelli had had for Aurelia a pale slight thing. That was but a shadow, this was the substance. Machiavelli, had he only known it, was enjoying the supreme happiness that man is capable of experiencing, the activity of creation.

"Look, Messere," cried his servant Antonio, riding up to come abreast of him. "Florence."

Machiavelli looked. In the distance against the winter sky, paling now with the decline of day, he saw the dome, the proud dome that Bramante had built. He pulled up. There it was, the city he loved more than his soul. . . . Florence, the city of flowers, with its campanile and its baptistery, its churches and palaces, its gardens, its tortuous streets, the old bridge he crossed every day to go to the Palazzo, and his home, his brother Toto, Marietta, his friends, the city of which he knew every stone, the city with its great history, his birthplace and the birthplace of his ancestors, Florence, the city of Dante and Boccaccio, the city that had fought for its freedom through the centuries, Florence the well beloved, the city of flowers. . . .

Spring had come early that year and the countryside, with the trees bursting into leaf, the wild flowers, the fresh green of the grass, the rich growth of wheat, was a joy to the eye. To Machiavelli the Tuscan scene had a friendly, intimate delight that appealed to the mind rather than to the senses. It had none of the sublimity of the Alps, nor the grandeur of the sea; it was a patch of the earth's surface, classical without severity, lightly gay and elegant, for men to live on who loved wit and intelligent argument, pretty women and good cheer. It reminded you not of the splendid solemn music of Dante, but rather of the light-hearted strains of Lorenzo de' Medici.

One March morning Machiavelli, up with the sun, went to a grove on his small estate that he was having cut. He lingered there, looking over the previous day's work, and talked with the woodsmen; then he went to a spring and sat himself down on the bank with a book he had brought in his pocket. It was an Ovid, and with a smile on his thin lips he read the amiable and lively verses in which the poet described his amours and, remembering his own, thought of them for a while with pleasure.

"How much better it is to sin and repent," he murmured, "than to repent for not having sinned!"

Biagio looked suspiciously at a pile of manuscript on his friend's writing table.

"What have you there?"

Machiavelli gave him a disarming smile.

"I had nothing much to do here and I thought I'd pass the time by writing a comedy. Would you like me to read it to you?"

"A comedy?" said Biagio doubtfully. "I presume it has political implications."

"Not at all. Its only purpose is to amuse."

"Oh, Niccolo, when will you take yourself seriously? You'll have the critics down on you like a thousand bricks."

"I don't know why; no one can suppose that Apuleius wrote his *Golden Ass* or Petronius the *Satyricon* with any other object than to entertain."

"But they're classics. That makes all the difference."

"You mean that works of entertainment, like loose women, become respectable with age. I've often wondered why it is that the critics can only see a joke when the fun has long since seeped out of it. They've never discovered that humor depends upon actuality."

"You used to say that not brevity, but pornography was the soul of wit. You've changed your mind?"

"Not at all. For what can be more actual than pornography? Believe me, my good Biagio, when men cease to find it so they will have lost all interest in reproducing their kind and that will be the end of the Creator's most unfortunate experiment."

"Read your play, Niccolo. You know I don't like to hear you say things like that."

With a smile Machiavelli took his manuscript and began to read.

"A Street in Florence. Enter Callimacao and Ligurio. . . ."

A Room with a View

E. M. Forster

It was pleasant to wake up in Florence, to open the eyes upon a bright bare room, with a floor of red tiles which look clean though they are not; with a painted ceiling whereon pink griffins and blue *amorini* sport in a forest of yellow violins and bassoons. It was pleasant, too, to fling wide the windows, pinching the fingers in unfamiliar fastenings, to lean out into sunshine with beautiful hills and trees and marble churches opposite, and close below, the Arno, gurgling against the embankment of the road.

Over the river men were at work with spades and sieves on the sandy foreshore, and on the river was a boat, also diligently employed for some mysterious end. An electric tram came rushing underneath the window. No one was inside it, except one tourist; but its platforms were overflowing with Italians, who preferred to stand. Children tried to hang on behind, and the conductor, with no malice, spat in their faces to make them let go. Then soldiers appeared—good-looking, undersized men—wearing each a knapsack covered with mangy fur, and a great-coat which had been cut for some larger soldier. Beside them walked officers, looking foolish and fierce, and before them went little boys, turning somersaults in time with the band. The tramcar became entangled in their ranks, and moved on painfully, like a caterpillar in a swarm of ants. One of the little boys fell down, and some white bullocks came out of an archway. Indeed, if it had not been for the good advice of an old man who was selling button-hooks, the road might never have got clear.

Over such trivialities as these many a valuable hour may slip away, and the traveler who has gone to Italy to study the tactile values of

Giotto, or the corruption of the Papacy, may return remembering nothing but the blue sky and the men and women who live under it. So it was as well that Miss Bartlett should tap and come in, and having commented on Lucy's leaving the door unlocked, and on her leaning out of the window before she was fully dressed, should urge her to hasten herself, or the best of the day would be gone. By the time Lucy was ready her cousin had done her breakfast, and was listening to the clever lady among the crumbs.

A conversation then ensued, on not unfamiliar lines. Miss Bartlett was, after all, a wee bit tired, and thought they had better spend the morning settling in; unless Lucy would at all like to go out? Lucy would rather like to go out as it was her first day in Florence, but, of course, she could go alone. Miss Bartlett could not allow this. Of course she would accompany Lucy everywhere. . . .

At this point the clever lady broke in.

"Being English, Miss Honeychurch will be perfectly safe. Italians understand. A dear friend of mine, Contessa Baroncelli, has two daughters, and when she cannot send a maid to school with them, she lets them go in sailor-hats instead. Every one takes them for English, you see, especially if their hair is strained tightly behind."

Miss Bartlett was unconvinced by the safety of Contessa Baroncelli's daughters. She was determined to take Lucy herself, her head not being so very bad. The clever lady then said that she was going to spend a long morning in Santa Croce, and if Lucy would come too, she would be delighted.

"I will take you by a dear dirty back way, Miss Honeychurch, and if you bring me luck, we shall have an adventure."

Lucy said that this was most kind, and at once opened the Baedeker, to see where Santa Croce was.

"Tut, tut! Miss Lucy! I hope we shall soon emancipate you from Baedeker. He does but touch the surface of things. As to the true Italy—he does not even dream of it. The true Italy is only to be found by patient observation."

This sounded very interesting, and Lucy hurried over her breakfast, and started with her new friend in high spirits. Italy was coming at last. . . .

Miss Lavish—for that was the clever lady's name—turned to the right along the sunny Lungarno. How delightfully warm! But a wind down the side streets cut like a knife, didn't it? Ponte alle Grazie—particularly interesting, mentioned by Dante. San Miniato—beautiful as well as interesting; the crucifix that kissed a murderer—Miss Honeychurch would remember the story. The men on the river were fishing. (Untrue; but then, so is most information.) Then Miss Lavish darted under the archway of the white bullocks, and she stopped, and she cried:

"A smell! a true Florentine smell! Every city, let me teach you, has its own smell."

"Is it a very nice smell?" said Lucy, who had inherited from her mother a distaste to dirt.

"One doesn't come to Italy for niceness," was the retort; "one comes for life. *Buon giorno! Buon giorno!*" bowing right and left. "Look at that adorable wine-cart! How the driver stares at us, dear, simple soul!"

So Miss Lavish proceeded through the streets of the city of Florence, short, fidgety, and playful as a kitten, though without a kitten's grace. It was a treat for the girl to be with anyone so clever and so cheerful; and a blue military cloak, such as an Italian officer wears, only increased the sense of festivity.

"*Buon giorno!* Take the word of an old woman, Miss Lucy: you will never repent of a little civility to your inferiors. *That* is the true democracy. Though I am a real Radical as well. There, now you're shocked."

"Indeed, I'm not!" exclaimed Lucy. "We are Radicals, too, out and out. My father always voted for Mr. Gladstone, until he was so dreadful about Ireland "

"I see, I see. And now you have gone over to the enemy."

"Oh, please—! If my father was alive, I am sure he would vote Radical again now that Ireland is all right. And as it is, the glass over the front door was broken last election, and Freddy is sure it was the Tories; but mother says nonsense, a tramp."

"Shameful! A manufacturing district, I suppose?"

"No—in the Surrey hills. About five miles from Dorking, looking over the Weald."

Miss Lavish seemed interested, and slackened her trot.

"What a delightful part; I know it so well. It is full of the very nicest people. Do you know Sir Harry Otway—a Radical if ever there was?"

"Very well indeed."

"And old Mrs. Butterworth the philanthropist?"

"Why, she rents a field of us! How funny!"

Miss Lavish looked at the narrow ribbon of sky, and murmured:

"Oh, you have property in Surrey?"

"Hardly any," said Lucy, fearful of being thought a snob. "Only thirty acres—just the garden, all downhill, and some fields."

Miss Lavish was not disgusted, and said it was just the size of her aunt's Suffolk estate. Italy receded. They tried to remember the last name of Lady Louisa someone, who had taken a house near Summer Street the other year, but she had not liked it, which was odd of her. And just as Miss Lavish had got the name, she broke off and exclaimed:

"Bless us! Bless us and save us! We've lost the way."

Certainly they had seemed a long time in reaching Santa Croce, the tower of which had been plainly visible from the landing window. But Miss Lavish had said so much about knowing her Florence by heart, that Lucy had followed her with no misgivings.

"Lost! lost! My dear Miss Lucy, during our political diatribes we have taken a wrong turning. How those horrid Conservatives would jeer at us! What are we to do? Two lone females in an unknown town. Now, this is what *I* call an adventure."

Lucy, who wanted to see Santa Croce, suggested, as a possible solution, that they should ask the way there.

"Oh, but that is the word of a craven! And no, you are not, not, *not* to look at your Baedeker. Give it to me; I shan't let you carry it. We will simply drift."

Accordingly they drifted through a series of those gray-brown streets, neither commodious nor picturesque, in which the eastern quarter of the city abounds. Lucy soon lost interest in the discontent of Lady Louisa, and became discontented herself. For one ravishing moment Italy appeared. She stood in the Square of the Annunziata and saw in the living terra cotta those divine babies whom no cheap reproduction can ever stale. There they stood, with their shining limbs bursting from the garments of charity, and their strong white arms extended against circlets of heaven. Lucy thought she had never seen anything more beautiful; but Miss Lavish, with a shriek of dismay, dragged her forward, declaring that they were out of their path now by at least a mile.

The hour was approaching at which the continental breakfast begins, or rather ceases, to tell, and the ladies bought some hot chestnut paste out of a little shop, because it looked so typical. It tasted partly of the paper in which it was wrapped, partly of hair oil, partly of the great unknown. But it gave them strength to drift into another Piazza, large and dusty, on the farther side of which rose a black-and-white facade of surpassing ugliness. Miss Lavish spoke to it dramatically. It was Santa Croce. The adventure was over.

"Stop a minute; let those two people go on, or I shall have to speak to them. I do detest conventional intercourse. Nasty! they are going into the church, too. Oh, che Britisher abroad!"

"We sat opposite them at dinner last night. They have given us their rooms. They were so very kind."

"Look at their figures!" laughed Miss Lavish. "They walk through my Italy like a pair of cows. It's very naughty of me, but I would like to set an examination paper at Dover, and turn back every tourist who couldn't pass it."

"What would you ask us?"

Miss Lavish laid her hand pleasantly on Lucy's arm, as if to suggest that she, at all events, would get full marks. In this exalted mood they reached the steps of the great church, and were about to enter it when Miss Lavish stopped, squeaked, flung up her arms, and cried:

"There goes my local-color box! I must have a word with him!"

And in a moment she was away over the Piazza, her military cloak flapping in the wind; nor did she slacken speed till she caught up an old man with white whiskers, and nipped him playfully upon the arm.

Lucy waited for nearly ten minutes. Then she began to get tired. The beggars worried her, the dust blew in her eyes, and she remembered that a young girl ought not to loiter in public places. She descended slowly into the Piazza with the intention of rejoining Miss Lavish, who was really almost too original. But at the moment Miss Lavish and her local-color box moved also, and disappeared down a side street, both gesticulating largely.

Tears of indignation came to Lucy's eyes—partly because she had taken her Baedeker. How could she find her way home? How could she find her way about in Santa Croce? Her first morning was ruined, and she might never be in Florence again. A few minutes ago she had been all high spirits, talking as a woman of culture, and half persuading herself that she was full of originality. Now she entered the church depressed and humiliated, not even able to remember whether it was built by the Franciscans or the Dominicans.

Of course, it must be a wonderful building. But how like a barn! And how very cold! Of course, it contained frescoes by Giotto, in the presence of whose tactile values she was capable of feeling what was proper. But who was to tell her which they were? She walked about disdainfully, unwilling to be enthusiastic over monuments of uncertain authorship or date. There was no one even to tell her which, of all the sepulchral slabs that paved the nave and transepts, was the one that was really beautiful, the one that had been most praised by Mr. Ruskin.

Then the pernicious charm of Italy worked on her, and, instead of acquiring information, she began to be happy. She puzzled out the Italian notices—the notices that forbade people to introduce dogs into the church—the notice that prayed people, in the interest of health and out of respect to the sacred edifice in which they found themselves, not to spit. She watched the tourists; their noses were as red as their Baedekers, so cold was Santa Croce. She beheld the horrible fate that overtook three Papists—two he-babies and a she-baby—who began their career by sousing each other with the Holy Water, and then proceeded to the Machiavelli memorial, dripping but hallowed. Advancing toward it very slowly and from immense distances, they touched the stone with their fingers, with their handkerchiefs, with their heads, and then retreated. What could this mean? They did it again and again. Then Lucy realized that they had mistaken Machiavelli for some saint, hoping to acquire virtue. Punishment followed quickly. The smallest he-baby stumbled over one of the sepulchral slabs so much admired by Mr. Ruskin, and entangled his feet in the features of a recumbent bishop. Protestant as she was, Lucy darted forward. She was too late. He fell heavily upon the prelate's upturned toes.

Aaron's Rod

D. H. Lawrence

In the morning it was still November, and the dawn came slowly. And through the open window was the sound of the river's rushing. But the traffic started before dawn, with a bang and a rattle of carts, and a bang and jingle of tram-cars over the not-distant bridge. Oh! noisy Florence! At half-past seven Aaron rang for his coffee: and got it at a few minutes past eight. The signorina had told him to take his coffee in bed.

Rain was still falling. But towards nine o'clock it lifted, and he decided to go out. A wet, wet world. Carriages going by, with huge wet shiny umbrellas, black and with many points, erected to cover the driver and the tail of the horse and the box-seat. The hood of the carriage covered the fare. Clatter-clatter through the rain. Peasants with long wagons and slow oxen, and pale-green huge umbrellas erected for the driver to walk beneath. Men tripping along in cloaks, shawls, umbrellas, anything, quite unconcerned. A man loading gravel in the riverbed, in spite of the wet. And innumerable bells ringing: but innumerable bells. The great soft trembling of the cathedral bell felt in all the air.

Anyhow it was a new world. Aaron went along close to the tall thick houses, following his nose. And suddenly he caught sight of the long slim neck of the Palazzo Vecchio up above in the air. And in another minute he was passing between massive buildings, out into the Piazza della Signoria. There he stood still and looked round him in real surprise, and real joy. The flat, empty square with its stone paving was all wet. The great buildings rose dark. The dark sheer front of the Palazzo Vecchio went up like a cliff, to the battlements, and the slim tower soared dark and hawk-like, crested, high above. And at the foot of the cliff stood the great naked David, white and stripped in the wet, white against the dark, warm-dark cliff of the building—and near, the heavy naked men of Bandinelli.

The first thing he had seen, as he turned into the square, was the back of one of these Bandinelli statues: a great naked man of marble, with a heavy back and strong naked flanks over which the water was trickling. And then to come immediately upon the David, so much whiter, glistening skin-white in the wet, standing a little forward, and shrinking.

He may be ugly, too naturalistic, too big, and anything else you like. But the David in the Piazza della Signoria, there under the dark great Palace, in the position Michelangelo chose for him, there, standing forward stripped and exposed and eternally half-shrinking half-wishing to expose himself, he is the genius of Florence. The adolescent, the white, self-conscious, physical adolescent: enormous in keeping with the stark, grim enormous palace, which is dark and bare as he is white and bare. And behind, the big, lumpy Bandinelli men are in keeping too. They may be ugly—but they are there in their place, and they have their own lumpy reality. And this morning in the rain, standing unbroken, with the water trickling down their flanks and along the inner side of their great thighs, they were real enough, representing the undaunted physical nature of the heavier Florentines.

Aaron looked and looked at the three great naked men. David so much white, and standing forward, self-conscious: there at the great splendid front of the Palazzo Vecchio: and at the fountain splashing water upon its wet, wet figures; and the distant equestrian statue; and the stoneflagged space of the grim square. And he felt that here he was in one of the world's living centers, here, in the Piazza della Signoria. The sense of having arrived—of having reached a perfect center of the human world: this he had.

And so, satisfied, he turned round to look at the bronze Perseus which rose just above him. Benvenuto Cellini's dark hero looked female, with his plump hips and his waist, female and rather insignificant: graceful, and rather vulgar. The clownish Bandinellis were somehow more to the point. Then all the statuary in the Loggia! But that is a mistake. It looks too much like the yard of a monumental mason.

The great, naked men in the rain, under the dark-gray November sky, in the dark, strong, inviolable square! The wonderful hawk-head of the old palace! The physical, self-conscious adolescent, Michel-angelo's David, shrinking and exposing himself, with his white, slack limbs! Florence, passionate, fearless Florence had spoken herself out. Aaron was fascinated by the Piazza della Signoria. He never went into the town, nor returned from it to his lodging, without contriving to pass through the square. And he never passed through it without satisfaction. . . .

Here men had been at their intensest, most naked pitch, here, at the end of the old world and the beginning of the new. Since then, always rather pulling and apologetic.

Aaron felt a new self, a new life-urge rising inside himself. Florence seemed to start a new man in him. It was a town of men. On Friday morning, so early, he heard the traffic. Early, he watched the rather low, two-wheeled traps of the peasants spanking recklessly over the bridge, coming in to town. And then, when he went out, he found the Piazza della Signoria packed with men: but all, all men. And all farmers, land-owners and land-workers. The curious, fine-nosed Tuscan farmers, with their half-sardonic, amber-colored eyes. Their curious individuality, their clothes worn so easy and reckless, their hats with the personal twist. Their curious full oval cheeks, their tendency to be too fat, to have a belly and heavy limbs. Their close-sitting dark hair. And above all, their sharp, almost acrid, mocking expression, the silent curl of the nose, the eternal challenge, the rock-bottom unbelief, and the subtle fearlessness. The dangerous, subtle, never-dying fearlessness, and the acrid unbelief. But men! Men! A town of men, in spite of everything. The one manly quality, undying, acrid fearlessness. The eternal challenge of the unquenched human soul. Perhaps too acrid and challenging today, when there is nothing left to challenge. But men—who existed without apology and without justification. Men who would neither justify themselves nor apologize for themselves. Just men. The rarest thing left in our sweet Christendom.

Altogether Aaron was pleased with himself, for being in Florence. Those were the early days after the war, when as yet very few foreigners had returned, and the place had a native somberness and intensity. . . .

Aaron and Lilly sat on Argyle's little loggia, high up under the eaves of the house, a sort of long attic-terrace just under the roof, where no one would have suspected it. It was level with the gray conical roof of the Baptistery. Here sat Aaron and Lilly in the afternoon, in the last of the lovely autumn sunshine. Below, the square was already cold in shadow, the pink and white and green Baptistery rose lantern-shaped as from some seashore, cool, cold and wan now the sun was gone. Black figures, innumerable black figures, curious because they were all on end, up on end—Aaron could not say why he expected them to be horizontal—like fishes that swim on their tails, wiggled endlessly across the piazza, little carriages on natural all-fours rattled tinnily across, the yellow little tram-cars like dogs slipped round the corner. The balcony was so high up, that the sound was ineffectual. The upper space, above the houses, was nearer than the undercurrents of the noisy town. Sunlight, lovely full sunlight, lingered warm and still on the balcony. It caught the facade of the cathedral sideways, like the tips of a flower, and sideways lit up the stem of Giotto's tower, like a lily stem, or a long lovely pale pink and white and green pistil of the lily of the cathedral. Florence, the flowery town. Firenze—Fiorenze—the flowery town: the red lilies. The Fiorentini, the flower-souled. Flowers with good roots in the mud and muck, as should be: and fearless blossoms in air, like the cathedral and the tower and the David.

"I love it," said Lilly. "I love this place. I love the cathedral and the tower. I love its pinkness and its paleness. The gothic souls find fault with it, and say it is gimcrack and tawdry and cheap. But I love it; it is delicate and rosy, and the dark stripes are as they should be, like the tigermarks on a pink lily. It's a lily, not a rose: a pinky white lily with dark tigery marks. And heavy too, in its own substance: earth-substance, risen from the earth into the air: and never forgetting the dark, black-fierce earth—I reckon here men for a moment were themselves, as a plant in flower is for the moment completely itself. Then it goes off. As Florence has gone off. No flowers now. But it *has* flowered. And I don't see why a race should be like an aloe tree, flower once and die. Why should it? Why not flower again? Why not?"

World So Wide

Sinclair Lewis

The railway station at Florence had a fine, flaring Mussolini touch, very spacious and inclined to marble and wood panels, but the piazza in front of it was of a suburban drabness, and the back of the church of S. Maria Novella was a mud-colored bareness, sullen with evening. He would not be staying here long! His taxi-driver was learning English, and was willing to make it a bilingual party, but as Hayden's Italian was limited to *bravo, spaghetti, zabaglione* and the notations on sheet music, this promising friendship did not get far, and he went to bed blankly at the Hotel Excelsior.

But in the bright morning of late autumn he looked from his hotel and began to fall in love with a city.

He saw the Arno, in full brown tide after recent mountain rains, with old palaces along it and cypress-waving hills beyond. On one side was the tower of Bellosguardo and a fragment of the old city wall, and on the other the marvel of the church of San Miniato, white striped with a dark green that seemed black from afar. Hayden saw a city of ancient reticences and modern energy, with old passageways, crooked and mysterious, arched over with stone that bore carven heraldic shields.

"I like this! Maybe I'll stay out the week."

There was then living in Florence a friend and classmate of Hayden's father: a retired American automobile-manufacturer, competent engineer and man of business, aged seventy-five or so, named Samuel Dodsworth. Hayden sent a letter up to him by hand at his Villa Canterbury on Torre del Gallo Hill, and the Dodsworth chauffeur brought down a note inviting Hayden to cocktails that afternoon. . . .

Unlike most Italian villas, which show to the passer-by only a plastered wall flush with the street and a small door that opens on the delights of garden and terrace within, the Dodsworth's Villa Canterbury, which had been built for Lord Chevanier in 1880, was set back from the street, with a lawn and an ilex alley. It was a timbered manor house, half-English and half-Yonkers. The interior was chintz and willow plate and Jacobean oak, and the chief change from his Lordship's day was that the Paris *Herald Tribune* had ousted the London *Times*, and the *Yale Alumni Magazine* the *Fortnightly Review*.

Not even yet was Hayden up to an eight-thirty-dinner schedule and, arriving at six, he was half an hour early for cocktails, which gave him a chance to study his hosts. Dodsworth was a tall, portly, gray-moustached man, given to quiet listening, and his wife, to whom he referred as Edith, looked somewhat Italian, though Hayden thought that she might have been born in Canada or Massachusetts.

Dodsworth, in his arm-chair, was a largeness and a solidity; he looked as though he would not willingly move from it. He asked of Hayden, . . . "How long you staying in Italy?"

"I can't tell yet. I had a motor smash, and I'm taking a few months off. I may stay in Florence for—for a fortnight."

"Don't stay in Italy too long—or anywhere else abroad. It gets you. Since I was fool enough to sell the Revelation Motor Company, Edith and I have drifted through India and China and Austria and God knows where all, and this time, we've been back in Italy for three years—course, Edith's been coming here off and on for many years. Well, we tried to go back and live in the States, in Zenith, but we're kind of spoiled for it. Everybody is so damn busy making money there that you can't find anybody to talk with, unless you're willing to pay for it by busting a gut playing golf. And I got to dislike servants that hate you and hate every part of their job except drawing their pay. I like having the girl here bring me my slippers without feeling so doggone humiliated that she rushes out and joins the Communist Party!

"And back home, this last time, I was bored listening to all the men I used to know talking about hunting and fishing and baseball and same old golf. Fishing! Hell, I used to skip down to Florida, one time, and enjoy yanking in a mean tarpon as much as anybody, but when you hear most of those old, gray-haired galoots, the way they talk about catching a vest-pocket black bass, you'd think the man was a ten-year-old brat that had just hooked his first crappie. Kind of immature, they struck me. . . .

"And then I like these hills in Tuscany and the monasteries and villas and the variety of it—get in your car and in an hour or so you're in San Gimignano, looking at those old towers. Starts your imagination working about the old wars and battles right there where you're standing. Or you're in Siena and have lunch out in that old square there and look at that big slender tower and wonder how the devil those old fellows managed to raise those enormous blocks of stone without any of our machinery.

"Afraid I'm not putting up any very good argument about chasing you back home, but I mean—that's what's so dangerous here; you do get to like it and hesitate to go back and face responsibilities, and that would be bad for a young fellow like you. Me—I never can learn this cursed Italian language; Edith has an awful time getting me to say *acqua fresca* when I want a glass of water. But I do like to have food that you can eat and wine that you can drink without paying four and a half bucks at a restaurant for a burnt steak and some fried spuds flavored with penicillin!" . . .

Guests were beginning to chatter in, but before the cocktails came, Mrs. Dodsworth led Hayden out on the terrace for the View which, by Florence custom, is advertised along with laundry equipment, garage, cost of upkeep and distance from Leland's Bar.

Although it was masked by the early darkness, Hayden was conscious of power in the aspect of Florence below them in its golden basket, between this hill range of Arcetri and, far across, the Fiesole Hill. Mrs. Dodsworth could point out the scarcely seen tower of the Bargello, Giotto's bell tower, the spire of Santa Croce, while, flaunting, soaring, even more whelming than by day in the floodlights which the mists turned to wreaths of floating rose, the tower of the Palazzo Vecchio dominated the world more than any bullying skyscraper of a hundred steel-strapped storeys.

As an architect, as a tongueless poet, Hayden was uplifted; as a lonely man on a voyage to find himself, he wondered if down there, in that pattern of sunken stars, he might not find a clue to his lost highway. He was in love, and if only with a city, he knew that he could still move to the magic of love for something.

And then he went in to say Yes, he thought an olive in his dry martini would be fine.

The guests were most of them from the Florentine Anglo-American Colony, which is united only in a firm avoidance of their beloved native lands. There were a few of the scholarly eccentrics for whom

Florence has been renowned ever since Dante, but the rest were of the active militia of card players. . . .

. . . Hayden had been looking past the others at a young woman of twenty-seven or -eight who seemed as out of place as Hayden himself. He thought of ivory as he noted the curious Mediterranean pale-dark hue of her oval face, of her competent hands, which would be smooth to the touch: her cheeks and brows and hands smooth as a horn spoon, as a tortoise-shell box, as an ivory crucifix. Her black hair was parted above the oval ivory face; over her head was a gold-threaded ivory-colored scarf, and her dress was of pure cream-colored wool with no adornment except a broad belt of golden fabric. There was something Latin, something royal in her, something almost holy, free from human vulgarity and all desire except for the perfection of sainthood.

Hayden asked Mrs. Dodsworth, ''Is that girl talking to Mr. Friar an Italian? She could be a *principessa.*''

''No, she's a plain Miss, and she's an American, but she does speak Italian almost well enough for a native. Her name is Olivia Lomond— Dr. Lomond, I suppose it is. She's a professor, or assistant professor or something, in the history department at the State University of Winnemac, of which my Sam is a trustee. That's how we happen to know her, because I imagine she looks down on us bridge maniacs. She's doing research on some manuscript records in the Laurentian Library for a year or so. Would you like to meet her?''

He earnestly would.

Olivia Lomond, when he talked to her, was a little blank; civil enough but not interested. Yes, she was collating some Machiavelli and Guicciardini manuscripts with early official records of Florence; a dusty job, not very rewarding. Yes, she taught at Winnemac: Early European History, especially the Middle Ages and the Renaissance in Italy.

Hayden tried, ''That's a period that, just now, I'd like to know more than anything in the world, and I'm as ignorant of it as a Colorado sheep-herder. It must have so much more than just sword-and-roses romance.''

She nodded and she said nothing, but her expression said clearly enough, ''Yes, of course you would be ignorant of it; you, the American businessman, the tourist!''

He was piqued, and he boasted, ''Naturally, as an architect, I suppose I could draw from memory the floor plans of the Riccardi-Medici palace.''

"Oh! Oh, you're an architect? In the States?"

"Out West. Newlife. Do you know it?"

"I'm afraid not—afraid not." Nor did she seem very much to want to know it. She was merely paying a conversational rent on her cocktail. "Do you speak any Italian?"

"I'm afraid not—no." He was determined to be as lofty as this goddess whose ivory veins were filled with ice-cold ink.

"You should speak it."

"Why?"

"If you ask that, you answer me."

"It's not a very important commodity in Newlife. But then, you probably don't think much of Newlife."

"How could I? It just hasn't entered my philosophy of life. I have no doubt it's a very friendly community, with lovely shade trees—one of the most enterprising spots in Nebraska." . . .

Uninterestedly continuing her social duty, Dr. Lomond droned at Hayden, "Are you staying here for some days?"

Astounded by his own news, he heard himself asserting, "I may stay here for some years!"

"No! Really?"

He had aroused her—to at least as much attention as she would give to a donkey-cart in the street, and as she said "Really?" he had perceived that her voice was beautiful: melodious, rather grave, suitable to a woman all of ivory.

She sounded almost half-interested with, "Are you to have an official position here?"

"No. No job. I shall just be studying—go back to school in my senility. I want to master your blasted Italian speech and history." . . .

He had meant it—for that moment he had. He would set up shop as a scholar; he would be an Erasmus, a Grosseteste, an Albertus Magnus, if only to *show* this intellectual snob of a lady professor. . . .

He would *show* her, and in her show the whole wide world. . . .

He sat in what was to become his favorite room in Florence, the bar of the Hotel Excelsior with its dark mirroring wood and its two bartenders, Enrico and Raffaele, the men in town most worth cultivating, and he contentedly planned to stay in Florence for a week, a month, a season. He would pray for a Biblical miracle: to become again as a little child, and go back to school.

Next morning he again climbed the Torre del Gallo Hill, to have by clear light the view he had seen in twilight enchantment. Below him he saw the bronze-red majesty of the cathedral dome, and Giotto's tower—as ivory as Olivia Lomond. Fiesole, across the valley, was sharply defined on a hill silver-gray with olive trees. Florence is a thousand years less old than Rome, yet in its medieval reds and yellows and dark passageways it seems older, as in New England a moldering gingerbread mansion of 1875 seems more venerable than a severe white parsonage of 1675.

"I'll do it. I'll stay. I'll hunt for Michelozzos, not mallards!" said Hayden.

PART 5

EPILOGUE

SAN MINIATO

See, I have climbed the mountainside
Up to this holy house of God,
Where once that Angel-Painter trod
Who saw the heavens opened wide,

And throned upon the crescent moon
The Virginal white Queen of Grace,
Mary! could I but see thy face
Death could not come at all too soon.

O crowned by God with thorns and pain!
Mother of Christ! O mystic wife!
My heart is weary of this life
And oversad to sing again.

O crowned by God with love and flame!
O crowned by Christ the Holy One
O listen ere the searching sun
Show to the world my sin and shame.

Oscar Wilde

The Nazi Destruction
of Florence

British War Office Report

The Allied forces in Italy are provided with booklets containing the official list of buildings of every sort which, on account of their artistic or historic interest, are exempt from military use and have to be protected against avoidable damage. Here under the heading "Florence," we read "The whole city of Florence must rank as a work of art of the first importance." Such is the Allied Army's estimate of a city which the Germans chose to violate.

The great monuments, nearly all of which lie north of the river, escaped practically undamaged because, though the enemy held the northern bank against our advance, our troops deliberately refrained from firing upon them.

No damage of any significance," states the official report, "is attributable to Allied action." But to the historic town of Florence the damage was very heavy.

On the north bank the heart of the old city round the Ponte Vecchio, with all its associations, is gone. The Ponte Vecchio itself is not seriously damaged, but the old houses on the bridge have suffered severely from blast, and the greater part of the series of old houses on the south bank is totally destroyed. The destruction is of a thoroughness out of all proportion to the military results achieved. That the Germans should blow up all the other bridges is understandable, and they blew up all of them (though a good deal of sculpture from the Ponte S. Trinità has been recovered from the river by divers) but the Ponte Vecchio, with its narrow footway between the old shops, was of no military value to us, seeing that no lorry could use it, and there the systematic destruction of its approaches had no practical object. Yet it had been planned long in advance, as early in March, 1944, they had made (cynically enough) a complete photographic survey of the precise area which they subsequently mined and ruined.

On the south side of the Arno the whole of the Via De'Guicciardini, from the Pitti Palace to the river, has gone; along the river front the zone of destruction spreads eastwards along the Via De' Bardi up to the Piazza Santa Maria Soprarno, and westwards along the Borgo San Jacopo to the Via Dei Giudici; the whole of the famous view looking up the river to the Ponte Vecchio, with the medieval houses reflected in the water, is lost for ever.

Here were destroyed three of the old Florentine towers, and of one that survived, the Torre Dei Marsili, the Della Robbia terra-cotta decorations have been smashed. The Uffizi Gallery suffered much damage from blast and the corridor linking it with the Pitti Palace was badly wrecked throughout its length and near the Bardi arch more than two hundred yards of it, together with the sixteenth-century Bagno Dei Medici, were completely destroyed.

Twelve palaces were either completely destroyed or remain but as partial ruins of no value; amongst the old houses the Casa Machiavelli and the Casa Del Giambologna are the most famous that have perished; the Casa Del Torre De' Bardi collapsed and buried in its ruins the Columbaria Library, with all its manuscripts and incunabula. This was one of the most serious losses suffered by the city, but fortunately about half of the manuscripts and the greater part of the ancient library have been saved through the prompt action of the Allied Monuments, Fine Arts and Archives officers who organized the excavation of the site.

On the north side of the river more of the old towers have gone, including the Torre Degli Amidei, the most beautiful and best preserved of all the towers of Florence; the Torre Dei Barbadori was in so dangerous a state that it had to be demolished. The front part of the Palazzo Acciaioli, with its frescoed hall, collapsed; the Palazzo De Angelis was utterly destroyed; the thirteenth- and fifteenth-century Palazzo Di Parte Guelfa and the Palazzo Buondelmonte are both severely damaged. But the real loss is that of the old houses—the Piazza Del Pesce, right up to the thirteenth-century Church of S. Stefano (which itself has suffered), the Via Por S. Maria, the Loggia Del Mercato Nuovo; all have gone, and with them all the most characteristic remains of medieval Florence.

In contrast to this lamentable record of German ruthlessness is the relative immunity of the principal monuments of Florence, *i.e.*, of the area which the Germans held against Allied attack. Even S. Maria Novella, close as it is to the railway yards, which were the target of our bombing attacks, was not hit; apart from broken windows and a few loosened tiles no real damage is reported from any of the great churches, palaces (other than those mentioned above) or monuments that make up the wealth of the city. The libraries and the archives have not suffered, except the Biblioteca Della Columbaria, as reported above.

From the galleries of Florence all the more important pictures had been removed to deposits outside the limits of the city. The principal private collection in Florence was that of Mr. [Bernard] Berenson. The best of the pictures had been stored in a villa at Careggi, where they were safely preserved in spite of the villa having been struck by numerous shells; the rest were left in Mr. Berenson's house in the Borgo S. Jacopo, which was destroyed by the German demolitions. From the ruins there have been recovered thirty-one paintings; seven are completely destroyed, a Madonna and Child of the school of Bellini, an Annunciation attributed to Francesco Gentile, a Madonna by Caprioli, a predella by Fungai, Two Saints of the Tuscan school, early fourteenth-century, a triptych of the Scuola Marchigiana, and a fifteenth-century Adoration of the Shepherds; badly damaged are fifteen paintings, which include a portrait by Sebastiano Del Piombo, a Madonna and Two Saints by Lorenzo Monaco, a Borgognone Madonna, a Holy Family by Paris Bordone, two predelle by Taddeo Di Bartolo, a S. Jerome by Basaiti, two predelle by Granacci and a Madonna by Neri Di Bicci; slightly damaged are a Bonsignori mythological piece, a Perugino Madonna, a tondo by Domenico Morone, a predella by Girolamo Di Benventuto, and works by Pesellino, Ortolano, Giovanni Francesco Di Tolmezzo, and a fourteenth-century Byzantine Saint and a Head of Christ of the school of Andrea Del Castagno.

Of the villas round Florence a good many suffered severe damage but the most important fared best on the whole. In the Villa Reale at Poggio a Caiano the frescoes by Andrea Del Sarto, Allori and Pontormo are intact; so are those by Poccetti in the Villa Torrigiani and those by Passignano in the Villa Artimino; the Ghirlandaio in the Villa Canucci, the Michelangelo fresco in the Villa Scopeto and the Pollaiolo fresco in the Villa La Gallina; the Volterrano frescoes in the Villa Reale Di Petraia were slightly damaged by flying glass and needed to be protected from the weather.

The Flood, November 4, 1966:
A Letter From Florence

Francis Steegmuller

The plain on both sides of the Arno which is today the site of the city of
Florence was said by Livy to have been so marshy in antique times as
to have impeded Hannibal during his march on Rome, and according
to Florentine legend it took Hercules himself (whose effigy appears in
one of the ancient seals of the city) to drain the swamp and make
possible the founding of a settlement. The plain has had to be kept
drained ever since, and, even so, the Arno has frequently flooded over
into it; there have been about sixty floods of various degrees of gravity
since the twelfth century, the worst until now having been those of
1333 and 1844. The summer tourist, who often sees the Arno at
Florence as a stony riverbed, can scarcely be expected to imagine its
sinister potentialities.

If Hercules had been available to repair the results of the mammoth
inundation of November 4, 1966, the worst disaster in the annals of
the city, his task would have closely resembled another of his exploits
—the cleansing of the Augean stables. Today, more than two months
after the event, men and women in high boots were still shovelling out
of cellars and other low-lying places in various quarters of Florence
deposits of greenish-gray, malodorous mud left by the receding Arno,
and, along with it, debris of all kinds—tree branches, other people's
furniture, clothing, window frames, splintered bric-a-brac—that
landed blocks, or even miles, from its place of origin after being swept
along at astonishing velocity (up to thirty-five miles an hour) by the
water in the streets. And everywhere one sees another characteristic
souvenir of this most modern of floods—the smeary brown-black
stain of oil, which came from thousands of smashed fuel tanks and was

carried on the surface of the flood. In many places, there is a high-water line of oil along a gray or pale-yellow Florentine façade; in others oil coats an entire surface—a door, the panes of a window or a row of windows (sometimes second-story windows)—and even the insides of houses and shops. . . .

It is not in the streets lined with shops that one realizes most clearly the hardships wrought by the flood. Four and a half thousand families lost their homes. Especially around Santa Croce and in the poorer districts . . . one sees row after row of empty, gutted flats on the first and second floors of tenement buildings; often entire houses, weakened by the flood, have had to be vacated, and numbers of them have been propped up with timbers, which close some of the narrower streets to traffic. Many families of slender means in these districts were provisionally moved to not yet completed city housing on the outskirts of the city. The municipality and private aid have given them subsidies, a little furniture, and, according to present ruling, three rent-free months. By the end of that time, it is hoped, their old homes, many of which were never very solid, will be dried out and repaired. Only forty or so Florentines died in the flood, but most of the deaths took place here in these tenements, where it was hardest to escape being trapped. One still sees more mud and oil here than elsewhere. The people evacuated were generally the lowest paid of all Florentines, ground-floor and second-floor rents being the most modest in the city, and now, because of flood damage to the companies that employed them, they are the most apt to be out of work. They are the indispensable hard-working "little" Florentines whom one reads about in the novels of Vasco Pratolini, and a consciousness of these dispossessed pervades the city. It is omnipresent, like the mold, and like the remains of the mud, which, even in the most carefully cleaned sections of Florence, has penetrated every crack, so that whenever rain comes, out it still oozes.

No official warning was ever given to the population, and although the river had been badly swollen for days, most Florentines slept through the night of November 3rd-4th ignorant of the imminent danger. The Mayor has declared that he and much of his official family were on watch throughout the night, keeping in touch by telephone as long as they could with engineers upriver; that the river was constantly expected to subside; and that when, on the contrary, it began to spill over into the city in the early-morning hours, it was already too late, and warning by loudspeaker, klaxon or the tolling of bells would have brought only panic. Some Florentines were awakened during the night by telephone calls from friends in the country who were alarmed by the appearance of the upper Arno; others, out late at night, drew their own conclusions from looking at the river. But not even the fire brigade or the military in local barracks was officially alerted.

The only Florentines to be warned as a group were the jewellers with shops lining the Ponte Vecchio and the streets adjoining it. These merchants employed a private night watchman. At about one in the morning, he telephoned to the homes of those whom he could reach, and a number came, unlocked their shops, and filled suitcases with what they could, the bridge trembling beneath them. Others, in the absence of any official warning, thought that their watchman was exaggerating, and went back to sleep. The jewelers who did come had to leave quickly; the water was already close, and, in addition to the trembling, there were frightening sharp reports, as though the bridge were cracking. The wife of one of the jewelers has said that when she and her husband arrived they found a number of noctambulous Florentines—some of them apparently hoodlums, some in cars with headlights pointed toward the scene—gathered at the end of the bridge, watching, as though hoping to see it break and collapse. The arrival of the jewelers with their suitcases was greeted with jeers. Two policemen were also standing there watching, and when the jeweler's wife angrily asked why they weren't out spreading the alarm, their answer was "We have no orders." The water continued to rise and about half the jewelry shops on the Ponte Vecchio are now gaping open—gutted by the tremendous force of a torrent that passed right through them. The worst damaged are those on the east side of the bridge; they took the full brunt of the current.

The flood damage to Florence has frequently been spoken of as "worse than the war." Apart from the physical differences of the two catastrophes, there can, of course, be no real comparison between deliberate destruction planned and executed by man against his fellows and a totally unlooked-for accident of nature. Even in the latter case, however, people are disposed to fix blame, at least for negligence. The knowledge that one small group of citizens was warned has done nothing to diminish the outcries of other Florentines, and charges are being loudly made in advance that the official investigations now under way will provide nothing but whitewash. But out of the mass of lamentations, accusations, and so-called "evidence" that inevitably accumulates in the wake of such a disaster, a few details seem to be incontrovertible. First, the position of Florence is obviously a highly vulnerable one. At the bottom of a bowl of hills, it is watered by a river that during periods of rain and melting snow has always been swollen by tributaries from the deforested mountains among which it flows before reaching the city. One of these mountain tributaries, the Sieve, is particularly dangerous and has given rise to a Florentine proverb: *"Arno non cresce se Sieve non mesce"*—"The Arno doesn't rise unless the Sieve rushes into it." The only way to be sure of avoiding Florentine floods, someone has said, would be to move Florence. Then, there is the question of dams. The abrupt opening of a hydroelectric dam at Levane, thirty-eight miles above Florence, on the night of November 3rd and the consequent release of millions of tons of water certainly aggravated the height and force of the flood. The dam apparently would have burst if it had not been opened, but some hydraulic experts believe that it could have been opened earlier and more gradually. At any rate, the timing of the opening of the dam at Levane and the degree of cooperation and communication that existed between the dam engineers and the officials of the great city downstream are naturally being much discussed in Florence and throughout Italy at this moment, with greatly varying proportions. A resurgence of the traditional Italian lack of confidence in governmental protection has reminded people of the years of flooding in the valley of the Po, the rate at which Venice is sinking into its own canals, and last year's landslide at Agrigento, caused by overbuilding. In such matters, the philosophical and stoical Italian acceptance of disaster is, ironically, thought to have contributed to official neglect. "This famous Italian patience of ours has become a vice," one Florentine remarked the other day.

The lack of official warning in Florence was followed, for a time, by a strange playing down of the extent of the disaster over the nationally owned Italian radio and television stations. A day or two after November 4th, one newscaster announced to a public still uninformed of the extent of Florence's submersion that "the situation in Florence is returning to normal." Premier Aldo Moro, when criticized in Parliament a week after the disaster for not having yet visited the stricken city, made a reply that has become famous: "My fourteen-year-old daughter is up there, helping save the books from the National Library." . . .

As for the casualties in paintings, books, manuscripts, and archives, one of the reproaches constantly heard since the flood has concerned the storage of so many of the city's treasures in low-lying places. The ancient printed volumes of the Palatine Collection, which were presented to the city in the eighteenth century by one of the last of the Medici, were kept in the basement of the Biblioteca Nazionale Centrale, a building constructed in this century—despite the warning provided by floods of other centuries—only a few feet from the bank of the Arno; these are the most celebrated of the millions of Florentine books that were immersed in water and emerged covered with mud and oil. The city archives, dating back centuries, are in shelves on the ground floor of the Uffizi, and the lower three or four shelves of the archives, including documents from the thirteenth century, were water-soaked. One reply to the reproaches on this subject is a reminder that at the time of the *last* Florentine disaster, the artillery bombardment of the city in 1944, the danger came from above, and at that time it was the treasures kept on *upper* floors that caused the greatest concern. Certainly it has been common for at least a generation now to think of safety as lying underground, man having become accustomed to regard himself, rather than nature, as his most likely destroyer.

. . . Pictures, which were in the process of restoration in the Uffizi gallery *Restauro*, in the basement and on the ground floor, were brought upstairs in time, early on the morning of November 4th. More than two hundred paintings on wood panels, including about forty that were not moved out of the Uffizi *Restauro* in time, are at present being treated, across the Arno, in the Boboli Gardens' *limonaia*—a vast greenhouse where the Gardens' hundreds of lemon trees usually pass the winter. (This year, they have been moved into a sheltered courtyard of the nearby Pitti Palace.) Inside the *limonaia*, on both sides of a long center aisle, as in a military hospital, are rows of metal frames with pictures lying prostrate on them like so many casualties on their beds. The patients are bandaged wholly or in part with rice paper, which holds the pigment down while the wood panels dry out. Each panel bears a tag like a fever chart—a carefully inscribed record of its decreasing degree of humidity. Overhead rumbles a huge machine that was rushed from Rome to control the humidity in the *limonaia*. Men in white jackets—the staff of the Uffizi Restauro—work on those pictures that have dried out sufficiently to be touched; with pincers they peel off the rice-paper bandages and perform other delicate operations. . . .

The largest, and also the most gravely maimed, of the patients in the *limonaia* is the great Cimabue "Crucifixion." For many years, although it is the property of the Franciscan friars of the Church of Santa Croce, which stands in a particularly low-lying part of the city, it hung in the Uffizi, up several long flights of stairs; a few years ago, the friars asked that it be returned to them, and they hung it in their museum, on the ground floor off their cloister. Among the most striking photographs of Florence at the height of the flood was one taken from the air that showed the cloister of Santa Croce filled with water nearly up to the top of its arcades; here the flood water was at its highest, remained longest, and left the most mud. The official statement is that the Cimabue is 'seventy per cent destroyed.''...The present opinion is that, for the most part, the picture is not restorable, and that it should be rehung, in its tragic state, as a memento of the flood, with, beside it, a photograph of it as it came down from the thirteenth century to November 4, 1966.

For centuries, students of the Italian Renaissance in any of its aspects have come to work in the libraries of Florence. These are the world's richest in this field—in printed books, manuscripts, and archives. Of them all, the Biblioteca Nazionale Centrale is the greatest—along with the library of the Vatican, the most renowned in Italy. The floding of the Nazionale and of other Florentine collections of books and documents has been, apart from human losses, the greatest blow suffered by the city. Florence's continued usefulness and reputation as an international scholarly center depend on the rapid recuperation of the damaged collections. It is estimated that close to two million volumes need restoration, including rebinding, before they can be returned to use. Drying out is the first step. Many of the water-soaked volumes are being interleaved with blotting paper at various treatment centers in Florence, and others are being given first aid—some of it necessarily a little rough—all over Tuscany and Umbria. Near Arezzo, some of the lofty barns used by the Italian state tobacco monopoly for the drying of tobacco leaves are now full of volumes hanging over poles, with tobacco-leaf caretakers acting as book nurses; brick factories, textile-drying sheds, and even heating plants have been pressed into service....

At the Baptistery, facing the Cathedral, five panels of Ghiberti's bronze "Gate of Paradise" were detached by the flood....Certain sculptures have emerged from their unaccustomed baths in a new guise; of the four horses in Ammanati's Neptune fountain beside the Palazzo Vecchio, for example, two have turned out to be of white marble and two of porphyry, instead of a general gray, as they had long seemed to be. The cleaning of large numbers of lesser sculptures often reveals the preferences of the cleaners; girls from all over Europe lovingly clean every square inch of the innumerable cupids, whereas stern, bearded Jupiters—harder to clean, anyway, because of their dense marble curls—are often neglected.

A hundred and fifty young people—principally from Italy, England, the United States, Holland, and Germany—have formed a group called Centro Operativo Firenze, with headquarters at present in a Via Ghibellina *palazzo* whose lofty rooms are empty except for cots and the few mud-caked belongings of the workers. These people have undertaken to do the hardest and most repugnant job of all, the emptying of mud-filled cellars, and are still receiving about forty requests a day from all over Florence. Their long days are spent heaving pails of stinking silt from icy, black basements up onto the streets, where the deposits are eventually taken away by the army, to be dumped outside Florence. For a short time after the disaster, this frightful task of cellar-cleaning was performed by the Army itself, under government orders. The high-spirited boys and girls on whom the job has now, unfathomably, devolved are paid a tiny stipend by the Commune of Florence and are fed, appropriately, in an orphanage.

The countless anecdotes one hears in Florence about "what I did the day of the flood" remind a New Yorker of those he has heard about "what happened to me during the blackout," and, indeed, the Florentines, who know all about that night in New York and have read about the population increase nine months later, are fond of saying, "What's going to happen here? We were without electricity for three weeks!" Dry Florentine humor has produced a number of flood jokes, sardonic, self-deprecating, often anticlerical. Like all disasters, the calamity attracted many curious out-of-town sightseers, and when the Pope came from Rome to say a midnight Mass on Christmas Eve it was remarked, "So even His Holiness has dropped in to see what the Boss has been up to!" . . .

Walking along the Arno these days, the visitor from abroad is apt to realize that his eyes turn upward less often than they used to toward the hills around Florence, with their woods and villas and castles. Instead, his attention is riveted to the devastated riverbanks and, above all, to details of walls. The action of the water and subsequent hand-scrubbing have caused the lower stories of many buildings to emerge a lighter color than the rest—below the dreadful, ever-present high-water line, which is already commemorated by a number of engraved plaques. Often, it appears, the oldest buildings—and the oldest furniture as well—resisted the flood best. Surveying the damage, one lover of this city (which was a massive fortress before, and even while, becoming an art center) remarked, "If Florence weren't so ancient, it wouldn't still be here."

Bibliography of Selections

Berenson, Bernard. *The Italian Painters of the Renaissance*. Oxford: Oxford
    University Press, 1930.
Boccaccio, Giovanni. "Account of the Divine Comedy." In Dante, *The
    Divine Comedy*. Translated by Henry Wadsworth Longfellow. Leipzig:
    Tauschnitz, 1867.
———. *The Decameron*. Translated by Richard Aldington, New York:
    Covici, Friede Publishers, 1930.
British Committee on the Preservation and Restitution of Works of Art,
    Archives, and Other Material in Enemy Hands, War Office Reports.
    Works of Art in Italy: Losses and Survival in the War. London: His
    Majesty's Stationery Office, 1945.
Browning, Elizabeth Barrett. *The Poetical Works of Elizabeth Barrett
    Browning*. London: Smith Elder, 1890.
Burckhardt, Jacob. *Civilization of the Renaissance in Italy*. Translated by
    S. G. C. Middlemore. London: Phaidon Press, 1940.
Byron, George Gordon (Lord). "Childe Harold, Canto IV," *The Works of
    Lord Byron*. Edited by Ernest Hartley Coleridge. New York: Scribner's,
    1899.
Cellini, Benvenuto. *The Life of Benvenuto Cellini Written by Himself*. Edited
    and translated by John Addington Symonds. New York: Brentano's,
    1906.
Clark, Kenneth. "Kenneth Clark on the Mona Lisa," *Burlington Magazine*,
    March 1973.
Cooper, James Fenimore. *Excursions in Italy*. London: Bentley, 1838.
Dante Alighieri. *The Divine Comedy*. Translated by Henry Wadsworth
    Longfellow. Leipzig: Tauschnitz, 1867.
———. *The Letters of Dante*. With introduction, translation and notes by
    Paget Toynbee. Oxford: Clarendon Press, 1966.

Eliot, George. *Romola*. Leipzig, Tauchnitz, 1863.

Forster, E. M. *A Room with a View*. New York: Knopf, 1923.

Foscolo, Ugo. "Boccaccio." *Critical Perspectives on the Decameron*, edited by R. S. Dombrowski. London: Hodder and Stoughton, 1976.

Galileo. *The Sidereal Messenger of Galileo Galilei*. Translated by Edward Stafford Carlos. London: Dawson's of Pall Mall, n.d.

———. "Sentence and Recantation." In Karl von Gebler, *Galileo Galilei and the Roman Curia*. Translated by Mrs. George Sturge. Merrick, N.Y.: Richwood Publishing Co., n.d.

Gilbert, Felix. Introduction to *History of Florence*, by Niccolo Machiavelli. New York: Harper and Brothers, 1960.

Guicciardini, Francesco. *History of Italy and History of Florence*. Translated by Cecil Grayson. Edited and abridged with an introduction by John R. Hale, London: New English Library, 1966.

Hawthorne, Nathaniel. *Passages from the French and Italian Notebooks*. Boston: Osgood, 1872.

Hawthorne, Sophia Amelia. *Notes in England and Italy*. New York: Putnam's, 1875.

Howells, William Dean. *Tuscan Cities*. Boston: Houghton Mifflin Co., 1885.

James, Henry. *Portraits of Places*. Edited by George Finch. New York: Lear Publishers, 1948.

Lawrence, D. H. *Aaron's Rod*. New York: Penguin Books, 1950.

Lewis, Sinclair. *World So Wide*. New York: Random House, 1950.

McCarthy, Mary. *The Stones of Florence*. London: William Heinemann, 1959.

Machiavelli, Niccolo. *History of Florence and of the Affairs of Italy from the Earliest Times to the Death of Lorenzo the Magnificent*. New York: Harper and Brothers, 1960.

Maugham, Somerset. *Then and Now*. New York: Doubleday, 1946.

Melville, Herman. *Journal of a Visit to Europe and the Levant*. Edited by Howard C. Horsford. Princeton, N.J.: Princeton University Press, 1955.

Michelangelo, Buonarroti. *The Sonnets of Michael Angelo Buonarroti*. Translated by John Addington Symonds. New York: Lear Publishers, 1948.

Ouida (Louise de la Ramée). *The Tower of Taddeo*. London: William Heinemann, 1899.

Pater, Walter. *The Renaissance*. With an introduction and notes by Sir Kenneth Clark. London: Fontana Library, 1961.

Steegmuller, Francis. "A Letter from Florence." *Stories and True Stories*. Boston: Little, Brown, 1972.

Stendhal (Marie-Henri Beyle). *Rome, Naples and Florence*. Translated by Richard N. Coe. New York: George Braziller, 1960.

Symonds, John Addington. *The Renaissance in Italy*. London: Smith Elder,
    1880.
Taine, Hippolyte Adolphe. *Italy: Florence and Venice*. Translated by J.
    Durand. New York: Holt, 1887.
Trollope, Thomas Adolphus. *A History of the Commonwealth of Florence*.
    London: Chapman and Hall, 1865.
Vasari, Giorgio. *Lives of the Painters, Sculptors and Architects*. Translated
    by A. B. Hinds. New York: E. P. Dutton, 1900.
Villani, Giovanni. "Eulogy." In Dante, *The Divine Comedy*. Translated by
    Henry Wadsworth Longfellow. Leipzig: Tauschnitz, 1867.

Index